A REPUBLIC, NOT A DEMOCRACY

A REPUBLIC, NOT A DEMOCRACY

How to Restore Sanity in America

ADAM BRANDON

Skyhorse Publishing

Skyhorse Publishing books may be purchased in bulk at special discounts for sales promotion, corporate gifts, fund-raising, or educational purposes. Special editions can also be created to specifications. For details, contact the Special Sales Department, Skyhorse Publishing, 307 West 36th Street, 11th Floor, New York, NY 10018 or info@skyhorsepublishing.com.

Skyhorse® and Skyhorse Publishing® are registered trademarks of Skyhorse Publishing, Inc.®, a Delaware corporation.

Visit our website at www.skyhorsepublishing.com.

10 9 8 7 6 5 4 3 2 1

Library of Congress Cataloging-in-Publication Data is available on file.

Cover design by Maddy O'Connor and Kai Texel

Print ISBN: 978-1-5107-5634-2
Ebook ISBN: 978-1-5107-5635-9

Printed in the United States of America

Table of Contents

To Joan Carter, Rob Lansing, and Frank Sands—
each of you believed in me when few did

*"It is not until a people lose their religion that they lose
their religious liberty, not until they cease to speak as free men and
women that they lose freedom of speech, not until they permit themselves
to be herded into a subservient rabble that they lose their freedom of
assembly—and, as businessmen, not until they begin to
rely on outside help, political or otherwise, that they lose
their freedom to manage their own establishments."*
—Harry Lynde Bradley[1]

1   Harry Lynde Bradley, *Allen-Bradley: An American Story*, Robert A. Smith, ed., written in 1957, unpublished manuscript published by Rockwell Automation, 2003. Uploaded to Scribd, Aug. 11, 2011. https://www.scribd.com/document/62118919/Harry-L-Bradley-Manuscript

Foreword

A s I write this, Christmas has passed and New Year's is a couple days away. For me, it is time to raise a pint of British ale to celebrate the culmination of Brexit. More than four years ago, voters in the United Kingdom passed a referendum to leave the European Union because of a strong desire to reclaim our sovereignty as a nation.

This task was all but impossible. For decades, political, academic, media, and economic elites in London thought what was good for them was good for Britain. The debate over Brexit was no different. Those who wanted the United Kingdom to remain in the European Union were influential and arrogantly believed they knew what was best for us all and had a certain measure of contempt for supporters of Brexit.

To the American reader, this must sound familiar. The elites in America are just as self-righteous as those in London. Whatever grows their power is the best course, even if it worsens the lives of others and further erodes the precious institutions that promote the rule of law, sovereignty, and liberty.

The great British philosopher John Locke wrote, "No man's knowledge here can go beyond his experience." The elites who supported remaining in the European Union could not understand the experience of those who wanted to leave. Similarly, the elites in Washington, D.C. who are ever fighting for more control over your life do not understand the experience of most Americans, who so desperately want to be left alone.

The Anglo-American democratic systems have their roots in the mists of time. From the Magna Carta to the Scottish Enlightenment to the American Revolution, we have believed in the rights of the individual to govern themselves and their destinies. Many may wonder how the Magna Carta, a document written during the thirteenth century, could have influenced eighteenth century America. The Magna Carta was the culmination of efforts to restrain King John and his arbitrary rule.

The Founding Fathers of America were heavily influenced by the Magna Carta in their quest for independence from Great Britain and the tyrannical reign of King George III. "No taxation without representation," the famous creed from Boston in protest of the Intolerable Acts, was taken from the Magna Carta. In The Rights of the British Colonies Asserted and Proved, the fierce American patriot James Otis wrote:

"[I]f it was thought hard that charter privileges should be taken away by act of parliament, is it not much harder to be in part, or in whole, disfranchised of rights, that have been always thought inherent to a British subject, namely, to be free from all taxes, but what he consents to in person, or by his representative? This right, if it could be traced no higher than Magna Carta, is part of the common law, part of a British subjects birthright, and as inherent and perpetual, as the duty of allegiance; both which have been brought to these colonies, and have been hitherto held sacred and inviolable, and I hope and trust ever will. It is humbly conceived, that the British colonists (except only the conquered, if any) are, by Magna Charta, as well entitled to have a voice in their taxes, as the subjects within the realm. Are we not as really deprived of that right, by the parliament assessing us before we are represented in the house of commons, as if the King should do it by his prerogative? Can it be said with any colour of truth or justice, that we are represented in parliament?"

Many of the protections of individual liberty that became part of the Bill of Rights were inspired by the Magna Carta. The very foundations of the American experiment are limited government and individual liberty, but those foundations are under attack by people desperate for political power in Washington, D.C.

Sovereignty in Britain rests in Parliament in Westminster. But in 1973, the United Kingdom joined the European community and surrendered much of its power to the seat of the European Union in Brussels. I am very supportive of trade and ongoing deep partnerships with our European neighbors. It is very important to maintain these relationships to grow our economies and prosper. I am not in favor of ceding nearly a thousand years of self-governance, the cost of which was steep and hard-fought, and our sovereignty to unaccountable bureaucrats in Brussels.

While the London-based elites enjoyed this arrangement, it did not travel well outside of London, where most Britons wondered whether we were an independent country or not. The elites in London, as well as those in Brussels, couldn't understand why Brits would want to leave the European Union. The elites backing the European Union talked of the supposed economic benefits and ease of travel throughout Europe, but most Britons were wary of such arguments. They wanted the United Kingdom to be governed by the United Kingdom.

What makes Britain is not the regulations and government programs, but the people. They do not want to be managed by faceless bureaucrats. These Britons wanted to restore self-government and the independence of the United Kingdom. Many pundits have opined that immigration was the primary reason for Brexit, not so subtly hinting at prejudice or xenophobia, but an exit poll found that "[n]early half (49%) of leave voters said the biggest single reason for wanting to leave the EU was 'the principle that decisions about the UK should be taken in the UK.'"[1]

How did it happen? Grassroots made Brexit possible. It started small, in pubs and in people's homes. Rather than being told what to think by the media, Britons took comfort in conversations with their neighbors. They chose independence from Brussels and the path of self-determination and self-government.

Grassroots is long hard work. It takes time. There are setbacks. But it also has the power of a glacier and is the only thing in nature that can move the establishment. The United Kingdom's membership in European Communities began in 1973 and was affirmed in 1975 with our first-ever national referendum, in which more than two-thirds of voters chose to stay in the European Communities. But public opinion began to change after the formation of the European Union in 1993. The skepticism of the European Union transcended party ideologies.

A small grassroots political party was formed to give voice to those who believed that leaving the European Union was the only means by which self-government could be restored. The UK Independence Party was formed in 1993 and it had no real money, no well-known personalities, but it did have a message that attracted grassroots campaigners. From a tiny vote share in the beginning, UKIP rose to win the European Parliament Elections in 2014. As I led the party through many of these years and spoke at over two thousand public events, the grassroots became taller. In the end, the Prime Minister, David Cameron, had no option but to concede a referendum, as we were destroying his vote.

We started with small victories, the most notable being Prime Minister David Cameron's promise for a referendum on the United Kingdom's membership in the European Union. Although he ultimately campaigned to remain in the European Union, Cameron made good on his promise after the Tories won the election in 2015.

---

1   Peter Roff, "Brexit Was About Britain," *US News*, June 30, 2016. https://www.usnews.com/opinion/articles/2016-06-30/poll-shows-brexit-vote-was-about-british-sovereignty-not-anti-immigration

Another small victory came in early 2016 when Boris Johnson, who is now the prime minister, lent his support to Brexit.

Every step of the way, we were doubted and mocked. And then we won. Even in victory, we had many setbacks as we left the European Union. But as I write this, the prime minister has secured a trade deal with the European Union that protects the United Kingdom's sovereignty, or, as the prime minister explained, a deal that allows us to "go our own way but also have free trade." We claimed our independence on June 23, 2016, with the Brexit referendum. On January 1, 2021, we formally reclaim our sovereignty with this new trade agreement.

None of this would have been possible without grassroots who had had the determination and strong desire to seek independence from the stranglehold of the European Union. Grassroots is when citizens seize the responsibility to be active participants in their government and political processes. It's when they no longer feel they need to "trust" the political and bureaucratic experts.

Politicians, pundits, and bureaucrats have only the power we give them. The power lies with you, the voter, who controls not only your vote but the influence you have on those around you. This is why it is important to arm yourself with knowledge and to learn what works to convince your friends and neighbors to come to your side.

We are at a time in history when our institutions are being challenged. The elites have clearly shown that they are not up for the challenges of today's world. The optimism is that the grassroots, inspired by their basic common sense of how the world actually works, will define the future.

In America today, those who favor centralized power are back in control. It is going to take a sustained grassroots campaign to overturn this in the years to come. The fight starts now.

—Nigel Farage

A REPUBLIC, NOT A DEMOCRACY

CHAPTER I
A Republic, If You Can Keep It

I t was a cooler summer than usual in Philadelphia when the Constitutional Convention was held in 1787.[1] For four months, some of the sharpest minds in history convened to eventually settle on their new nation's founding constitution.

Only ten years before, Philadelphia was occupied by British forces led by General William Howe. The occupation of the City of Brotherly Love was symbolic for the British. Philadelphia was the capital of the new nation fighting for its independence from a tyrannical king. It was also where the Second Continental Congress met and debated the Declaration of Independence. Boston may have been the spirit of the American quest for independence, but Philadelphia was its cradle.

A decisive Patriot victory in Saratoga, New York in October 1777 marked a turning point in the war for independence. Americans would soon form an alliance with France. With a formidable French naval presence soon to challenge British supply chains, the British abandoned Philadelphia in June 1778. The war for independence

---

1   "Appendix: The Weather during the Convention," Supplement to Max Farrand's *The Records of the Federal Convention of 1787*, Yale University Press, 1987. https://www. consource.org/document/appendix-the-weather-during-the-convention-1787/

ended in 1783, with the former British American colonies becoming free and independent states.

Since 1781, the thirteen states had been bound together by the Articles of Confederation and Perpetual Union. This governing document had flaws that hampered the development of the new nation. A new charter was needed.

The Founding Fathers were learned men. They had studied classical Athenian and Roman history and were heavily influenced by the rhetorical styles of Aristotle, Cicero, Demosthenes, and many other classical statesmen and philosophers.[2] Benjamin Franklin, James Madison, Alexander Hamilton, and the other delegates to the Constitutional Convention had studied and learned from history's best and worst examples of governance and tried to incentivize man's best traits while limiting the abuse of power.

Striking the right balance to limit the size and scope of the federal government was crucial. Delegating authority, separating powers, and providing necessary checks and balances was paramount.

So, when Benjamin Franklin was asked by Elizabeth Willing Powel what kind of a government he and the other delegates at the Constitutional Convention had crafted in Philadelphia, he famously said, "A republic, if you can keep it."[3]

The Tyranny of Pure Democracy

What Franklin meant is that truly free men and women should beware of pure democracy. This sentiment penetrated everything the Constitution's collaborators did in the summer of 1787.

---

2   James M. Farrell, "Above all Greek, above all Roman fame: Classical Rhetoric in America during the Colonial and Early National Periods," *International Journal of the Classical Tradition* 18:3, 415-436, September 2011. https://scholars.unh.edu/cgi /viewcontent.cgi?article=1003&context=comm_facpub

3   James McHenry, "Papers of Dr. James McHenry on the Federal Convention of 1787," Journal, Yale Law School's Avalon Project, May 14, 1787. https://avalon.law .yale.edu/18th_century/mchenry.asp

The American colonists had just left one form of tyranny, a monarchy, but knew better than to replace a king with pure democracy. The Founders were very familiar with the history of ancient Athens and its true, direct democracy, in which a simple majority vote of the populace decided most questions of governance. This beautiful experiment in Athens devolved into mob rule, minority rights trampled by the whims of the majority.[4]

My friend Dr. David Hoinski is a philosophy professor at the University of West Virginia. We've been close friends since our freshman year in high school, but we've gone our separate ways when it comes to politics. Dr. Hoinski teaches philosophy and is an expert on Plato. During the winter of 2019, he encouraged me to read Plato's *Republic*. The thing that hit me most about studying Plato, who wrote more than two thousand years ago, was his observation that right before you have tyranny, you have a pure democracy.

That's part of what Benjamin Franklin meant. We throw around the term "democracy" so loosely in reference to America, but we're actually a republic. There is a big difference between the two. A pure democracy ends up becoming mob rule. A republic has an entire system of checks and balances to prevent that. It's our republican form of government that makes America so durable.

In our system, the business interests in New York City are checked by the political interests in Washington. You have the state interests checking federal interests. You have all of this separation in our system of government that is, by design and quite literally, a republic (if you can keep it) through consistently checking power. Because the Founders gave us a system in which power could be checked by other sources of power, that gave space for liberty to flourish.

What I worry about today is that we're finally devolving into the breakup of the republic that the Founding Fathers warned us about. James Madison described this as the problem of "faction."[5] Writing in 1787, as New York was deciding whether or not to ratify

---

4   Jim Huntzinger, "Why the Founding Fathers Despised Democracy," Townhall, Dec. 8, 2018. https://finance.townhall.com/columnists/jimhuntzinger/2018/12/07/why-the-founding-fathers-despised-democracy-n2537155

5   James Madison, *The Federalist Papers*, No. 10

the Constitution, Madison explained that the benefit of a republican form of government was that it would undercut faction.

Madison described faction as "a number of citizens, whether amounting to a majority or a minority of the whole, who are united and actuated by some common impulse of passion, or of interest, adversed to the rights of other citizens, or to the permanent and aggregate interests of the community." He surmised that there were "two methods of curing the mischiefs of faction." The first was "removing its causes," which he rejected because that meant "destroying the liberty which is essential to its existence" and "giving to every citizen the same opinions, the same passions, and the same interests." This solution, he noted, "was worse than the disease."

The other method of curing the mischiefs of faction was "controlling its effects." This is why Madison and the framers of the Constitution chose to make America a republic. In fact, Madison explicitly rejected direct democracy. He wrote, "[D]emocracies have ever been spectacles of turbulence and contention; have ever been found incompatible with personal security or the rights of property; and have in general been as short in their lives as they have been violent in their deaths."

Once we take that road, you're going to see a significant step toward that pure democracy of the Founders' nightmares. This kind of hyper-democratization of society used to be far-left, pie-in-the-sky thinking. Such conversations weren't remotely considered part of the mainstream debate. No longer. Many Americans were talking about socialism seriously before the global pandemic, and that event has encouraged some of them to push even harder for a more collectivist and pure democratic system.

Now we're actually talking about universal basic income. It's not a punchline. That's where our country is. When she served as a senator, Kamala Harris introduced a proposal that's very similar to universal basic income.[6] The Committee for a Responsible Federal

---

6   Bailey Steen, "Kamala Harris introduces $2 trillion basic income-style bill to combat US poverty," *Medium*, Nov. 1, 2018. https://medium.com/@TrigTent/kamala-harris-introduces-2-trillion-basic-income-style-bill-to-combat-us-poverty-ba391b9d6dbb

Budget estimated that Harris's proposal would cost $3 trillion.[7] To put that in some perspective, the net worth of the wealthiest person in the world, Amazon CEO Jeff Bezos, is around $200 billion, only one fifteenth of what Harris' plan would spend.[8]

If you combine direct democracy with universal basic income, the republic is over. The country will just descend into voting for "who is going to give me more free stuff."

If we devolve into such a sad state, the main and perhaps only purpose of the government at that point will be redistributing free stuff and suppressing those who disagree with the whims of the mob. That's when you have a tyranny of the majority.

In his 1859 essay *On Liberty*, philosopher John Stuart Mill wrote, "The will of the people . . . practically means the will of the most numerous or the most active *part* of the people; the majority, or those who succeed in making themselves accepted as the majority; the people, consequently, *may* desire to oppress a part of their number; and precautions are as much needed against this as against any other abuse of power."[9]

If America takes such a path, we're setting ourselves up for a very dangerous situation that is reminiscent of Germany in the 1930s. Throughout history, you have seen this problem: that within systems where winners have all the control, you start to see a battle between the military juntas on the right and left-wing juntas on the other side.

It goes back and forth. When you empower the mob in such a fashion, it actually brings about violence. So we are at risk. It's disturbing. Our republic is a constant balance. If you have these checks and balances, we have a system that is capable of fixing

---

7   "Kamala Harris's LIFT the Middle Class Act," Committee for a Responsible Federal Budget, Oct. 1, 2019. https://www.crfb.org/blogs/kamala-harriss-lift-middle-class-act

8   Michelle Toh, "Jeff Bezos is now worth a whopping $200 billion," *CNN Business*, Aug. 27 2020. https://www.cnn.com/2020/08/27/tech/jeff-bezos-net-worth-200-billion-intl-hnk/index.html

9   John Stuart Mill, *On Liberty, and Other Writings*, ed. Stefan Collini, Cambridge University Press, 1989. pg. 8

problems. If you do away with our system and the Constitution, we're really in trouble.

Democracy Is Temporary

One of the greatest quotes I've ever read about why democracies rise and fall is one that usually gets attributed to British historian Alexander Tytler. It's been invoked by the likes of Ronald Reagan and P. J. O'Rourke, and although it turns out that no one really seems to know whether Tytler actually wrote it, it resonates with everything I know about history.

"A democracy is always temporary in nature; it simply cannot exist as a permanent form of government," Tytler said. "A democracy will continue to exist up until the time that voters discover that they can vote themselves generous gifts from the public treasury. From that moment on, the majority always votes for the candidates who promise the most benefits from the public treasury, with the result that every democracy will finally collapse due to loose fiscal policy, which is always followed by a dictatorship."

Tytler added, "The average age of the world's greatest civilizations from the beginning of history has been about two hundred years. During those two hundred years, these nations always progressed through the following sequence: From bondage to spiritual faith; From spiritual faith to great courage; From courage to liberty; From liberty to abundance; From abundance to selfishness; From selfishness to complacency; From complacency to apathy; From apathy to dependence; From dependence back into bondage."[10]

I believe we are in the midst of or are getting close to the abundance-selfishness-apathy phase of this cycle. We could argue where in this cycle the US actually lands at the moment. It's clear, though, that too many have taken the liberty that we have enjoyed for so long for granted.

---

10 Loren Collins, "The Truth about Tytler," LorenCollins.com, Updated Jan. 25, 2009. https://www.lorencollins.net/tytler.html

Keeping Our Republic in a Post-COVID-19 World

In the 2020 COVID-19 pandemic, America saw an unprecedented and historic closure of small businesses. Many of those small businesses that closed during the pandemic won't reopen. There continues to be a tremendous amount of insecurity and unease in our society. So-called "progressives" saw this as an opportunity to tear down America's entire system. They have an idealized version of something else they believe they can put in its place.

That's putting a lot of faith in men, something our Founders meticulously tried to avoid. Society is a balancing act between freedom and safety. When we're in good times, we want more economic and personal freedom. During bad times, we want more safety. The problem that comes from the desire for more security during bad times is that the growth in government never goes away.

Those who are using this crisis to tear down America's system reject our constitutional form of government. Even if they intend to do good things, the law of unintended consequences, particularly in or post-pandemic chaos, could bring about all sorts of unimagined problems.

History is littered with problems that arise from disrupting this balance. In her 2006 book, *Liberty for All: Reclaiming Individual Privacy in a New Era of Public Morality*, law professor Elizabeth Price Foley explains it this way: "America started with a concept of limited government, designed to protect and improve the life, liberty, and property of citizens, and has ended with a concept of unlimited government, capable of restricting our life, liberty, and property in the name of protecting us from ourselves."[11]

During a discussion on her book, Foley further explained, "The morality of American law has been abandoned by all branches when certain exigencies and pragmatic considerations have arisen . . . a desire to avoid civil war; followed closely by a desire to avoid another civil war; a desire to protect the United States from dangers

---

11　Elizabeth Price Foley, *Liberty for All: Reclaiming Individual Privacy in a New Era of Public Morality*, Yale University Press, 2006.

of socialist and, later, communist thought; a desire to pull this coun-try out of a severe economic depression; and...a desire to protect America from terrorism."[12]

The pendulum has consistently swung toward security, be it eco-nomic security in the case of the Great Depression, or more security to protect the homeland in the case of the post-September 11 world.

Franklin's quip, "a republic, if you can keep it" also meant that our founders designed the system to be kept and maintained by an engaged citizenry. The majority of Americans do want to keep their country's long-standing system. They might want to improve it. They certainly want to improve the lives of their fellow countrymen. They want to make sure this generation is working to solve big problems.

Americans aren't looking to tear down the system. That means they must be engaged. The power of the citizen is what maintains this important balance. The Founding Fathers intentionally created a system that was supposed to keep power from being centralized. This was their legacy to all Americans.

The founders knew, as Lord Acton told us, "absolute power cor-rupts absolutely."[13] The nature of government, though, isn't to be idle and do nothing. We have to heed Thomas Jefferson's warning in 1788 that "[t]he natural progress of things is for liberty to yield, and government to gain ground."[14]

Each generation has to decide what government they want. They have to decide whether they will fight the centralization of power at the hands of political elites. We also have to remember that silence is often viewed as consent. Citizens can fight the centralization of power, growth of government, and loss of economic and personal liberty, but they first have to participate.

---

12   Elizabeth Price Foley, "Liberty for All: Reclaiming Individual Privacy in a New Era of Public Morality," Cato Institute, October 31, 2006. https://www.cato.org /multimedia/events/liberty-all-reclaiming-individual-privacy-new-era-public-morality

13   John Emerich Edward Dalberg (Lord Acton), "Letter to Archbishop Mandell Creighton," Hanover College, April 5, 1887. https://history.hanover.edu/courses /excerpts/165acton.html

14   Thomas Jefferson, "From Thomas Jefferson to Edward Carrington, 27 May 1788," National Archives, May 27, 1788. https://founders.archives.gov/documents /Jefferson/01-13-02-0120

An Engaged Citizenry

Participating in our republic doesn't mean simply watching Fox News and voting. It doesn't mean only voting. Participating means educating yourself and your friends and neighbors. Participating is going to visit your congressmen and senators' offices either in your district and state or in Washington, D.C.

Think of this book as a call to arms. The amount of power in your voice is why you need to be involved. My goal is that you become a more active and engaged citizen. Doing so is a crucial check on power that gives space for human liberty to flourish and endure. The alternative is to lie back and let the Washington so-called "experts" take full control. We saw what a disaster that was with the global pandemic.

The response to the COVID-19 crisis did immeasurable harm to our economy. We needed to be safe, but we also needed to be smart. We knew who was the most vulnerable to the virus, the elderly and people with serious pre-existing conditions, and that those of us who were healthy needed to take the actions necessary to make consumers comfortable by practicing social distancing.

Governors, rarely with any check on their power, acted unilaterally to partially shut down state economies. The goal was to prevent health care providers from being overrun, but these actions were neither safe nor smart for millions of businesses and individuals.

That is why it's important that we hold our leaders accountable. President John F. Kennedy famously said, "Ask not what your country can do for you, ask what you can do for your country." What every American should be doing for their country is making sure that we continue to achieve this important constitutional balance in the name of keeping this republic.

America is the sum of all of our individual efforts to fan the flames of freedom and to chase our dreams in our own specific ways. But if we begin to see the US government merely as a tool for redistribution and giving us things that would completely erode the heart of the system that was bequeathed to us—we're through.

What We're Up Against—The Cloward-Piven Strategy

Professors Richard Cloward and Frances Fox Piven came up with a strategy in 1966 that they believed would force the federal government to enact socialist policies. The vehicle for these policies would be the Democratic Party.

Known as the Cloward-Piven strategy, the idea was to overwhelm local governments and budgets by getting as many people on welfare as possible. After the system collapsed, the federal government would be forced to take action, which would lead to the adoption of socialist policies. The two professors explained:

> *Widespread campaigns to register the eligible poor for welfare aid, and to help existing recipients obtain their full benefits, would produce bureaucratic disruption in welfare agencies and fiscal disruption in local and state governments. These disruptions would generate severe political strains, and deepen existing divisions among elements in the big-city Democratic coalition: the remaining white middle class, the white working-class ethnic groups and the growing minority poor. To avoid a further weakening of that historic coalition, a national Democratic administration would be constrained to advance a federal solution to poverty that would override local welfare failures, local class and racial conflicts and local revenue dilemmas. By the internal disruption of local bureaucratic practices, by the furor over public welfare poverty, and by the collapse of current financing arrangements, powerful forces can be generated for major economic reforms at the national level.*[15]

What might have sounded too radical five decades ago doesn't sound too radical to many in America now, particularly in today's Democratic Party.

---

15   Frances Fox Piven and Richard A. Cloward, "The Weight of the Poor: A Strategy to End Poverty," *The Nation*, May 2, 1966. https://www.thenation.com/article/archive/weight-poor-strategy-end-poverty/

I always thought Cloward-Piven sounded like a crank strategy, but then I recalled seeing a photograph from when President Bill Clinton signed the Motor Voter Act, which loosened voting standards. Professors Cloward and Piven were there looking over President Clinton's shoulder as he signed the bill into law. Why? They helped craft the legislation that would take us one step closer to a purer democracy.[16]

Every US citizen has the right to vote. That's something generations have fought for and one of our sacred rights as Americans. At the same time, it needs to be easily understood who is legal to vote and who isn't so that everyone trusts the process. The more you water it down, as Motor Voter sought to do, the more confusing and convoluted the process can become. Fewer people will trust our government and institutions if the voting process begins to appear farcical. The system eventually collapses.

In the 2020 election, Democrats wanted to loosen voting rules and restrictions even beyond what the Motor Voter Act attempted to do a decade-and-a-half ago under President Clinton by allowing same-day voter registration and expanding access to absentee voting and voting by mail.[17] Cloward-Piven strategy, anyone?

Today, it's not hard to imagine the far left of the Democratic Party endorsing Cloward-Piven, now that even members of Congress openly call themselves socialists and push for extreme expansion of government programs, and more influence in virtually every aspect of our lives.

In fact, today, Frances Fox Piven is in her late eighties and is a hero of sorts to many of the new crop of far-left radicals. In May 2019, a *New York Times* profile on Piven set the scene, which sounds like Congresswoman Alexandria Ocasio-Cortez and Senator Bernie

---

16 "TWO COLUMBIANS HELP DRIVE HOME 'MOTOR VOTER' BILL," *Columbia University Record*, Vol. 19 No. 2, September 10, 1993. http://www.columbia .edu/cu/record/archives/vol19/vol19_iss2/record192.25

17 "Summary of Elections Provisions of H.R. 6800, The Heroes Act," Committee on House Administration (accessed Sept. 21, 2020). https://cha.house.gov/sites /democrats.cha.house.gov/files/HEROES%20Act%20election%20provision%20 2-pager.pdf

Sanders's dream setting—and a nightmare for the future of American liberty.

> *On a recent afternoon, a crowd had gathered in the auditorium of the People's Forum, a new event space in Midtown Manhattan. There was a picture of Lenin tacked on the wall, a shelf of books about Che Guevara and a cafe serving avocado toast. The young true believers and rickety old militants in attendance were learning history and strategy from Frances Fox Piven, a distinguished professor of political science at the Graduate Center of the City University of New York.*
>
> *"Since the 1970s, everything has gotten worse and worse," said Ms. Piven, who is now 86. There were very clear reasons for this. "Poor people," she said, had been "humiliated" and "shut up." Those in power now are "crazy."*
>
> *"But they're also evil," she continued. "And they will be evil because they are greedy." Only one thing would stop them, she said. "We have to be noisy, and difficult and ungovernable."*[18]

The characterization that "everything has gotten worse and worse" since the 1970s is patently absurd. I don't understand how one could come to that conclusion. We have this thing called the internet, which brings the world to us from the comfort of our homes. We have smartphones that make our lives so much easier. Airline deregulation made flights cheaper. Once a death sentence, AIDS is treatable today. Although things did get worse during the pandemic, in 2019, household income hit a record high[19] and the poverty rate fell to a record low.[20]

---

18 Alex Traub, "This 86-Year-Old Radical May Save (or Sink) the Democrats," *The New York Times*, May 10, 2019. https://www.nytimes.com/2019/05/10/nyregion/frances-fox-piven-democratic-socialism.html

19 Susan Heavey, "US median income hit record in 2019, Census data shows," *Reuters*, September 15, 2020. https://www.reuters.com/article/us-usa-economy-census-idUSKBN2662EY

20 Jeanna Smialek, Sarah Kliff, and Alan Rappeport, "US Poverty Hit a Record Low Before the Pandemic Recession," *The New York Times*, September 15, 2020. https://www.nytimes.com/2020/09/15/business/economy/poverty-record-low-prior-to-pandemic.html

A freer economy, lower taxes, and deregulation led to better lives for Americans. How can that possibly mean that things have "gotten worse and worse"? The only possible way to explain this is that in the mind of Piven, as well as the minds of Ocasio-Cortez and Sanders, the government didn't create this; a freer economy did.

If you're a socialist, it's a difficult pill to swallow. A freer economy has improved the lives of Americans and reduced poverty. Yes, we still have a safety net for those who need it, but incomes rising and poverty declining means that fewer people are relying on the government, which is an unacceptable outcome for today's Democratic Party.

How the Republic Will Be Lost, If We Don't Keep It

The United States isn't going to be defeated by a foreign power. We are only going to lose our republic if we reject the legacy left to us by our Founders. As long as we preserve those bedrock principles, they will be there for our kids and grandkids and future generations.

If we reject the legacy left by the Founders, then history will repeat itself. We know that when democracies go down the road of becoming mere redistribution centers, it will be the end of the America we know and love. And it won't be pretty. History isn't pretty.

What protects us in the end is the Constitution. It protects our system of government. It protects our checks and balances. As long as citizens are engaged and work to protect our constitutional structure, the Constitution will forever be the greatest bulwark against any person, group, or idea that threatens our system of government.

The threats to the republic are real. We're seeing the Left mobilize to change the rules of the game. After the death of Justice Ruth Bader Ginsburg in September 2020, weeks before the presidential election, Democrats began making a lot of threats. Senator Ed Markey of Massachusetts, who is the chief sponsor of the Green New Deal in the Senate, tweeted, "Mitch McConnell set the precedent. No Supreme Court vacancies filled in an election year. If he violates it, when Democrats control the Senate in the next Congress, we must abolish the filibuster and expand the Supreme Court."[21]

Ending the filibuster in the Senate, packing the Supreme Court, and making the District of Columbia and Puerto Rico states are ways to enhance the Democrats' power in Washington.[22] Each of these ideas have been floated by Democrats for years. They're not new threats. In the states, Democrats are trying to do away with the Electoral College.[23] Democrats don't like the rules, so they change them; constitutional norms be damned.

We are rapidly moving toward a parliamentary-style system with an upper and lower house based on simple majorities like the United Kingdom. A parliamentary system also wouldn't work in the United States. America is a continental-sized country. We have a society that is very multicultural. We're not a country based on more than five thousand years of common history and traditions.

In the parliamentary system, minority rights don't exist in any meaningful sense. Until recently, the Senate has generally respected minority rights such as the filibuster, but those rights have been chipped away by both parties out of political convenience.

Democrats are trending toward eliminating the filibuster for legislation, one of the last vestiges of minority rights in the Senate. Without the filibuster, the majority may pass whatever legislation they wish with a simple majority. That legislation will be whatever the hot topic of the day is as lawmakers respond to the whims of the mob. This means a government-run health care system like "Medicare for All," a federal takeover of elections, adding new states to the Union, and much more that will destroy the republic and

---

21   Ed Markey (@EdMarkey), Twitter, September 18, 2020. https://twitter.com/EdMarkey/status/1307122232850870274

22   Mike Allen, "Democrats' Armageddon option," *Axios*, September 20, 2020. https://www.axios.com/democrats-supreme-court-ginsburg-options-871f3e66-e7a4-4f40-9691-d20de1f4be61.html

23   Nathanial Rakich, "The Movement To Skip The Electoral College Is Picking Up Steam," *Five Thirty Eight*, May 29, 2019. https://fivethirtyeight.com/features/the-movement-to-skip-the-electoral-college-is-picking-up-steam/

leave our children and grandchildren facing more debt than they already are.

Some, like former President Obama, decry the filibuster as a "relic of Jim Crow" because it was used decades ago to block civil rights legislation.[24] Of course, those who tried to block those bills were on the wrong side of history, but the filibuster is ultimately a tool to build consensus in a chamber that has been called the "world's most deliberative body."

Adding the District of Columbia, Guam, the US Virgin Islands, and Puerto Rico to the Union would add two senators and new representatives for each new state. It's not about representation; it's about pure politics and power. Congress Democrats' incentive in creating new states is that it's likely that these new senators and representatives would be members of their party.

The frequent overtures to make the District of Columbia a state are disingenuous. Although license plates have "No Taxation Without Representation" on them, a throwback to the American colonists who didn't have representation in the British Parliament, residents of the District of Columbia do have representation.

Congress could just retrocede much of Washington, D.C. into Maryland and leave a much smaller federal district. There's precedent for this. Alexandria and Arlington were originally part of the District of Columbia. Congress allowed Virginia to retrocede the two cities in 1846.[25] It's a much easier solution, but it doesn't increase Democrats' power in Congress, so they don't have any interest.

Packing the Supreme Court, much like Franklin D. Roosevelt attempted in 1937 before the Supreme Court ended the *Lochner* era in *West Coast Hotel Co. v. Parrish*, could serve as a way for a Democratic administration to ensure that its agenda survives legal

---

24 Max Cohen, "Obama calls for end of 'Jim Crow relic' filibuster if it blocks voting reforms," *Politico*, July 30, 2020. https://www.politico.com/news/2020/07/30/barack-obama-john-lewis-filibuster-388600

25 Robert Brownell, "The Alexandria Retrocession of 1846," WETA *Boundary Stones Blog*, July 8, 2016. https://boundarystones.weta.org/2016/07/08/alexandria-retrocession-1846

challenges and aids Democrats as they force America into a direct democracy.

We don't know where Joe Biden stands on court packing. During the 2020 presidential campaign, he repeatedly refused to say.[26] Kamala Harris has expressed openness to the idea.[27] We do know that many Democrats were floating the idea long before Amy Coney Barrett was confirmed to the Supreme Court in October 2020. As *The Hill* noted, court packing had become a "litmus test" for the Left.[28]

Democrats have already tried to confuse Americans about what packing the Supreme Court means by saying that Republicans have packed the federal courts with conservative and constitutional justices and judges. Filling legitimate vacancies on federal courts isn't court packing. The Supreme Court has had nine justices since 1869.[29]

Democrats' problem is with the Constitution, which provides a president with the authority to fill vacancies on courts and other posts with advice and consent from the Senate.

Trying to change the definition of court packing is essentially trying to ignore the past. We know the history of Roosevelt's court packing scheme. He wanted to add one new justice for each one over the age of seventy, expanding the Court to a maximum of fifteen justices.

We also know that the scheme backfired on Roosevelt. Everyone knew what his intentions were. Writing in the *Washington Post* in 1937, Franklyn Waltman explained, "Mr. Roosevelt's real objective is to make the Supreme Court amenable to his will, either by forcing

26 Caitlyn Oprysko, "After dodging questions about court packing, Biden floats commission to study judicial reform," *Politico*, Oct. 22, 2020. https://www.politico .com/news/2020/10/22/joe-biden-court-packing-judicial-reforms-commission-431157

27 Burgess Everett and Marianne Levine, "2020 Dems warm to expanding Supreme Court," *Politico*, Mar. 18, 2019. https://www.politico.com/story /2019/03/18/2020-democrats-supreme-court-1223625

28 Jordain Carney and Rachel Frazin, "Court-packing becomes new litmus test on left," *The Hill*, Mar. 19, 2019. https://thehill.com/homenews/senate /434630-court-packing-becomes-new-litmus-test-on-left

29 "The Court as an Institution," Supreme Court of the United States website, accessed 10 Nov., 2020. https://www.supremecourt.gov/about/institution.aspx

from that tribunal some of those who have disagreed with him, or by permitting him to offset their votes with men of his own choosing."[30]

The Electoral College is also under attack. As it stands, sixteen states, representing 196 electoral votes, have entered the National Popular Vote Interstate Compact. Under this clever yet unconstitutional initiative, states that are part of the compact would award their electoral votes to the winner of the popular vote.[31]

Kamala Harris, ever one to kowtow to the Left, has spoken favorably about eliminating the Electoral College. No kidding, Harris said, "There's no question that the popular vote has been diminished in terms of making the final decision about who's the president of the United States and we need to deal with that, so I'm open to the discussion [of the Electoral College]."[32] The popular vote doesn't matter in presidential elections. It has never mattered. That's a feature of our constitutional structure, not a bug.

The Left has coalesced behind the National Popular Vote Interstate Compact. This compact, which takes effect when states representing 270 electoral votes have approved it, would put immense power into the hands of the most populated areas of the country.

There are more than three thousand counties in the United States. Looking back at the data from the 2016 presidential election, the hundred counties with the most votes cast in the presidential election represented 40.5 percent of the votes cast.[33] These counties include Los Angeles County; the five boroughs that make up New York City; King County, Washington (Seattle); and Cook County,

30 Gillian Brockell, "Dear Democrats, FDR's Court-packing Scheme Was a 'Humiliating' Defeat," *The Washington Post*, Mar. 12, 2019. https://www. washingtonpost.com/history/2019/03/12/dear-democrats-fdrs-court-packing-scheme-was-humiliating-defeat/

31 Norman R. Williams, "The Danger of the National Popular Vote Compact," *Harvard Law Review*, March 13, 2019. https://blog.harvardlawreview.org /the-danger-of-the-national-popular-vote-compact/

32 Rachel Frazin, "Kamala Harris says she is open to abolishing the electoral college," *The Hill*, Mar. 20, 2019. https://thehill.com/homenews /campaign/434870-kamala-harris-says-she-is-open-to-abolishing-electoral-college

33 These figures are based on a review of county-by-county data available through Dave Leip's Atlas of US Presidential Elections. Accessed Aug. 8, 2020. https:// uselectionatlas.org/

Illinois (Chicago). Good luck seeing a presidential candidate campaign in Colorado or Ohio ever again.

As of the 2020 election, the National Popular Vote Interstate Compact is nearly 75 percent of its goal of 270 electoral votes.

The Constitution, already in peril, would become a meaningless document. The republic would effectively end. We may someday look back at this time as the good old days of institutional stability. The Left is trying to overload and crash the system that gives us that stability.

We can't expect someone else to step up and protect the Constitution. As Jonah Goldberg writes, "[T]he Constitution isn't magic. Its power derives from the power we invest in it."[34] We all have to be involved in the system. This is one of the reasons I love studying history. It's so important to put the United States and what it stands for in the proper historical context. We also must identify the threats and begin to engage our fellow citizens.

---

34   Jonah Goldberg, "An American Parliamentary System Won't Fix Our Problems," *National Review*, November 2, 2018. https://www.nationalreview.com/2018/11/us-politics-polarized-parliamentary-system-will-not-fix/

CHAPTER 2

When I Taught History

M y experience shaped my worldview. My family is the classic-
story of the American dream. My ancestors were poor Czech
immigrants who settled at the foot of the steel mills in Cleveland.
The experiences of my family gave me an understanding of what
it means to those who are truly seeking to make the words of the
Declaration of Independence—"life, liberty, and the pursuit of happiness"—a reality.

Growing up, I saw how people in my community were impacted
because of an evolving global economy. Many were struggling to
afford health care and college. It was obvious to me as a young kid
when I would go to downtown Cleveland and drive through some
of the old neighborhoods that many in the black community were
caught in cycles of intergenerational poverty. I wondered how they
could best break the cycle and realize the American dream.

I grew up in a mixed political community and was exposed to the
influence of blue-collar Democrats and hardcore Republicans. I saw
firsthand which policies helped and which held people back from
achieving their version of the American dream.

We all start at different places in life, where some might have
advantages since birth, and some might have to struggle harder.

Luckily, I didn't have to struggle, but that was only thanks to my parents' sacrifices and those in our family who came before them.

Dad always told some pretty horrible stories about his upbringing. He grew up in a poor Czech neighborhood at the base of Cleveland's Republic Steel, where he was raised in an abusive household. He came of age around old-school men, who drank, smoked, and fought a lot. Physical abuse surrounded him, out on the street or at home. This was his community normal.

My father associated the city with all the hardships of his childhood. He spent his life striving to escape it. Meanwhile, I was lucky enough to grow up in the suburbs, and always wanted to move closer to the action in the city. Dad would always ask me, "Why?" After growing up on the wrong side of the tracks where coal smoke would settle, Dad didn't understand why I would want to leave the safety and comfort of the suburbs.

Despite so many obstacles, Dad ended up going to college and marrying Mom. When he later attended dental school, he also worked at a tool shop that made airplane landing gear. He worked in the daytime and went to school at night. Thanks to his hard work, and unlike his own upbringing, I got to grow up in a comfortable suburb.

In my family, I was constantly surrounded by my great uncles and other relatives who would tell tales about settling in Cleveland, fighting in World War II, and other hardships their generation experienced that mine didn't. I would hear about the pioneers who first arrived in the area. My mother's side of the family had been in the United States for some time, but Dad's side was all blue-collar Czech immigrants.

Their story told me so much about this country. Their struggles taught me about how special this place is that I call home. This country has been very good to me, and I've been blessed to have the opportunity to live the American Dream.

When I graduated college, I cycled through a variety of jobs that I found boring and wasn't particularly skilled at. I was going to graduate school but needed a job to pay the bills. One night I came up with the genius idea that I might make a decent high school teacher.

Ironically, I found a job teaching history and government classes at a school in Washington, D.C. It still ranks as one of my favorite jobs. A few weeks before school started, I was given the textbook, and it was awful. You couldn't have done a better job of making American history boring and irrelevant.

I started reflecting on how I learned history. My favorite teacher at Walsh Jesuit High School in Cuyahoga Falls, Ohio was Father Jim Prehn. He had a passion for understanding the tides of history and how they made the world we live in today. He made history not an abstract part of the past, but the base for the present world.

I called Father Prehn, and he gave me some great advice: Don't teach specific subjects using large themes. Start small in order to lead students to considering larger ideas. It was great advice. To accomplish what he suggested, I first flipped the script and started to teach the present day, moving backward through history. In other words, we would end at Jamestown, not start. It was definitely novel.

The first half of the year was themed "Who are Americans?" and the second half of the year was "How did we get this way?" I taught the textbook, but also supplemented it with reading from conservative and libertarian authors, along with socialist historian Howard Zinn's *A People's History of the United States*. Right, left, and center.

The first assignment to my new students was to interview a veteran to make history real. Students interviewed family members about historical events like the President John F. Kennedy assassination and the Great Depression. My goal was to bring history alive and help them understand that they are part of an incredible tradition.

One major theme that I learned from Father Prehn was that history is a study between the balance of liberty and security. That concept has always stuck with me. The more liberty you have, the less security you have. I decided in high school that I would always err on the side of liberty.

I enjoyed the year and hope I was able to share my love for the study of history with my students. And I hope it gave them a better appreciation of why their country was worthy of their pride.

We Need to Know and Understand America's History—All of It

I consider myself an amateur student of history, and one thing I've learned is that it's always dangerous when you judge a man or woman outside of their time. Realize this: Our Founding Fathers *Were. Not. Perfect.* America's history *Is. Not. Perfect.*

Full stop.

Slavery was our country's original sin. It should never be forgotten. What happened to the Native Americans can only be described as genocide. It's a tragic history that will and should always remain with us. It happened and it's shameful.

It's important to keep perspective that all countries, in their history, have atrocities. Russia has the decossackization, the Great Purge, the Holodomor, and many others under Soviet rule. Germany has the Holocaust and genocide of Poles. China has the Great Leap Forward and famine. Japan has the rape of Nanking. Belgium has the genocide in the Congo. Turkey has the Armenian genocide. France has the French revolution. Pointing out these tragedies in our countries doesn't mean that we shouldn't understand our history, but we aren't unique in having stains on our past.

We could spend an endless amount of time going decade by decade through American history and finding groups and individuals who were treated unbelievably poorly. All we can do is strive to be better.

I've always found it interesting that when we teach history in our schools, after the Civil War, we don't really pick up again until World War I. I think it's largely due to the fact that we're embarrassed to talk about Jim Crow in the South. We had a whole period—and still do this today—where we were not living up to our nation's ideals. But that's what America and her history has always been—a constant challenge to live up to and improve the values of liberty and justice we hold dear.

Looking back to the American Revolution, it's important to remember that the first abolitionist organization was founded in 1775 in Philadelphia.[1] Founding Fathers like Thomas Paine, Benjamin Franklin, and Benjamin Rush were abolitionists.

In fact, Paine strongly condemned slavery as a "wicked practice" and that governments should "punish those who hold [Africans] in slavery."[2] Franklin was elected president of the Pennsylvania Abolition Society in 1787.[3] In 1790, Franklin petitioned Congress to abolish slavery.[4] Rush served as secretary of the Pennsylvania Abolition Society.[5]

When we start to erase history of any era in its totality, we are also erasing those people.

When you start erasing the Founding Fathers from history, any of them, you're also doing away with Crispus Attucks, who was one of five people killed by British soldiers outside the Old State House in Boston in 1770. That was the Boston Massacre. The first man to die in the American Revolution was a man of African and Native American ancestry who had escaped slavery.[6] Why Attucks was at the Old State House isn't known, but we do know that he was angry at British soldiers, who sought work to supplement their wages, because they were taking away job opportunities.[7]

The "woke" mobs and ANTIFA extremists got so out-of-control during the 2020 riots that swept the country nationwide that they

---

1   "First American abolition society founded in Philadelphia," history.com, April 13, 2020.   https://www.history.com/this-day-in-history/first-american-abolition-society-founded-in-philadelphia

2   Moncure Daniel Conway, ed. "The Writings of Thomas Paine," Online Library of Liberty, accessed Aug. 10, 2020. https://oll.libertyfund.org/titles/paine-the-writings-of-thomas-paine-vol-i-1774-1779

3   "Officers, members and supporters of the Pennsylvania Abolition Society," Pennsylvania Abolition Society, accessed Sept. 21, 2020 http://www.americanabolitionists.com/pennsylvania-abolition-society.html

4   "Benjamin Franklin's Anti-Slavery Petitions to Congress," National Archives, August 12, 2019. https://www.archives.gov/legislative/features/franklin

5   Pennsylvania Abolition Society, Op. cit.

6   "Who was Crispus Attucks?" Crispus Attucks Museum, accessed Sept. 21, 2020. http://www.crispusattucksmuseum.org/crispus-attuck/

7   Patrick J. Kiger, "8 Things We Know About Crispus Attucks," history.com, February 11, 2020. https://www.history.com/news/crispus-attucks-american-revolution-boston-massacre

attempted to remove the Lincoln Emancipation statue in our nation's capital. Many wanted it taken down.[8] This statue honors President Abraham Lincoln for liberating more than three million souls from the horrible clutches of slavery. Known as the Emancipation Memorial, the statue was funded by emancipated slaves. The unveiling ceremony's keynote speaker in 1876 was abolitionist and former slave Frederick Douglass, who put history in its context:

> *Though he loved Caesar less than Rome, though the Union was more to him than our freedom or our future, under his wise and beneficent rule we saw ourselves gradually lifted from the depths of slavery to the heights of liberty and manhood; under his wise and beneficent rule… under his rule we saw for the first time the law enforced against the foreign slave-trade, and the first slavetrader hanged like any other pirate or murderer; under his rule, assisted by the greatest captain of our age, and his inspiration, we saw the Confederate States, based upon the idea that our race must be slaves, and slaves forever, battered to pieces and scattered to the four winds; under his rule, and in the fullness of time, we saw Abraham Lincoln, after giving the slaveholders three months' grace in which to save their hateful slave system, penning the immortal paper, which, though special in its language, was general in its principles and effect, making slavery forever impossible in the United States. Though we waited long, we saw all this and more.[9]*

This is the history these woke Leftists want erased.

History is exceedingly complicated. That's why it needs to be studied. I had an ancestor who fought to preserve the Union during the Civil War. I can't run around pretending that I somehow own his glory and have some measure of moral superiority. What your past looks like depends on where you live in this country. It's important

---

8   Aishvarya Kavi, "Activists Push for Removal of Statue of Freed Slave Kneeling Before Lincoln," *The New York Times*, June 27, 2020. https://www.nytimes.com /2020/06/27/us/politics/lincoln-slave-statue-emancipation.html

9   Frederick Douglass, "Oration by Frederick Douglass Delivered on the Occasion of the Unveiling of the Freedmen's Monument, April 14, 1876," Smithsonian, accessed Sept. 21, 2020. https://transcription.si.edu/project/12955

that we learn about this national history that belongs to all of us, including the tragic parts. There are so many lessons that need to be learned there. Those lessons give us an opportunity to correct the future.

At the same time, this is an incredible country. The Founders decided, for the first time since the ancient Greeks, to govern themselves. In addition to the concept of self-government, another major component of my definition of American exceptionalism—what makes us different from other countries—is the notion that you are born with your rights. They are not granted to you from your government.

These American ideals that the Founders laid down, we have been striving to live up to for almost 250 years. The minute you start ripping up history without an appreciation for the entire breadth of it is when you fail to learn from it. If we begin to erase our history, the good and the bad, there is no way we're going to be able to understand what this country is or what we stand for. Then we become what, exactly? I don't know. I would be afraid to know.

Our history is violent. It's bloody. It's something that much of, for any American living in any generation, would be hard to stomach. Our history is also wonderful. There are so many stories of unbelievable courage and historic heroics. Every generation has its bad actors, but this is a country that has infinitely more heroes than villains. We need to understand our failures, but also celebrate victories and the opportunities they produced. I look forward to a future of the United States that's not defined by our past. We are defined by our dreams, not our failures.

If we live up to our nation's founding principles, this gives me hope for liberty. If we fail to live up to them and begin to devolve into mob rule, where all rights are subject to the plenary power of the legislature, or the way of China, where individual liberty is violently suppressed, freedom could vanish from the planet.

If that happened, it might be another thousand years before you have a re-emergence of liberty in some place. Like America, that emergence would be an incredibly violent birth. If we lose our commitment to liberty, which in large part comes through a commitment to understanding our history—our entire history—there are no guideposts for us going forward.

If we lose this, the world loses hope.

The American Experiment Has Been Glorious

History is both ugly and beautiful, filled with heroes and villains. Obviously, the history of human beings is going to be complex. Again, as Americans, we should strive to hold up the good and learn from the bad in the interest of never repeating it. The past is also our common heritage. It's what drives progress.

We have lost a sense of balance when we teach our children about American history. There may have been a time when we whitewashed history to make it one positive vision, but we've over-corrected it now. It seems that the younger generations are only being taught the Howard Zinn version, that America is fundamentally flawed and has a history to be ashamed of. This is a mistake. Our country has an incredible story.

America's economic innovation has been a beacon for the world, where our free market system has created a superior quality of life for more people than any other country in history. Our scientists and innovators have been second to none—from Thomas Edison inventing the light bulb to Jonas Salk eradicating polio to Steve Jobs giving Apple to the world.

America's unique arts revolutionized the globe—and you can say this looking at music alone. Jazz, country, the blues, and hip-hop all originated in the United States. All mixed together, America gave the world rock n' roll, a genre that would dominate the globe decades after Chuck Berry duck walked, Little Richard wailed, and Elvis Presley shook his hips. None of our great music would have been possible without our unique melting pot.

We are the most successful multi-ethnic country in world history. Throughout our country's history, immigrants from all over the world have come to America to seek a clean slate. They've come here for economic opportunities for themselves and their families, religious liberty, and more political freedom.

It's a lot easier to be a small homogenous country where trust is higher across society. But America has never taken the easiest path. We are an experiment, governed out of a compact that limits the size and scope of government, protects our cherished freedoms, and leaves us to govern ourselves.

We should be proud to be patriots. We are an aspirational nation, as defined in the Declaration and the Constitution. We have often failed to live up to those aspirations, but we remain an experiment in the works. In the musical *1776*, Ben Franklin says, "We've spawned a new race here. . . . Rougher, simpler; more violent, more enterprising; less refined."[10]

We are still those things, but we are a continuing work in progress. The American story continues. It has been told in the past and will continue to unfold in the future through the millions of different individual experiences. Including mine.

America Really Is the Land of Opportunity

I enjoyed growing up in a solid, tight-knit community in Cleveland. When I see people out in Washington, D.C. and elsewhere in my travels wearing a Cleveland Browns hat, we hug. This exercise is *really* annoying to my wife. I watched the last game of the NBA Finals at the Little Bar in Cleveland when the Cavaliers won the 2016 NBA Championship. I hugged and celebrated until almost dawn with complete strangers. I experienced what America would be like without racial issues. Everyone was peaceful. We were all united. We had a common experience.

When I went to college, I wanted to do something to preserve that for others and expand it. I'm fully aware that there are other families in the United States who didn't have the same opportunities I did. All of us have different backgrounds and experiences in life

---

10   Jack Warner, et al. *1776*, Columbia TriStar Home Entertainment, 2002.

that shape our worldview. But I would like everyone to have those same opportunities. That's the entire point of my work.

I didn't grow up in a political family at all. I have to thank my sister for getting me interested in politics and current events as a young kid. I didn't get put in timeout when I got in trouble; my sister punished me by making me read George Will columns. I didn't like being punished, but those columns were thought-provoking and helped me understand why the Founders' vision of limited government needed to be protected.

But when I study issues today, my worldview is informed by my family's experience. When I study history and economics, I lead not with political ideology, but with what works. What I have personally seen work. What my family has seen work.

I remember one night having a few beers with an old high school friend who stressed that growing up where we did and how we did, we were lucky. We knew people in our families, only a generation before, whose upbringing was really rough, but we also got to interact with kids in our communities who were from wealthy families.

Our families' experience shaped ours and gave us perspective. We were a step away from the factory floor, but we were both lucky we had the opportunity to attend a Catholic high school where we received a great education. We met interesting people attending that school that we likely wouldn't have crossed paths with otherwise.

This sense of community and the cooperation of people from differing socio-economic statuses was part of what made Americans different from Europeans. In Europe, social class was something inherited and rigged, but in America, our ambitions were our only limitation.

In Charles Murray's *Coming Apart*, he details the decay of our social institutions, such as religious groups or civic associations, which allowed people from all walks of life to share in the same American experience. This divergence has created two distinct social classes, what we might call "coastal elites" and "average Americans," and might help to explain the growing disconnect between Washington and the rest of the country.

The COVID-19 pandemic has only exacerbated this divide. Economic hardship was most felt by those who could not simply plug in a computer, join a Zoom meeting, and work from home. Third places, which constitute the locations outside of the home or workplace where people gather, are permanently disappearing and with them, their essential contributions to our shared American culture.

To anyone reading this believing some of the hopes I have for myself and my fellow countrymen are easy to subscribe to as a white guy in the suburbs, my aspiration is that all families have the same opportunities. I can't change the past, but we can all be part of building a strong country in the future. We all want a safe home and community, good schools to send our children, and economic opportunities.

I don't believe and advocate my principles just because they are good for my family, but because they are good for everyone. Our system has proven to be the best system at generating prosperity and giving space for "life, liberty, and the pursuit of happiness." Our country's prosperity is no accident. It's precisely our founding values that paved the way for our prosperity. They outline the keys to our culture of liberty and rule of law to our success.

My own experience has informed my worldview from a young age. In today's world, where we have so many unforeseen problems—like global pandemics—it is still the lessons I have learned from my own unique journey in this country that give me hope for the future.

I'm just one of millions of Americans who have different stories and yet have come to similar conclusions that only deepen their love of country. It's easy to love. Our history has been one of fighting for and keeping our freedom, however imperfect. This hasn't been true for many other countries.

CHAPTER 3

I Was Eleven When I Learned Socialism Doesn't Work

M y first experience with socialism came when I was a kid. It was 1991, my parents had grounded me, and I had been sent upstairs to clean my room. I don't even remember what I did wrong. I do remember my Dad, who was pretty angry with me at the time, coming into my room carrying a black and white TV. It was an old television with bunny ears that made a loud click when you changed the channel with the dial. Some of you my age or older probably remember those. He set the old television up on top of my dresser, plugged it in, and turned it on.

It was live coverage of the fall of the Berlin Wall. I was curious, but I began to soak it all in. What was happening? Who were all these people? What were they smashing with those hammers? What did all that graffiti mean? There was dancing and cheering everywhere.

The Berlin Wall created a physical barrier between East Germany and West Germany. It was a way to close off East Germany from western influence. With Soviet dictator Nikita Khrushchev pulling the strings behind the scenes, construction of the wall began in August 1961. It separated families, generally cut off commerce, and it highlighted the stark differences between the two nations divided by nearly one hundred miles of concrete and ideology.[1]

Although the exact number is in dispute, at least 140 people were killed trying to cross the Berlin Wall.[2] Most were killed by guards patrolling the wall or from other circumstances while trying to evade patrols. Guards were given express permission to kill those attempting to cross. The order read: "Do not hesitate to use your firearm, not even when the border is breached in the company of women and children, which is a tactic the traitors have often used."[3]

Musicians like David Bowie[4] and Bruce Springsteen played concerts in front of the Berlin Wall. Both are credited for roles in the fall of the wall and reunification of Germany.[5] Politicians like John F. Kennedy and Margaret Thatcher[6] spoke against what the wall represented. In June 1987, roughly two years before the fall of the wall, Ronald Reagan made a plea for freedom in East Germany.

We welcome change and openness; for we believe that freedom and security go together, that the advance of human liberty can only strengthen the cause of world peace. There is one sign the Soviets can make that would be unmistakable, that would advance dramatically the cause of freedom and peace. General Secretary Gorbachev, if you seek peace, if you seek prosperity for the Soviet Union and eastern Europe, if you seek

1 Nate Barksdale, "How long was the Berlin Wall," history.com, Nov 5, 2014. https://www.history.com/news/how-long-was-the-berlin-wall

2 "Victims of the Wall," Berlin.de, accessed July 25, 2020. https://www.berlin.de/mauer/en/history/victims-of-the-wall/

3 "E German 'licence to kill' found," BBC, August 12, 2007. http://news.bbc.co.uk/2/hi/europe/6943093.stm

4 Blake Stilwell, "This is how David Bowie helped bring down the Berlin Wall," wearethemighty.com, August 20, 2018. https://www.wearethemighty.com/music/david-bowie-berlin-wall

5 Stephen Evans, "How Bruce Springsteen rocked the Berlin Wall," BBC, October 21, 2014. https://www.bbc.com/culture/article/20130626-how-springsteen-rocked-the-wall

6 John Tagliabue, "Mrs. Thatcher's Visit to the Berlin Wall," *The New York Times*, October 30, 1982. https://www.nytimes.com/1982/10/30/world/mrs-thatcher-visits-the-berlin-wall.html

liberalization, come here to this gate. Mr. Gorbachev, open this gate. Mr. Gorbachev, tear down this Wall![7]

I had never witnessed anything like it before. Most in America of my generation had not. I watched entire sections of the Berlin Wall be torn down in a peaceful quest for freedom. People were crying tears of joy, hugging, and celebrating. Dad told me not to change the channel. He wanted me to watch history unfold before my eyes. He couldn't have been more right.

The Dreariness of Socialism

The images on my screen seemed so foreign to a kid like me. Eastern Europe was a distant place where my family came from a long, long time ago. It was unlike anything I had ever seen or experienced growing up in Cleveland. Obviously, people were happy as they celebrated bringing down this physical symbol of oppression. Yet, I couldn't shake my focus from the fact that what they were tearing down was so dark and cold.

I had seen old videos of communist orphanages in Romania, with so many poor souls standing in long lines, but perhaps what stuck with me most was how gray everything was. There were children in these videos who had never known a loving touch. I couldn't fathom living so drearily. After all, I was an American kid growing up in the 1990s. But watching the Berlin Wall fall at a young age, I began to have a curiosity about what socialism is.

I will always be grateful to Dad for making me watch. That moment was a big part of what sparked my interest in politics and history. I'm in my early forties now, so I'm younger than the Baby Boomers, but slightly north of Millennials. For many younger Americans today, the COVID-19 crisis and the nationwide protests will be a defining

---

7   Peter Robinson, "Tear Down This Wall: How Top Advisers Opposed Reagan's Challenge to Gorbachev—But Lost," *National Archives Prologue Magazine*, Vol. 39, No. 2, Summer 2007. https://www.archives.gov/publications/prologue/2007/summer /berlin.html

moment. Before that, the terrorist attacks on September 11, 2001 that resulted in the destruction of the Twin Towers had a similar impact for many in their twenties and thirties today. I obviously went through that horrific time too.

But in recent years I have come to the conclusion that being a certain age and having lived through all of these events gives one a unique perspective, one that is significantly different than just experiencing one of these historic moments.

For example, if you are young enough to only recall September 11 and not the fall of the Berlin Wall—someone who came of age after the Cold War had ended—you are much less likely to understand socialism and how intrinsically evil it is. It's one thing to be told that these old communist regimes were rotten. It's quite another to witness it, as I did from the comfort of my childhood bedroom.

It's hard to fathom how bad socialism is without context. The Cold War gave Americans of a certain age an understanding of the true nature of that dangerous collectivist ideology most young people simply haven't been able to experience. When young Americans today see the havoc caused by Venezuela's socialist government, I think they dismiss it as just poverty in a backwards country that can never be the United States. Many don't comprehend that there was an intentional economic system that caused their plight. They don't see the hunger, chaos, and human rights abuses, or, to the degree that they are aware of these horrors, don't necessarily attribute them to socialism, per se.

Most people don't realize that Venezuela was once a rich country, the wealthiest in South America,[8] with the world's largest proven oil reserves.[9] It was also a popular vacation destination. Socialism has nearly destroyed the country. Only in recent years, there were

---

8   Brian Clark, "Venezuela was once the wealthiest country in South America— Here's how it descended into turmoil," CNBC, March 1, 2019. https://www.cnbc .com/2019/03/01/venezuela-juan-guaido-nicolas-maduro-south-america.html

9   Steven John, "9 mind-blowing facts about Venezuela's economy," *Business Insider*, March 23, 2019. https://markets.businessinsider.com/news/stocks /venezuela-economy-facts-2019-5-1028225117

reports of toilet paper shortages[10] and people eating pets[11] and rats so they wouldn't starve.[12] Venezuela has also faced a dire health care emergency[13] and an energy crisis.[14]

Back in August 2011, Senator Bernie Sanders republished an editorial from a Vermont-based newspaper in which the editorial board criticized America and claimed that "the American dream is more apt to be realized in South America, in places such as Ecuador, Venezuela and Argentina, where incomes are actually more equal today than they are in the land of Horatio Alger."[15] No kidding, this editorial board had the audacity to rhetorically ask, "Who's the banana republic now?"

In 2019, I worked with Project Arizona to interview some young people who shared their stories about where they're from and how they discovered liberty. Project Arizona is an amazing organization that brings young people from other countries to the United States to engage in different volunteer opportunities and continue to develop their leadership skills.

One of the people I interviewed from Project Arizona was Jorge Andrés Galicia Rodríguez, who is from Venezuela. The picture that

---

10 Mike Bird, "An economist just explained Venezuela's chronic shortage of toilet paper," *Business Insider*, November 15, 2015. https://www.businessinsider.com /why-venezuela-is-running-out-of-toilet-paper-2015-11

11 Yesman Utrera, "Pets on the Menu as Venezuelans Starve," *Daily Beast*, November 4, 2017. https://www.thedailybeast.com/zoo-animals-on-the-menu-as-venezuelans-starve

12 Alastair Tancred, "Zoos are forced to slaughter animals to feed others in Venezuela, where bone-thin pumas have become the face of the crisis," *Daily Mail*, March 1, 2018. https://www.dailymail.co.uk/news/article-5449023/Venezuelans-eat-rats-dogs-economy-nosedives.html

13 Melody Schreiber, "Researchers Are Surprised By The Magnitude Of Venezuela's Health Crisis," National Public Radio, April 5, 2019. https://www.npr.org/sections/goatsandsoda/2019/04/05/709969632/researchers-are-surprised-by-the-magnitude-of-venezuelas-health-crisis

14 Sam Meredith, "'The electric war': Major power failure in Venezuela leaves much of the country in the dark," CNBC, March 8, 2019. https://www.cnbc.com/2019/03/08 /venezuela-crisis-power-failure-leaves-much-of-the-country-in-the-dark.html

15 Valley News Editorial Board, "Close The Gaps: Disparities That Threaten America," *Valley News*, August 5, 2011. Republished by Senator Bernie Sanders, https://www.sanders.senate.gov/newsroom/must-read/close-the-gaps-disparities-that-threaten-america

Jorge painted of the devastation shows how dangerous socialism really is.

> *The situation right now in Venezuela is really awful. I think we have lost many of the good things that you have here in North America. And I'm talking about the basic things. For example, in my house there has been like 20 or 21 days without any kind of water supply. So if you go to your pipe or try to open, you will have like nothing, right. No electricity. Lines to get food. You have to be dependent on government to try to do your living and to try to survive. I mean, it's a tragedy. For young people like me, it's really depressing because you don't get to plan, you don't get to think about the big things—like I want to study a career, I want to be someone, I want to accomplish this in life, I want to have my own house, I want to have my own family—because you're no longer an individual but more like an asset of the state, of the totalitarian state.*[16]

Based on my life's experience, as well as the life experiences of people like Jorge, I unquestionably see socialism as a failed and discredited form of government. This might not be the case with younger generations, but it's also true they can't authentically embrace an ideology if they don't really know what it is.

When some of today's American politicians chat up "socialism" in a positive way and polls show young people warming to that message, I don't think they connect that word with a country like Venezuela. Or China. Or Cuba. Or the old Soviet Union. Or Poland.

Lessons from Poland

I decided to attend grad school to study economics, and my childhood curiosity about the other side of the Iron Curtain took me to Eastern Europe. I attended Jagiellonian University in Krakow in

---

16   Adam Brandon, "The Freedom Files with Adam Brandon Ep 45: Jorge Andrés Galicia Rodríguez," *FreedomWorks*, June 12, 2019. https://www.freedomworks .org/content/ep-45-freedom-files-adam-brandon-jorge-andre%CC%81s-galicia-rodri%CC%81guez

2000 to study economics at the master's level. A little over a decade removed from the fall of the Soviet Union, the situation was still pretty raw there. Old cars lined the streets. People were still struggling. That dreariness that had resonated with me so much as a kid when the Berlin Wall came down still haunted Poland at that time.

Communism might have been over, but people were still suffering from the damage done. Thanks to my stay there almost two decades ago, I have had the educational benefit of seeing the stark difference between socialism and freedom, both as a child, on my TV screen, and as an adult, up close.

I remember my girlfriend at that time would get a few pieces of clothing a year. That's it. Most American women, and most men for that matter, can't fathom this. I remember commenting to her that everything she wore was a basic color. I asked, "Don't you want to buy something pink?" She explained to me that every piece of clothing has to go with everything else, because you only get one.

We too often take for granted the freedoms and particularly the civil liberties we enjoy in America. Under Poland's communist regime, the government kept secret files on everyone. I asked my girlfriend then if she and her family had ever looked at each other's files. I quizzed her, "Aren't you curious what the Ministry of Public Security was saying about you?" She said they decided as a family not to look. They knew it would be people talking about other people in the family and would rather not know. They just let it all go.

She came from a good family, but they had all been forced to live in a dwelling that was built in the 1930s and never had any major renovations. The entire family lived in only a couple of rooms. They didn't have a lot of hot water. In the wintertime, they had this little device that heated the water, which gave you just enough for rinsing your face and backside, but you couldn't take a full shower. There simply wasn't enough water for a proper cleaning. I also remember they had one coal stove that was used to heat the entire house. Central heating and air would have been a pipe dream. They stole electricity off the power line.

Remember, this was all happening in the *year 2000!* Not 1956 or even 1986. This was happening in Y2K. This was the legacy of socialism. There were constant reminders of the past and how things used to be done in Poland. Poland had a similar history to the rest of Western Europe. If the Iron Curtain had been on the right side of Poland, not the left side, they would've had the same living standards as Germany, Italy, and the United Kingdom.

When I had to pay my bills in Krakow, I would have to go to their post office, stand in line with everyone and then pay the bill in cash. I first had to stand in a line so they could stamp a piece of paper, and then go to another line to actually pay the bill. It was all so tedious. It was very time consuming. I had to take a couple days a month to take care of these basic things. It was absurd. Still, it was an improvement for Poles over how they had lived before. I could only imagine how bad things were in 1989.

I would hear stories from my girlfriend's family about them having no meat for months. Think about it: Americans, then and now, can get a burger for next to nothing nearly anytime they like. But imagine if you couldn't? Imagine if this was a major chore or not even attainable at all?

Returning to Poland in 2018

When I returned to Poland in 2018, it had all changed. The cars on the streets were new. Buildings were being redone. The ugly, grey concrete coatings had been taken down to show the beautiful, pre-communist brick and wood facades. The clothes were bright. There were people smiling. The restaurants were full. People were optimistic.

I even had the best gin and tonic of my life! It was almost as though the years 1948 to 1989 didn't happen. It had taken fifteen years of freedom to get to this better place. The difference from the last time I had been in the country was stark. The people, working in a free market, solved Poland's ills very quickly.

There is a generation of young Poles today who have zero recollection of communism. They have no memory of the meat shortages and food rationing that caused demonstrations.[17] To them, it was just this funny or odd thing in their past. Their parents, and grand-parents' tales about what they endured likely sound like our parents' stories about walking miles to school in the snow. Unfortunately, these stories become more of a punch line than lessons to be learned.

For so many of today's Polish kids and young adults, socialism was a long time ago, even though most of them have relatives who lived under that system. If young Poles can't understand, imagine how dis-tant socialism seems for young Americans.

Young people today, when they say "socialism"—and maybe I'm being too soft on them, but I don't think so—simply don't have a historical reference point for what it really means. They assume that with some new socialism in America, they will have all the blessings and comforts of consumer capitalism, but the rich will pay for every-one to have everything they need.

They think that the iPhones, cheeseburgers, and reality TV shows they have at their fingertips today will also be available under socialism; only someone else will pay for them. Poles of any age as late as 2000 could tell them that is not how socialism really works.

Today's liberal politicians try to sell free universal health care, education, housing, basic income, and everything else you can imag-ine, without ever explaining how these programs will be paid for. This is quite literally Kamala Harris's agenda if she ever becomes president.[18] Of course, this sounds good to young people and others. But there does exist this thing called "math."

Self-described socialist and New York Congresswoman Alexandria Ocasio-Cortez's $94 trillion "Green New Deal" is a

---

17   Michael Dobbs, "Poland Announces Near-Total Rationing of Food," *The New York Times*, April 15, 1981. https://www.washingtonpost.com/archive/politics/1981/04/15/poland-announces-near-total-rationing-of-food/dd054608-dab0-40fb-81b1-7a9695f59490/

18   Meera Jaggannathan, Jacob Passy, and Jillian Berman, "Kamala Harris on student-loan forgiveness, Medicare, universal basic income, credit scores—and a tax on trading stocks," *MarketWatch*, Aug. 16, 2020. https://www.marketwatch.com/story/kamala-harris-on-student-loan-forgiveness-medicare-universal-basic-income-credit-scores-and-a-tax-on-trading-stocks-2020-08-12

smorgasbord of every big government program you can think of.[19] Most of the Democrats who ran for president in 2020 had nothing but praise for this plan. Like court packing, the Green New Deal has become something of a litmus test for many Democrats, particularly with the party's hard left base.

Joe Biden may not support the Green New Deal, but one radical environmental activist called Biden's plan "a damn good start."[20] Biden plans to pull America back into the costly Paris Agreement and push burdensome environmental regulations.[21] Kamala Harris was a cosponsor of the Green New Deal.

Yet, a *conservative* estimate puts the cost of Ocasio-Cortez's supposed "deal" at $93 trillion.[22] Think about that. America's Gross Domestic Product is about $20 trillion. Our national debt is currently higher than our GDP, approaching $30 trillion. The estimated GDP of *every nation on the planet* in 2019 was $87.7 trillion.[23]

How does any adult honestly believe such a program could be paid for? And yet in Washington and beyond, there are plenty of adults peddling socialist fantasies right now and young people who honestly don't know better are buying what they're selling.

Conservatives and libertarians believe in freedom over totalitarianism. Free markets have been the answer to fixing these old communist countries and it's still the bulwark against any new danger that we might ever go down this oppressive path in our own country.

Liberty works. Every time. It's up to us to use it.

---

19 Elizabeth Harrington, "Study: New Green Deal would cost up to $94 trillion," *The Washington Free Beacon*, Feb. 25, 2019. https://freebeacon.com/issues /study-green-new-deal-would-cost-up-to-94-trillion/

20 David Roberts, "What Joe Biden was trying to say about the New Green Deal," *Vox*, updated Oct. 7, 2020. https://www.vox.com/energy-and-environment/21498236 /joe-biden-green-new-deal-debate

21 Umair Irfan, "How Joe Biden plans to use executive orders to fight climate change," *Vox*, Nov. 9, 2020. https://www.vox.com/21549521/joe-biden-transition-climate-change-senate-runoff

22 Douglas Holtz-Eakin, et al. "The Green New Deal: Scope, Scale, and Implications," *American Action Forum*, February 25, 2019. https://www.americanactionforum.org /research/the-green-new-deal-scope-scale-and-implications/

23 "GDP (current US $)," The World Bank, accessed Nov. 12, 2020. https://data. worldbank.org/indicator/NY.GDP.MKTP.CD

Why the Left Wants to Change America

The Left believes the United States would be rich no matter what. They seem to believe that national prosperity is inevitable and changes that are made are simple addition and subtraction, the taking from some and redistributing to others that will have no impact on anyone. They don't understand that the prosperity we've seen as a nation is a direct result of our constitutional structure and economic system.

Look at Latin America. These countries are probably more resource-rich than the United States. Latin America has gold, silver, copper, iron, oil, coal, and natural gas. Yet, countries like Argentina and Venezuela, as well as many other Latin American countries, are incredibly poor and have rates of poverty that are unthinkable to those of us in the United States. The Left has learned absolutely nothing from Latin America's experiment with socialism.

That's probably one of the most frustrating things about those in the United States who speak favorably about socialism. They constantly deny the record of failure and misery that socialism has. "That's not real socialism," the Leftist apologist for socialism will say. It's easy to mock, but it shows the across-the-board failure of our education system.

We like to think that we beat socialism at the end of the Cold War. The socialists just went underground into education. My friend, Dr. Hoinski, always says, "People say that colleges are making kids liberal. That's not true. They show up that way." He appears to be right.

Each year, the Victims of Communism Memorial Foundation releases a survey of Americans' opinions about socialism. The most recent survey found that 49 percent of Americans between the ages of sixteen and twenty-three (Generation Z) have a favorable view of socialism and 31 percent from this same age group want to phase out capitalism in favor of socialism.[24] Fully 30 percent of Generation Z has a favorable view of Marxism. This is mind-boggling.

---

24 "2020 Annual Poll: US Attitudes towards Socialism, Communism, and Collectivism," Victims of Communism Memorial Foundation, Oct., 2020. https://victimsofcommunism.org/annual-poll/2020-annual-poll/

The Left believes we can have prosperity and innovation if we socialize risk. Innovators taking risks is what has created the opportunity and prosperity that we have as a nation. If there's no risk, those who would innovate won't be incentivized to do so.

The Left believes that capitalism is rigged and that the rich only get wealthy through corruption. They believe we can afford free health care, free education, and a carbon-free world, that there's an endless supply of money and resources that are just being hogged by the rich.

If all the wealth of every billionaire in the United States was confiscated, the roughly $3.8 trillion[25] taken by force would have covered a little more than ten months of federal spending in FY 2019. That's only the static effect of such a tyrannical action. Never mind the impact on stocks, collapse of retirement accounts, and the loss of millions of jobs that would come as a result.

The Left believes that the founding system and the Constitution are inherently bad and that we can't overcome the legacy of racism without blowing up the entire system. It certainly appears that this is the goal of the Left. It's a fundamental remaking of our constitutional structure, moving to a direct democracy in which the mob rules.

What a Socialist America Would Look Like

"There is nobody in this country who got rich on their own. Nobody."
—Senator. Elizabeth Warren[26]
*"If you've got a business, you didn't build that. Somebody else made that happen."***—President Barack Obama**[27]

---

25 Calculated by adding up the wealth of all billionaires in the United States and comparing the sum to federal outlays for FY 2020. Source: "The World's Real-time Billionaires," *Forbes*, accessed Nov. 10, 2020. https://www.forbes.com /real-time-billionaires/#405fed2f3d78

26 Joey Clark, "Elizabeth Warren's Selective Outrage," Foundation for Economic Education, September 23, 2016. https://fee.org/articles/elizabeth-warrens-selective-outrage/

27 Barack Obama, "Remarks by the President at a Campaign Event in Roanoke, Virginia," obamawhitehouse.archives.gov, July 13, 2012. https://obamawhitehouse.archives .gov/the-press-office/2012/07/13/remarks-president-campaign-event-roanoke-virginia

I don't know about you but watching the youth of America flirt with socialism—in recent elections and in general—really pisses me off.

Remember what I said about actually living through the experience of seeing the Berlin Wall fall versus not? Gallup says nearly half of Millennials and Generation Z hold a positive view of socialism, compared to only 39 percent of Generation X and 32 percent of Baby Boomers.[28] We could blame this gap on the naïvety of youth, but the oldest members of the Millennial generation turned forty in 2020. Hard to believe, right?

These aren't just kids anymore. Millennials are buying houses, paying taxes, and having children of their own. They should know better than to believe the broken promises of socialism. But clearly, they don't. To steal a line from the classic movie *Cool Hand Luke*, "What we've got here is a failure to communicate." We—as parents, teachers, and neighbors—are doing a bad job explaining to younger generations how socialism kills and plunders societies. Young Democrats think socialism in practice looks like Denmark or Sweden, not Venezuela or North Korea.

Denmark's former prime minister, Lars Løkke Rasmussen, has rejected the notion that his country is socialist. In 2015, he said, "I know that some people in the US associate the Nordic model with some sort of socialism. Therefore, I would like to make one thing clear. Denmark is far from a socialist planned economy. Denmark is a market economy."[29]

Economist Johan Norberg, a Swede, has resoundingly debunked the myth of socialism in Sweden. He writes, "Laissez-faire economics turned a poor backwater into one of the richest countries on the planet. Then it experimented with socialism briefly in the 1970s and 1980s. This made the country famous, but it almost destroyed it. And learning from this disaster, the left and the right have, in

28   Lydia Saad, "Socialism as Popular as Capitalism Among Young Adults in US," Gallup, November 25, 2019. https://news.gallup.com/poll/268766/socialism-popular-capitalism-among-young-adults.aspx

29   Lars Løkke Rasmussen, "Nordic Solutions and Challenges—A Danish Perspective," Harvard Kennedy School, October 30, 2015. https://www.youtube.com/watch?v=MgrJnXZ_WGo

relative consensus, liberalized Sweden's economy more than other countries, even though it's still far from its classical liberal past."[30]

Similarly, Carl Bildt, who served as prime minister of Sweden from 1991 to 1994, mocked America's most famous socialist on Twitter, writing, "Bernie Sanders was lucky to be able to get to the Soviet Union in 1988 and praise all its stunning socialist achievements before the entire system and empire collapsed under the weight of its own spectacular failures."[31]

Although Denmark and Sweden aren't socialist countries, they do have large welfare states,[32] high income taxes and value-added taxes,[33] and higher gas prices ($6.51 per gallon in Denmark and $6.04 in Sweden).[34] The suburbs, as we know them in America, are also impossible in these countries. Home sizes are also not nearly as large as they are in the America, where the average home size is 2,467 square feet[35] compared to 1,173 square feet in Denmark[36] and 1,313 square feet for a one- or two-dwelling building in Sweden.[37]

---

30   Johan Norberg, "Sweden's Lessons for America," Cato Institute, January/February 2020. https://www.cato.org/publications/policy-report/swedens-lessons-america

31   Carl Bildt (@carlbildt), Twitter, February 25, 2019. https://twitter.com/carlbildt/status/1100039769810235393

32   James Rolfe Edwards, review of "Scandinavian Unexceptionalism: Culture, Markets, and the Failure of Third-Way Socialism," by Nima Sanandaji, *Cato Journal*, 2017.   https://www.cato.org/sites/cato.org/files/serials/files/cato-journal/2017/5/cj-v37n2-16.pdf

33   Elke Asen, "Insights into the Tax Systems of Scandinavian Countries," Tax Foundation, February 24, 2020. https://taxfoundation.org/bernie-sanders-scandinavian-countries-taxes/

34   "Gasoline prices, liter, 21-Sep-2020," globalpetrolprices.com, accessed Sept. 21, 2020. https://www.globalpetrolprices.com/gasoline_prices/

35   Mark J. Perry, "New US homes today are 1,000 square feet larger than in 1973 and living space per person has nearly doubled," American Enterprise Institute, June 5, 2016. https://www.aei.org/carpe-diem/new-us-homes-today-are-1000-square-feet-larger-than-in-1973-and-living-space-per-person-has-nearly-doubled/

36   Hans Kristensen, "Housing in Denmark," Centre for Housing and Welfare, September 2007. http://boligforskning.dk/sites/default/files/Housing_130907.pdf

37   "Nearly 4.8 million dwellings in Sweden," Statistics Sweden, April 20, 2017. https://www.scb.se/en/finding-statistics/statistics-by-subject-area/housing-construction-and-building/housing-construction-and-conversion/dwelling-stock/pong/statistical-news/dwelling-stock-2016-12-31/

Young Democrats believe socialism is just a "nicer" version of capitalism. It's not. Socialism is responsible for the deaths of nearly 100 million people worldwide. According to *The Black Book of Communism*, the body count from socialism is unprecedented in world history.[38] Some 65 million people were killed in China, 20 million in the Soviet Union, two million in Cambodia, and two million in North Korea. These weren't only people killed during purges or deemed to be enemies of the state but also were people who died during famines caused by central planning.

That is what socialism looks like in its tragic conclusion. Somewhere in the middle, it looks like Poland in the 1990s. But in the beginning, it looked something more like the Democratic presidential debate stage in 2020. With Kamala Harris as the vice president in the Biden administration and likely the frontrunner for the Democratic nomination in 2024, Democrats are likely to keep flirting with socialist policy ideas.

Socialism would not come to the United States through a violent coup d'état, or some sort of Orwellian conspiracy where the United Nations swoops in and takes all our guns away. I really doubt it. Most likely, socialism would advance in the United States the way it's doing right now—slowly, incrementally, and over the span of generations.

Socialism begins with a lot of promises: tax the rich, feed the poor, equal outcomes for all, rules to keep corporations honest, and lots of free stuff. In return, the government asks for control over the means of production and the flow of capital throughout society. Maybe not all at once, but a little at a time.

Socialists point fingers at the most dishonest and unlikeable titans of industry and declare them morally unfit to operate the companies they have created. In the name of protecting society's most vulnerable, they call for the nationalization of health care, utilities, news, education, banking, and other major industries.

The proposal is simple:

---

38   Jean-Louis Panné, et al. *The Black Book of Communism: Crimes, Terror, Repression,* Harvard University Press, 1999.

We are but humble servants to the public. Unlike those greedy business-men, we have the knowledge and the moral compass needed to manage the market responsibly. Let us be central planners of the economy, and we can improve society without changing your own living standards. If you like your life, you can keep your life. We just want to level the play-ing field for everybody else.

Sounds pretty great, doesn't it? After all, who cares about boring, unrelatable metrics like "growing the economy" when we already live in tremendous material abundance compared to the rest of the world? Socialism begins with a society that takes its own success for granted. It begins with forgetting what systems and values got us this far in the first place.

Socialism Would Change the DNA of America

If the United States embraces socialism, it won't be a simple policy decision. Socialism isn't "nice capitalism." It's not a matter of tak-ing the system we have and making it better. You can have freedom or socialism, but you can't have both. Embracing socialism would change the DNA of who we are as a country.

The Founders created a system of government that protects the rights and liberties of the smallest minority group—the individual. In our republic, the rights of the individual are prioritized over the group. People are free to determine their own lives, work hard, and keep the fruits of their labor. These freedoms are rights given by God, not government.

Socialism would flip America's founding promise on its head. It puts boundaries around American creativity and dynamism and pri-oritizes the interests of the group over the rights of the individual. Under socialism, our rights come from government. Personal wealth is collected and redistributed according to "need," and that need is determined by the people in power.

Keep in mind—these people in power are not altruistic robots. They all have their own set of biases and incentives that guide their behavior.

Like Milton Friedman said, there are no magic angels who are going to organize society for us. Still, we would put our fate in their hands.

Socialism would require us to forfeit our self-governance and redefine the American promise.

Socialism Would Neuter Our Republic

The United States has a representative democracy, which means we elect people who *promise* to use their vote to get these things done, but the general principle is the same. Our rights and liberties are written in stone, and everything else we vote for the government to provide is a privilege. We can grow or shrink the government to provide these privileges—or not—every few years, although history shows it's a lot harder to get rid of a government program than it is to create one.

Now here's the problem. Socialism turns these privileges into rights that can't be voted away. It gives everyone the "right" to a college education, shelter, or job. Each new entitlement sets government at a larger minimum size beyond which it cannot be reduced. You are no longer free to choose whether or not these tax-funded programs should exist.

At best, you might get some input into what these programs do. Being a voter in a socialist democracy would be like owning a house in one of those fancy private communities. Sure, you can choose how to paint your house—as long as your choice is one of these three government-approved colors.

A house divided between democracy and socialism cannot stand. By the time people begin to realize this, it's usually too late. And in my personal reading, as a student of history, I have yet to find a single example of the government responding peacefully to the unrest that follows.

Socialism Would Destroy the US Economy

For the sake of argument, let's say I'm wrong. Let's pretend someone found a peaceful and democratic way to implement socialism in the

United States. For the sake of this exercise, the American people know they are playing second fiddle to the "common good" and they are super fine with it.

What happens next? The government would begin increasing the levels of oversight they hold over private businesses, and maybe even nationalize some industries entirely. We don't need to use our imagination to picture how the government would flex its muscles in this scenario. All we need to do is look at what Democratic primary candidates have been saying on the 2020 presidential debate stage and take them at their word.

During the Democratic primaries—and no doubt still—Senator Elizabeth Warren called for massive tax increases on the wealthy to pay for social programs. She wanted to raise the minimum wage, provide Medicare for All, and break up the Big Banks. Senator Sanders called for those same things, plus a national rent control, free college, and implementation of the Green New Deal.

A 2020 Democratic White House hopeful, Andrew Yang wanted to give a universal basic income of $1,000 per month to all US adults.[39] He also wanted to require tech companies to get approval from the government before making any changes to their algorithms.[40]

Disaster would ensue if these power grabs were to become a reality, and here's why. A healthy market economy depends on a few things:

- **Private property:** When people own their property, not the government. Individuals have the right to sell or rent their property for a profit.
- **Free choice and competition:** When businesses are free to sell goods and services to anyone they want (as long as they don't steal or hurt anyone), and individuals are free to purchase goods and services from anyone they want.

---

39 "The Freedom Dividend, Defined," yang2020.com, accessed Sept. 21, 2020. https://www.yang2020.com/what-is-freedom-dividend-faq/

40 "Regulating Technology Firms in the 21st Century," yang2020.com, November 14, 2019. https://www.yang2020.com/blog/regulating-technology-firms-in-the-21st-century/

- **Prices set by supply and demand**: When prices are not determined by the government. Instead, they are determined by the availability of the good or service, how many people want to buy it, the costs of production, and how much consumers can afford.
- **Informed consumerism:** The expectation that people understand what they are buying and what prices are competitive and will use that information to make good decisions.
- **Profit motive:** The understanding that people are motivated by self-interest. Businesses want to make a profit. Buyers want to get a deal. Employees want to get paid as much as possible. Volunteers want to feel good about themselves. When given a choice, people choose to enrich their lives.

A socialist economy doesn't abide by a single one of the factors listed above. In fact, it attempts to ignore them. It takes the very framework that built and powered the largest market economy the world has ever known and turns it inside out.

Can you imagine if Andrew Yang or other Democrats got their way, and tech companies had to obtain government approval before making any changes to their algorithms? It would kill tech innovation in the United States. The digital world moves at a rapid pace. The government moves at the pace of a snail. By the end of the approval cycle, the technology would be obsolete.

Under the rules of socialism, nobody has any skin in the game. People don't really own their property—after all, businesses and properties would be seized by the government when deemed necessary. Business owners wouldn't really care about profits, because they know the government would decide how the money gets spent. And when profits don't matter, there is little motivation to keep efficiency high and costs low.

Public officials would set prices and control the supply of goods and services. Despite their best efforts, prices would be set somewhat arbitrarily, since these officials would lack the data and expertise necessary to understand all the complicated economic variables that impact demand in every location across America in real-time. (To be fair, nobody can.)

Individuals would need permission from the government to create new businesses. In fact, we might be prohibited altogether from competing with newly nationalized industries. With no competition, there would be no incentive to keep customers happy—and anyone who has ever interacted with the Department of Motor Vehicles knows what it's like when there's no incentive to keep customers happy.

On its best day, socialism can't change the laws of human behavior. It can't change the fact that incentives matter, people are self-interested, and central planning always fails. So, even if you *could* find a way to peacefully and democratically implement socialism, it would lead us on a path to economic destruction.

Socialism Would Explode the National Debt

As I write this, the US national debt is approaching $30 trillion.[41] As of the third quarter of 2020, the Bureau of Economic Analysis estimates that the total gross domestic product of the United States is $21.1 trillion. Put another way, our national debt is larger than the US economy.

That is only the tip of the iceberg. When you combine the federal debt with the money owed for Social Security and Medicare, the United States holds a grand total of $83.2 trillion in unfunded liabilities. Eighty-three trillion dollars. And that's a conservative estimate.

Let that number sink in for a minute.

It's not possible for the rich to pay for everything—even if we wanted them to pay for it all. The math just doesn't allow for it. According to the Brookings institution, the top "1 percent" of

---

41   "The Debt to the Penny and Who Holds It," treasurydirect.com, accessed August 11, 2020. https://www.treasurydirect.gov/govt/reports/pd/pd_debttothepenny.htm

Americans held $25 trillion of wealth in 2016.[42] The richest man in the world, Jeff Bezos, has an estimated net worth of about $200 billion.[43] Those aren't salaries that will be replenished every year. Those are measurements of a lifetime of accumulated wealth.

The government could seize the entire personal fortune of Jeff Bezos, and the best they could do with his money is fund 28 percent of the defense budget, one time.[44] The math just doesn't work. When it comes to the government, we are talking about spending on a completely different order of magnitude.

Now, let's put the cherry on top. Democratic presidential hopefuls in 2020 wanted:

- Student loan forgiveness: $1.6 trillion
- Medicare for all: $34 trillion
- Social Security expansion: $1.5 trillion
- The Green New Deal: $94 trillion
- Affordable housing for all: $2.5 trillion
- Universal basic income: $3 trillion
- Tax subsidies: $2.5 trillion

These are only a handful from the policy wish list of Democratic presidential candidates. Yet, all of these were serious proposals on the campaign trail. An analysis conducted by the *Washington Free Beacon* found that together, the 2020 Democratic candidates called for more than $210 trillion in new spending.[45] Remember when I said the US holds a grand total of $83.2 trillion in unfunded liabilities

---

42 Isabel V. Sawhill and Christopher Pulliam, "Six facts about wealth in the United States," Brookings, June 25, 2019. https://www.brookings.edu/blog/up-front/2019/06/25/six-facts-about-wealth-in-the-united-states/

43 Jonathan Ponciano, "Jeff Bezos Becomes The First Person Ever Worth $200 Billion," Forbes, August 26, 2020. https://www.forbes.com/sites/jonathanponciano/2020/08/26/worlds-richest-billionaire-jeff-bezos-first-200-billion/

44 Projected defense discretionary outlays for FY 2020 are $715 billion.

45 Charles Fain Lehman and David Rutz, "Analysis: Dem Candidates Call For More Than $200 Trillion in Spending," The Washington Free Beacon, July 31, 2019. https://freebeacon.com/politics/analysis-dem-candidates-call-for-more-than-200-trillion-in-spending/

and national debt? To put that into perspective, that's nearly four times larger than America's entire gross domestic product and 416 times the net worth of Jeff Bezos.

Democratic presidential candidates wanted to nearly double that amount in *new* spending. Biden may not necessarily push these specific policies, but at the very least he'll push aspects or forms of them to keep the Left happy and implement what he can through regulation. This trend must be rejected and stopped full force. Our liberty depends on it.

CHAPTER 4

Socialism Doesn't Work—Freedom Does

There is no such thing as freedom without free markets, to which private property is integral. You could even say it's divinely ordained. Here is my evidence that God believes in private property: Thou shall not steal. Stealing implies ownership.

I'm saying this tongue-in-cheek, in part, but it's also genuine. One of your most fundamental rights is to your property. You have, or should have, the basic right to your own labor.

What is your labor worth? Whether it was thousands of years ago and you worked all day to grow wheat to make bread, or one hundred years ago you made shoes, or today you design computer programs— in any age, whatever you do provides some form of currency. That currency allows you to do what you choose in pursuit of your own version of happiness.

Private property is essential to this basic human function. If you don't control your labor, who does? When you look at totalitarian systems, every restriction on your ability to consume what you want, and how you want it, is a form of tyranny. These important decisions are being made not by you, but for you. You have no agency. It's dehumanizing. Choice is essential to our humanity.

Some of my favorite people are those who have weird but interesting hobbies. They are part of what makes this world so amazing. I have my own hobby, namely Revolutionary War reenactments. Most people wouldn't be interested in this niche passion and they certainly aren't going to spend a dime on it. I also like to spend money on Cleveland Browns football. (That last one is probably a really bad example of a "good use" of money.) These things give me happiness and connection with others.

Under oppressive systems where you don't have control of your own labor, people have to spend so much time simply trying to get their basic necessities. When you have to spend a lot of time getting bread and potatoes, you really don't have a lot of time to get a hobby. This also means you don't really have time to truly develop your personality, deciding and expressing your own likes and dislikes. When you have to worry about eating, day to day, you never really fully become yourself.

The notion of the individual is suppressed in oppressive systems over the goals of the state. The individual exists for the benefit of the collective. This is the antithesis of freedom. But the individual works toward innovation because he or she is incentivized to do so. As Ludwig von Mises wrote, "All rational action is in the first place individual action. Only the individual thinks. Only the individual reasons. Only the individual acts."[1]

My experience in Poland, seeing and talking to people about how they lived under communism, made it clear that socialism changed these people's circumstances for the worse and that oppressive regimes are inherently anti-human.

When you earn your dollars, you should be able to use them however you want. This is not "greed," no matter how much some like to spin it that way. History shows—Poland showed me—that forced government redistribution of money isn't always "compassion" either.

If you want to build a business, if you want to invest in a hobby, if you want to give your money to your family, if you want to blow it all on beer—whatever you could possibly want to do with your

---

1   Ludwig von Mises, *Socialism: An Economic and Sociological Analysis*, Liberty Fund, 1981. pg. 97

labor—I'm not going to tell you how to spend it. I'm not equipped to make that judgment. I'm me. You're you.

I know that anyone who doesn't spend their money on Revolutionary War reenacting and who doesn't spend their money on the Cleveland Browns is misspending their money. No doubt most believe the same about my decisions. That's how freedom works. How many people are there in this world that share my similar interests? My wife doesn't even share them. That's the point. We're all individuals.

Money and property are the cornerstones of a free society. We control our own ability to work or even not to work. But if you decide not to work, you shouldn't expect to be able to take the labor of others. That's theft. Private property is a moral argument. When societies observe basic free market principles, whether that means employing thousands or merely collecting stamps, all of this human action benefits our fellow man. And besides, isn't freedom of choice and pursuing our own happiness what it means to be alive?

A speech I heard once that stayed with me describes ancient paintings from thousands of years ago in the Chauvet Cave in France. The images showed, and the speaker expressed, that every human generation seeks more happiness and joy than what came before them. They strive for more joy in their own experience on this earth. This only happens through private exchange in a free market. It only comes when people have the freedom to decide what they want to do on their own.

When I first lived in Poland in 2000, the only cars you saw on the road were Ladas, a Russian car; Polonez, a Polish make; and the Czech-made Skoda. They all looked exactly the same. They were all variations of the same piece of junk car. Clunky boxes.

A car is a great example of the principle that you should be able to get whatever you like: You want a more practical car? Have at it. Do you want to work harder for a more expensive car? The choice is yours. When you limit people's choices in the name of some ostensible collectivist humanitarianism, you always end up with a system that squelches what makes us human.

I will always err on the side of freedom. Because without it, there is no innovation. A perfect example is the cars you see on the streets of Poland today compared to what I experienced back in 2000. Today, the only time you might see some throwback Cold War-era Lada or Skoda on the road in Poland, is if some kid has souped it up with a huge engine! Talk about innovation! These days you can't count all the different cars Polish people drive on their roads since they have had the freedom to choose.

Some Poles like sporty cars. Some have a big station wagon for their family. Some have vans they can work out of. These cars represent different personalities. They are a symbol of the triumph of individualism. You can see the happiness on Poles' faces compared to the way things once were.

It's a true masterpiece of the human spirit. You could even call it spontaneous art. It's rewarding to see people who once had little to no freedom now flourishing since they have been allowed to make the same kinds of choices with their labor that we in America have enjoyed since day one. Which boggles my mind as to why anyone would want to tear down this country.

Freedom Is "Progressive"

I have always resented the term "progressive." I'm a progressive person. Like most people, I look forward to a better future. I like change. In fact, I *love* change. It's part of the reason I favor a free market economy.

Austrian economist Joseph Schumpeter described capitalism as "creative destruction." Schumpeter wrote that free markets were the "process of industrial mutation… that incessantly revolutionizes the economic structure from within, incessantly destroying the old one, incessantly creating a new one." He considered the creative destruction "the essential fact about capitalism."[2]

---

2   Joseph A. Schumpeter, *Capitalism, Socialism, and Democracy*, Harper & Bros., 1947. Pg. 83

This is exactly what we're all trying to do in a free society. You want this sort of positive "destruction" in society. We should want to be ripping and tearing our ideas up all the time and creating better products. Free markets also help determine what we might need and at what cost. What capitalism and a functioning market economy do is rationalize price. When you have the market, it's unbelievably efficient in delivering the right goods at the right cost. If you get rid of it, you're not going to get any of these goods.

Refrigerators that were built today are better than ones that were built a few years ago. They are always getting better. This is why I resent the term "progressive." Capitalism has given the world the most progress in world history, and yet the politicians and left activists who identify as "progressives" want to smash the free market.

There are certain fundamental human truths that give people the space for that creativity and the destruction that goes along with it. Politicians like Congresswoman Alexandria Ocasio-Cortez or Senator Bernie Sanders can promise complete support and safety for citizens via the government, but that collectivist thinking throughout history has always led to citizens becoming collectively miserable.

I always go back to Father Prehn during my freshman year of high school in 1992. He said that society is a debate between liberty and security. The more liberty you have, the less security you have. The more security you have, the less liberty you have. At fifteen years old, I thought that was a pretty good way to look at things. Today's self-described socialist politicians seek a lot more security, absolute security really, which would come at the expense of liberty.

How is that "progressive"? Wouldn't losing liberty be regressive? Such an agenda, if successful, would be incredibly stifling, at a bare minimum. Through confiscating vast amounts of the nation's wealth for government purposes, these would-be saviors would destroy the freedom of choice that inspires innovation and that truly moves society forward.

America Has Always Been a Beacon of Hope—Which Everyone Needs

America has always been about opportunity. What we saw growing up in Cleveland was that as more people became successful, they would move to different and better neighborhoods. Each generation would get better. The first generation would work three janitor jobs. The next generation would have more leisure but still worked hard. The next might see their kids go to college or open a business.

That cycle is so healthy and important for society. When that cycle stratifies and people can't move up, and worse, start moving down, that's when we begin to have a lot of social problems. People need hope.

People left Europe because they made shoes because their grandfather made shoes, and their grandfather made shoes because his ancestors made shoes. That was the old system that generations for centuries considered the norm. That's not the story of America. It's embarrassing that we have poverty-ridden neighborhoods in America precisely because that's not supposed to happen here. This permanent cycle of poverty is aided and abetted through mass public assistance.

Look at the Great Society programs from the 1960s. During his State of the Union address in January 1964, Lyndon B. Johnson "declare[d] unconditional war on poverty in America."[3] As Michael Tanner of the Cato Institute notes, all levels of government have spent "more than $23 trillion" fighting poverty.[4] When Johnson declared the "war on poverty," the poverty rate was 19 percent. Before COVID-19 struck America, the poverty rate had declined to 10.5 percent.[5]

---

3   Lyndon Baines Johnson, "First State of the Union Address," Jan. 8, 1964. Transcript hosted by the American Rhetoric Online Speech Bank, updated Oct. 14, 2019. https://www.americanrhetoric.com/speeches/lbj1964stateoftheunion.htm

4   Michael D. Tanner, "What's Missing in the War on Poverty?" Cato Institute, Jan. 23, 2019. https://www.cato.org/publications/commentary/whats-missing-war-poverty

5   Jessica Semega, et. al, "Income and Poverty in the United States: 2019," US Census Bureau, Report No. P60-270, Sept. 15, 2020. https://www.census.gov/library/publications/2020/demo/p60-270.html

The recent drop in poverty rate has little to do with the Great Society. It's true that the poverty rate had been on the decline, but the tax cuts passed in 2017 and deregulation helped improve the outlook for many Americans quicker than maintaining the status quo of higher taxes and overregulation.

Too many of our programs are one-size-fits-all. Social workers should be incentivized to get more people off of the system. Case workers should get bonuses every time someone they are trying to help moves off of food stamps, instead of trying to get as many people to join into public assistance as possible. The goal is to help people stand on their own two feet.

We need a social safety net for those who make mistakes and those who are unable to work because of a disability. But the idea of the social safety net—and this is important—is to help you get on your feet when you find yourself in a terrible situation. It's not to create dependency. Most of the welfare problems that we have relate to people getting stuck in generational poverty because they have never known any other life than to rely on a system that was meant to help those in temporary need.

We incentivize people to stay in this rut. You always hear stories about Americans beginning to become more successful, but when they begin to earn a higher amount of money and reach a threshold that if they get $1 more, they lose their welfare benefits. So, they logically don't want to move forward.

I believe that for many people who are trapped in our welfare programs, it's not that they're lazy and don't want to try. They have given up hope. Once you've given up on that, all is lost. All people need hope, but it's never something the government can provide for you. It's about you having something you are passionate about in your life and having the opportunity to pursue it. This is uniquely American.

Hope also means responsibility. Not everyone is born with the same opportunities. Not everyone was born with the same capabilities. But the point of America is that you shouldn't be limited by anything except the size of your dream.

Our ideas matter because they work. In a free society, you're going to be able to choose what kind of education you get and have flexibility. The economy will improve, thus allowing Americans to move up the ladder.

The least happy people I've met are those who have the least control over their lives. Don't most people hate days when they have back-to-back meetings because you don't really own your time and don't accomplish anything? Happy people have control over owning or chasing their dreams. I want a society that supports that in every scenario imaginable. If we give up on that, we lose everything.

With our ideas, Americans are also allowed to fail. It's integral to the system. Amazon CEO Jeff Bezos has said, "I predict one day Amazon will fail. Amazon will go bankrupt. If you look at large companies, their lifespans tend to be thirty-plus years, not a hundred-plus years."[6]

I'm old enough to remember when Walmart was the bad guy. Now, Amazon has taken Walmart's place. But Bezos knows that customer satisfaction is the key to Amazon's success. "If we start to focus on ourselves, instead of focusing on our customers, that will be the beginning of the end. We have to try and delay that day for as long as possible." He has taken that risk, and it's paying off.

Anyone in the US is allowed to take a risk and fail. It's part of the reason we're so successful. For every big, new, and shiny corporation that exists, in its wake is wreckage of thousands of failed ones. Every day, entrepreneurs tear businesses apart and rebuild them. That's what helps bring about progress. You have to take risks. If you get rid of failure, you also throw out success. They are Yin and Yang.

If you take away the downfalls of capitalism that come with taking risks, you also lose the overwhelming benefits that system gives us. We don't want to become "mother, may I" with the government, constantly haggling with the state for our different parts and pieces of taxpayer funded "help."

---

6   Eugene Kim, "Jeff Bezos to employees: 'One day, Amazon will fail' but our job is to delay it as long as possible," CNBC, Nov. 15, 2018. https://www.cnbc.com/2018/11/15/bezos-tells-employees-one-day-amazon-will-fail-and-to-stay-hungry.html

It's our responsibility to protect freedom. Modern technology will also make it possible for our world to become better or worse at a pace like never before in human history. One example: The advent of 3D printing makes it possible for anyone to have a manufacturing plant in their home. Many might not realize this, but many of the parts for Boeing airplanes are 3D printed. In the future, when you design a car, it's going to come from a manufacturing facility that will look very unlike those in which Ford and Chevrolet have always built their products.

These processes are going to become radically decentralized and ultra-competitive. I won't be surprised in the decades to come to see Apple as a major car manufacturer. The entire system of producing goods is going to change.

There will also be tremendous opportunity in that change. When you have change, the best way for creative destruction to work is for a lot of capital to be floating around. Creative destruction without capital is just destruction. This is why it's so important to let free markets flow unfettered as much as possible. We never want to end up in a situation where we are taking from the future to subsidize the present, which is what so many who push socialism are hell-bent on. That's a one-way street to poverty for everyone.

I don't pretend to have all the answers for a healthy economy and freer country. Anyone who does pretend to have them is a liar or a fool. That's why I believe in the power of free markets. I know right now there are countless Americans working hard to solve my problems for their own advantage. The free market incentivizes them to do so. Most problems or inconveniences we have at this moment will be solved so long as government stays out of the way. Competition is crucial.

This is part of why harping on "income inequality" is such a dead end. We need wealthy people who will invest in new ideas. If you are Elizabeth Warren and want to punish and choke off wealth, there isn't going to be any capital for innovation.

If that innovation is successful—and it helps thousands, if not millions of Americans—some people will become incredibly rich. That's how it works. When Elizabeth Warren comes out and says that for entrepreneurs there will be a profit limit, she doesn't acknowledge that if people aren't allowed to make profits, innovation will die.

Going back to America's founding, we have always had risk. If you have liberty in our markets, yes, there will always be certain dislocations, but that will always work itself out.

Anti-free market collectivist mentality isn't exclusive to the Left. There are good and bad populisms. The Tea Party was populist. Populism that seeks to challenge an entrenched incumbency that's taking advantage of average Americans is always good. But populist movements again, Left or Right, that seek to outdo each other in redistributing wealth, are really just a faux activist version of what elites in both parties want to do anyway. It's a charade.

A concern of mine is that we get into a cycle of competing left- and right-wing populist efforts that see government as the solution to everything. Some conservatives in recent times have misinterpreted the Trump phenomenon as evidence that the US should emulate some of the big government right-wing movements in Europe. This would be a huge mistake and we would lose what makes us uniquely American.

We have to be careful of big government solutions from either party. I've never thought that top-down solutions from government work. Too often, when a top-down policy solution comes from a Republican administration, conservatives ignore it.

I remember when George W. Bush tried to use the ultimate top-down solution by going to war in Iraq. That top-down idea became such a boondoggle. Of course, there are other examples from recent years—No Child Left Behind, Medicare Part D, Dodd-Frank Wall Street Reform and Consumer Protection Act, and the Affordable Care Act. Each of these are great examples of purported top-down solutions that ended up not working. Top-down solutions don't work abroad, nor do top-down solutions work domestically.

CHAPTER 5

Why Identity Politics Is So Dangerous

―――――――

"Kids today" is a cliché that older generations have used to criticize their younger counterparts probably since the days humans first developed spoken language. Sometimes, there's some truth to it. I actually believe young Americans today are starting off with some significant disadvantages and lack basic development tools that their parents and grandparents took for granted.

If you go back to the dawn of time, most children learned by being in very close proximity to their parents and loved ones, whether it was hunting, being on the farm, or just living together in small townships. As children became young men and women, there were certain rites of passage. It was an ideal and natural way for generations to transfer knowledge to one another.

We are living in an interesting era now, both in the US but also in many societies around the world, where young people simply don't have those same rites of passage anymore. In fact, today, it's fairly easy for many people to stay in that adolescent stage well into their thirties and even forties. More people no longer necessarily have to learn certain tough lessons or face hardships that helped turn previous generations of young people into functioning and responsible adults.

Simultaneously, we have the erosion of grounding institutions. Whether it's family, the church, or last but not least, patriotism, each has withered to a degree in recent decades. As the definition of what constitutes a family evolves and as fewer people attend church, inevitably many Americans feel less patriotic than their parents or grandparents did. Too often we take for granted today, or even dismiss, these intellectual and emotional building blocks that past generations considered essential to maturity and stability.

One of the things you learn within your family, church, and community institutions is to agree to disagree and be tolerant. Human beings are always in danger of breaking down into sectarian violence. But in a genuine community you learn how to avoid that by talking to folks.

That is part of our national ethos. Coming from the Midwest that is made up of all these ethnic enclaves, they still formed a certain unity that is the American character and identity. Those bonds are what allow us to have conversations with each other. That has always been the strength of our society. The moment we start to believe, "If you're not in my tribe, then you're no good" would be the beginning of the end.

If I moved to China today, I could never be Chinese. No matter how hard I tried. The reverse isn't true. If you're Chinese and move to the United States, you and your family can easily become American in a relatively short period of time. That's our strength. If we ever lose that, then the America we know will be finished.

And yet, we are losing a lot of patriotism today. I'm definitely not a "Get off my lawn!" guy, but I do think a lot of younger Americans might not have that patriotic spirit in the same way their parents and grandparents did. We seem to be becoming a less religious society than we once were. We are less family-oriented than we have probably ever been. We've lost our connection to community. All of it creates a misunderstanding of what freedom truly is.

Freedom comes with a tremendous amount of responsibility. Freedom means taking care of yourself. Feeding yourself. Clothing yourself. Getting a job. It means figuring out what you have to offer that is materially useful for society so that you can become a full member of it. Some people are great athletes. Some are great doctors. Others are great barbers. The list of talents and options is endless. You have to figure out what you are good at.

Freedom also means respecting other people's freedoms. They can succeed or fail on their own, but the same goes for you. Freedom means taking responsibility for your life.

If You Feel Isolated, You Won't Be Happy

A major problem that arises with the erosion of integral societal institutions is that people become lost. We have seen studies showing that Millennials are one of the loneliest generations in American history. Too many people today feel isolated and lonely. This isn't healthy. And this phenomenon was happening before the COVID-19 pandemic.

College students are more stressed and depressed than ever. *The New York Times* reported in February 2019, "More than 60 percent of college students said they had experienced 'overwhelming anxiety' in the past year, according to a 2018 report from the American College Health Association. Over 40 percent said they felt so depressed they had difficulty functioning."[1]

"Money problems are exacerbating their worries," the *Times* continued. "Mental health professionals say college students have experienced financial burdens on a different scale than many of their predecessors. They grew up during the Great Recession and have seen family members lose jobs and homes. They have great uncertainty about their career prospects and feel pressure to excel academically or risk losing job opportunities."

In other words, combined with less societal nurturing than their predecessors might have had, today's young people feel like the future is bleak. They've lost hope.

---

1   Brad Wolverton, "As Students Struggle With Stress and Depression, Colleges Act as Counselors," *New York Times*, February 21, 2019. https://www.nytimes.com/2019/02/21/education/learning/mental-health-counseling-on-campus.html

The majority of the school shooters that have caused so much tragedy in recent years are completely lost. Most of them come from fatherless homes.[2] When parents are involved and active in their kid's life, and the child understands and appreciates this love, that means something to them. Kids don't feel alone. They are able to overcome hardships as a family.

We also don't do enough to encourage young people to think. Everything is just pushed on kids and they are supposed to like it, no questions asked.

When an entire generation is largely Balkanized, it's hard to feel like you are a part of anything. When you don't feel like you're a part of anything, you don't take responsibility for anything. You don't care if the country is doing well. It doesn't matter to you so much how your neighbors are doing. You stop caring about multiple things, but probably still expect someone else to. All of this creates a huge vacuum for the government to step in.

One part of modern life that has contributed to the disintegration of community—look at how much time we spend on our phones. This is addicting in a similar way that alcohol and cigarettes are.[3] When we see a text, email, or a reply on social media, our brain releases dopamine.[4] We crave more of it. It has meant that we all spend less time with each other. That's damaging to society.

I'm not going to tell you or anyone else what religion they should be, or even criticize them should they choose not to be a person of faith. I'm not going to demand that you be patriotic. I'm not going to insist that you have a family.

---

2   Emilie Kao, "The Crisis of Fatherless Shooters," Heritage Foundation, March 14, 2018. https://www.heritage.org/marriage-and-family/commentary/the-crisis-fatherless-shooters

3   Shamani Joshi, "Smartphone Addiction Affects Your Brain in the Same Way as Drug Addiction, Study Finds," *Vice*, February 19, 2020. https://www.vice.com/en_in/article/qjdzx5/smartphone-addiction-affects-your-brain-in-the-same-way-as-drug-addiction-study-finds

4   Trevor Haynes, "Dopamine, Smartphones & You: A battle for your time," Harvard University, May 1, 2018. http://sitn.hms.harvard.edu/flash/2018/dopamine-smartphones-battle-time/

I don't care what you do. It doesn't change the fact that I have observed that the people who are happiest have strong social networks and community bonds. Not telling people what to do is part of the libertarian in me. But being libertarian should also mean that we understand that human beings need to belong to some sort of community. Private individuals banding together in some form is what prevents the growth of the state.

Real Community vs. "It Takes a Village"

What I've noticed about libertarians, or at least the majority that I have known or worked with, is that they tend to be incredibly social. There's this myth that a libertarian is a weird psycho with a shotgun on a hilltop somewhere in rural Texas.

Libertarians believe and encourage human interaction—it's a prime basis of our philosophy—but that interaction has to be voluntary. I'm now, and forever will be, about the individual first. Yet, it is also true that individuals belong in communities. Just the same, we also believe in a family nucleus.

This is something very different than Hillary Clinton's concept of "It Takes a Village." Clinton's book of that title that many recall from years ago was really just a call for government to step in and take the place of the institutions that arise organically in any genuine community.[5] The freedom lover's view is that individuals acting voluntarily create communities that will create better kids and later, adult citizens, than any government scheme ever could.

Hillary wants government to raise your kids. In fact, this is a constant mantra from the Left today. The national Black Lives Matter (BLM) organization's original guiding principles stated, "We are committed to disrupting the Western-prescribed nuclear family structure requirement by supporting each other as extended families and 'villages' that collectively care for one another, and especially 'our' children to the degree that mothers, parents and children

---

5   Hillary Clinton, *It Takes a Village*, Simon and Schuster, 1995.

are comfortable."[6] Those principles were mysteriously deleted from BLM's website in September 2020.[7]

There's not one aspect of a young American's life that many politicians aren't eager to intervene in with some government policy, as if the state could know what's best for kids better than their parents.

I'm not sure if Mrs. Clinton would agree, but the only people who need to have a say in how a child is raised are the child's parents. Raising kids right within a community creates happy and productive adults. It's people coming together because they want to, not because government coerces them to.

Voluntary Association vs. Identity Politics

A big part of why I love watching the Cleveland Browns is that I know that when I'm sitting home alone watching the game, across the country there are tens or hundreds of thousands joining me at that moment. I'm in a community. What's even better is when I go to a game, and especially an away game, I start hugging and high-fiving people that I have never met before. These fans are older, younger, fatter, thinner, blacker, lighter—it doesn't matter what they are— but everyone is on the same team.

I'm not just talking about what's happening on the field. Some might criticize such sports camaraderie as being tribalistic, but everyone has some tribe they roll with. These voluntary "tribes" have a sense of camaraderie. Your sports team. Your church. Book clubs. *Star Wars* fans. Even when it comes to political philosophy, your fellow libertarians or conservatives or progressives. The list is endless. Still, again, these associations are voluntary.

A voluntary association is the opposite of identity politics, which is based on race or gender or some other biological fact the individual had no choice in. The tribes that fuel identity politics represent

---

6   James Freeman, "Black Lives Matter and the Family," *Wall Street Journal*, July 23, 2020. https://www.wsj.com/articles/black-lives-matter-and-the-family-11595530123

7   Conn Carroll (@conncarroll), Twitter, September 21, 2020. https://twitter.com /conncarroll/status/1308014176493801473

voluntary communities. I didn't decide to be born a white man. No one decided to be born female, black, tall or bald. You had nothing to do with these outcomes.

A so-called "community" that is based on nothing more than the physical circumstances of your birth is not a real or strong community. But a group that you choose to participate in because of shared values is something genuine.

This goes back to my upbringing in Ohio and America's melting pot. The fact that my dad wasn't taught Czech in my grandparents' home, that they insisted he speak English, was so that he and his family could voluntarily join a different tribe. They yearned to become Americans.

Very few people ever learn to speak Czech. You are either born speaking Czech, or you're not. Yet, those who do are likely welcomed into that community, but it's not in any way the melting pot we have in the US. If I learned to speak Czech and went to Prague, I would only be an American who spoke Czech.

In America, you can eat Indian food at home because that's what you grew up doing. You can have an Indian accent and even wear traditional Indian dress. And yet you can still assimilate into American society. You can become an American. But when any person or group puts any of the unique identities that are America in its totality ahead of others, that's when we arrive at an unhealthy tribalism.

The military is another great example of the difference between voluntary association and identity politics. You have a bunch of men and women who sign up, who have never met each other, and yet in a short period of time will risk their lives to save one another.

That's the strength of America. People coming together. No normal American of any stripe, much less a soldier, says, "Oh, that person is black, or that person is Muslim; I'm going to let them die." No, they have their American uniform on. They're going to fight for each other and for all Americans.

Our identity as a country is our greatest strength. When we focus on what divides us, things that we had no choice in, that's where it gets dangerous. That's why identity politics is so dangerous.

We Are Not as Divided as the Media Makes Us Appear

Bad news, political turmoil, and protests have a market. The media milks it for all it's worth. Whenever I turn on the television to watch cable news, divisiveness dominates the airwaves. It's far past the normal disagreement between Republicans and Democrats in Congress.

America has seen tense political divisions throughout our history, and the press has always had a major role in propaganda. In the early days of the Republic, newspapers did the dirty work of political parties. There were newspapers that promoted Alexander Hamilton's Federalist propaganda and ones that promoted the agenda of Thomas Jefferson's Democratic-Republicans.

During the election of 1800, James Callendar, a journalist hired to promote the campaign of Jefferson, wrote horrible things about the incumbent president, John Adams. Callendar called Adams a "hideous hermaphroditical character, which has neither the force and firmness of a man, nor the gentleness and sensibility of a woman."[8]

A surrogate of Adams' campaign, pastor and president of Yale University, Timothy Dwight, speculated in a sermon that Jefferson would bring a godless anarchy to America. Dwight suggested that "we may see the Bible cast into a bonfire" and "we may see our wives and daughters the victims of legal prostitution; soberly dishonoured; speciously polluted; the outcasts of delicacy and virtue, and the lothing of God and man."[9]

The *Connecticut Courant* suggested that under a Jefferson administration, "Murder, robbery, rape, adultery, and incest will all be openly taught and practiced; the air will be rent with the cries of the

---

8   "Hideous hermaphroditical character (Spurious Quotation)," monticello.org, accessed Sept. 24, 2020. https://www.monticello.org/site/research-and-collections/hideous-hermaphroditical-character-spurious-quotation

9   Timothy Dwight, "The Duty of Americans, at the Present Crisis," ConSource, July 4, 1798. https://www.consource.org/document/the-duty-of-americans-at-the-present-crisis-by-timothy-dwight-1798-7-4/

distressed; the soil will be soaked with blood, and the nation black with crime."[10]

In May 1856, Preston Brooks, a southern House Democrat who strongly supported slavery, caned Charles Sumner, a Republican senator from the north and abolitionist, in the Senate chamber for Sumner's comments about a fellow senator, Andrew Butler of South Carolina. Butler coauthored the Kansas-Nebraska Act, which allowed settlers to determine whether slavery would be allowed in these territories.

Two days before Sumner was assaulted by Brooks, Sumner gave a speech in the Senate in which he rebuked Butler.[11] The incident was one of several precursors of the tensions that would boil over into the American Civil War, in which as many as 850,000 people died. The stains of the horrible practice of slavery and the crimes of the Jim Crow era are forever in our history. There is no shortage of examples of hostilities, both wars of harsh words and uses of violence, since our founding.

The late 1960s were particularly trying for America. Martin Luther King Jr. was assassinated in March 1968 in Memphis, Tennessee. Robert F. Kennedy, who was campaigning for the Democratic presidential nomination, was assassinated a few months later. In May 1970, the Ohio National Guard opened fire on protesters at Kent State University, killing four people and injuring nine others. I grew up with people whose parents were there when this happened.

In recent years, political tensions have boiled over into violence and intimidation, in some cases. The shooting committed by a Bernie Sanders supporter before the 2017 Congressional Baseball Game that seriously injured Steve Scalise of Louisiana, at the time third highest ranking House Republican, and three others is one example. Another is the disgusting incident that took place in

---

10   Dick Polman, "You want to see ugly politics: Jefferson vs. Adams," Trib Live, August 31, 2012. https://archive.triblive.com/opinion/featured-commentary/you-want-to-see-ugly-politics-jefferson-vs-adams/

11   Mark Jones, "May 19, 1856 - The road to succession," *Charleston Post and Courier*, May 19, 2020. https://www.postandcourier.com/350/articles/may-19-1856---the-road-to-succession/article_bd3a18d6-8bc4-11ea-b241-9f233c446855.html

Charlottesville, Virginia, where buffoonish white supremacists and neo-Nazis seemingly sought out racial tension that resulted in the tragic death of a young woman.

More recent examples are protests that we have witnessed since the death of George Floyd. The actual protests are understandable and should spark a conversation. Unfortunately, agitators took advantage of the situation and instigated riots, violence, and looting, damaging businesses—including minority-owned businesses—in the process. They aren't seeking justice; they are seeking chaos. These agitators have allowed people to retreat to their partisan corners, giving them an excuse not to address the real issues that have always been around but should finally be addressed.

The protests outside the White House in August 2020 during which Senator Rand Paul and his wife, Kelley, were attacked by a mob of people is a more recent example. I was also there that night and experienced this firsthand. From the second I stepped out past the White House barricades, an angry mob targeted, descended upon me, spit on me, and tried to intimidate me. I could see the cold anger and hatred in their eyes. I witnessed full grown adults regress into the ugliest, most primal forms of themselves.

It seems like we are hopelessly and irreparably divided. We assume the worst about those who have differences of opinion on hot-button political issues. The fact is, we aren't as divided as the political class and the media make us out to be.

A recent study by Beyond Conflict and the University of Pennsylvania learned that the Republicans and Democrats believe that they dislike and disagree with each other more than they actually do.[12] Although the study didn't ask about policy specifics, researchers did ask about positions on hot button issues like immigration and guns. They found significant overlap on these issues.

I may not agree with or endorse everything in this study, but I do believe that we are less divided than we believe we are. The study

---

12 "AMERICA'S DIVIDED MIND: Understanding the Psychology That Drives Us Apart," *Beyond Conflict*, June 2020. https://beyondconflictint.org/wp-content /uploads/2020/06/Beyond-Conflict-America_s-Div-ided-Mind-JUNE-2020-FOR-WEB.pdf

found that 65 percent of Republicans and 60 percent of Democrats oppose putting party interests over what is best for America. Only 28 percent of Democrats and 23 percent of Republicans believe that party interests should come before what is best for the country.

Many of my friends and neighbors have different views on culture and political issues. Some even have extreme left-wing views. We are able to talk about our differences of opinion respectfully, without calling each other names, because we respect each other. But we are able to separate our differences and view each other as people and enjoy a drink together. We don't isolate ourselves in an echo chamber. We find our common interests, whether it's sports, history, life at home, or some other topic.

In some ways, the very tools that have brought the world within our grasp, such as the internet and social media, have also allowed us to hide behind a keyboard while we demean and denigrate those with whom we disagree. The problem isn't these tools; rather, the way we view each other is. Disagreements over policy issues are healthy. Reducing each other down to our politics or ideological viewpoints is unhealthy.

We have to get out of our echo chambers and respectfully engage in discourse with those with whom we disagree. It's all about the experiences in our lives that shape our worldviews. Understanding why someone views the world in a certain way and giving them the same insight in your mind may foster a healthier political discourse.

Chapter 6

Taking on the Swamp
Through Grassroots

A t the end of the day, my goals are simple—to protect the system and values of our constitutional republic, the rule of law, and free market economy for the next generation. Thomas Jefferson once said, "The natural progress of things is for liberty to yield, and government to gain ground."[1] I hear you, Mr. Jefferson. It's up to us to pass the "shining city on the hill" on for posterity.

Here's what I do know: It takes a lot more than money and marketing to drain the Swamp. Winning in politics is hard, but making an impact is policy change is even harder. You will never outspend the deep-pocketed special interests of the Beltway, and if you believe in limited government, you are never going to make Hollywood like you. Instead, you need to get comfortable with being uncomfortable in Washington and build a community too big to ignore.

Throughout my years at FreedomWorks, I've seen how grassroots helped to develop trusted relationships with the most powerful force in Washington: the American voter. Former congressman and acting

---

1   Thomas Jefferson, "From Thomas Jefferson to Edward Carrington, 27 May 1788," National Archives, May 27, 1788. https://founders.archives.gov/documents /Jefferson/01-13-02-0120

White House Chief of Staff Mick Mulvaney once described how important these relationships with individual voters are:

We had a hierarchy in my office in Congress. If you were a lobbyist who never gave us money, I didn't talk to you. If you were a lobbyist who gave us money, I might talk to you. If you came from back home and sat in my lobby, I talked to you without exception, regardless of the financial contributions.[2]

When even a single citizen shows up in the office of a representative, they can influence legislative policy and regulations. Now imagine what millions of organized and engaged citizens can do. FreedomWorks helps propel the only force that will ever truly effect political change in this country: America's grassroots. If we lose this, this precious American freedom that past generations fought so hard for, it would probably take a hundred years and some catastrophic crisis to get the concepts of liberty back.

I'm not looking to solve all the problems of the world. No one can do that. But the amount of new problems we would face if we ever lost this exceptional country would crush the dilemmas we face today. I fight because it's my way of giving back to a country that has given me so much. Plus, it's a lot of fun. I get to meet activists, congressmen, and other leaders of different stripes. I get to watch, for good or ill, how this whole political machine works. I feel really blessed to battle for good at FreedomWorks and do my part in my role.

I used to think I joined this fight to do it for the United States, but it has since dawned on me that I'm actually doing it for Western civilization. I'm doing it for the cause of reason. If we lose the United States, we lose Western civilization. If the enemies of freedom prevail, we could see a bleak Orwellian world right around the corner. I

---

2   Glenn Thrush, "Mulvaney, Watchdog Bureau's Leader, Advises Bankers on Ways to Curtail Agency," *The New York Times*, April 24, 2018. https://www.nytimes.com/2018/04/24/us/mulvaney-consumer-financial-protection-bureau.html

want to do something every day to pass off these concepts of liberty to another generation.

But that's part of what our generation is tasked with doing—to continue to strive toward those ideals. This country was born of a grassroots revolution against an oppressive government in far off England, and today, regular, hardworking people from across the fifty states speak out against Washington and the establishment's agenda.

Washington doesn't get to decide alone what America is or should be. We do.

How the Swamp Fights Back

It's important to me to illustrate in no uncertain terms how the corrupt Washington system works. Let's start with career politicians. They don't constitute all of the Swamp but have always been the primary actors. Career politicians are the people the entire corrupt system operates around. These are the politicians who are the most excited to be in Congress and who plan on staying forever. This is their dream job. They love feeling important and they feed on it.

Although they cloak much of what they do in the language of civic duty, it's really just a power trip. We saw plenty of this during the COVID-19 pandemic. And it's a dream job. No CEO of a major company is catered to the way congressmen are. A congressman has an entire taxpayer-funded staff that waits on them hand and foot to take care of their every need, from morning to evening. Talk about stroking your ego.

Also at their service is the establishment media. The overwhelming majority of reporters and journalists reside in New York City, Los Angeles and Washington, D.C. These hubs of media and political elites all reinforce each other. Doing what's right or telling the truth is never as important as watching each other's back.

Then there is the army of bureaucrats. Congress doesn't give these people the power to regulate, nor does the Constitution. There is no real reason for them to even exist, and yet there they are, unelected officials who man the bureaucracies where they wield too much power.

These technocrats have moved from administering the necessary branches of government to becoming a shadow government. The decisions they make affect the country and our lives and yet the vast majority of them are never held accountable. They really are what many refer to as the "Deep State."

Then, you have the lobbyists. A lobbyist is just trying to figure out a way to benefit whatever group they work for. Right and wrong, or what's best for the country, have little to do with how they operate. When you walk through the halls of Congress and you see some of these grungy looking people lining up to get into a committee hearing, these are people who are paid to stand in place of the actual lobbyist—then the person in the nice suit shows up right before the chairman or chairwoman gavels in the hearing.

Let's not forget the political consultants. A political consultant's job is to continuously run in a campaign cycle. They feed off of the tribalism. They are rarely or never in the political game to promote ideas or principles, but to win the next election at any cost.

Career politicians who are desperate to hang on to power at the expense of taxpayers. The media who look down on us. Bureaucrats who think they know what's best for us. Technocrats who constantly push their "expert" opinions on us. Lobbyists who constantly want bailouts and subsidies funded by taxpayers. Consultants who are constantly seeking their cuts from ad buys even though fewer Americans are watching television.

They are all DC-based critters. This is the Swamp.

How the Swamp Grinds You Down

When people talk about "draining the Swamp," what that means in real world terms is challenging these elitists by undoing the networks they use to support each other.

One of the lessons I've learned is that these people are absolutely addicted to power. You have US senators who should have been out of office years ago, and are perhaps today dealing with senility issues, who simply won't let go. Why is it, after such a long time, that they still fight so hard to remain in office? Why not let someone else with fresh ideas come in?

They don't know any other way of life. They're entrenched. They have all had a dozen chiefs of staff and even more communications directors. The next thing you know, you have thirty to forty people with incredibly well-paid jobs who pay for their mortgages and kids' colleges based on the favors and influence they have though the senator or congressman they used to work for.

These are the DC professionals that exist because they are wrapped up behind this one person. Their livelihoods rely on the access they get to power. The way this cycle of corruption gets short-circuited is through the grassroots disrupting it. That's the goal.

To be very clear, the Swamp isn't partisan. It's bipartisan. The Swamp will go to any length to ensure that the status quo is protected and that the corrupt system we have today continues indefinitely. If any changes do come about, their priority is making sure their piece of turf is protected. The Swamp doesn't look at the long-term trends of the nation. They just want to manage. It does not make a difference to them if they are managing a country that is on the rise or one that is in decline.

Because they never get hurt. The rest of the country could be suffering due to the Swamp's policies and Washington elites never feel a thing. They are often not even aware. Because of the Swamp's power structure, Washington is recession proof. While the rest of the nation struggles, DC chugs along fine with no real incentive to help their fellow countrymen.

"The spectacle of Washington's free spending while virtually every other region has had to cut back—increasing prosperity in the capital in the midst of the worst recession since the Great Depression—has engendered public resentment and a pronounced anti-Washington sentiment that is now playing out in the midterm election cycle," *The Washington Times* reported in 2010, in the wake of the Great Recession. "While the nation's workforce took a body blow, losing 8.3 million jobs—5.5 percent of the jobs available before the recession—Washington suffered no more than a surface wound. It reported a loss of about thirty-five thousand jobs, or 1.1 percent of the jobs available—mostly in real estate and construction businesses hurt by the housing collapse."[3]

The Swamp is insulated from the economic woes the rest of America has to endure. No wonder they don't want anything to change.

What Happens to Those Who Dare Challenge the Washington Elite?

If you're an elected official in Washington, there is no advantage to being a courageous leader like a Rand Paul, Mike Lee, or Jim Jordan because you get shunned by your party leadership. You get treated like crap by the media because they don't understand who this interloper is who is trying to mess up Washington elites' way of life. The media and political class label such types rebels or rabble rousers— and they are! That's the whole damn point. That's the only reason anyone *should* come to Washington—to change it.

Anyone who actually fights the system gets cut off from the lobbyists' money. I remember former Congressman Ron Paul of Texas used to say that lobbyists didn't even bother knocking on his door because they knew they weren't going to get anywhere. What could Washington influencers possibly seek to trade with people who only want to upend the system and limit government?

Some actively avoid the political games that Washington plays. It may surprise you to learn that committee assignments are often not based on merit; it's all about how much money you can raise and the dues you pay to the National Republican Congressional Committee (NRCC). As perverse as it may sound, committee assignments are essentially rented. Congressman Thomas Massie of Kentucky calls

---

3   Patrice Hill, "In throes of recession, D.C. stands apart," *Washington Times*, October 17, 2010. https://m.washingtontimes.com/news/2010/oct/17/in-throes-of-recession-capital-stands-apart/

it "extortion."[4] Massie has received notices reminding him that he is behind on his dues. That may eventually cost him a committee assignment.

Some of the best leaders you would want in the thick of things in Washington are completely shut out of the system precisely because you can't bribe them. The regulatory bureaucracy doesn't want anything to do with them. For the campaign consultants, these rebels can't raise money in the same way career politicians can, so they're not as much fun to deal with.

The Swamp fights back by grinding you down. Anyone who seeks to come to Washington to actually do some good is fought tooth and nail by the entire system at every juncture. The Deep State pulls out all the stops to pull the rug out from anyone who dares challenge it.

Look at the ridiculous Robert Mueller investigation. It's not so much that they went after President Trump, but they targeted so many mid and lower-level people and ground them down with $50,000 to $100,000 legal bills where those accused have to sell their home or liquidate their kid's college fund just to pay for representation.[5] That's how the system works. They know that anyone principled may win an election here or there, but they will keep coming after you until you can't take it anymore.

I look at some of these congressional staffers who, the moment they pass a significant bill, where do they go next? If they pass a finance bill, they go work for the big banks. If they pass a health care bill, they go work for the health care companies.

If you show even a hint of a challenge to the Swamp and expose to the country how these people truly operate, you are branded a threat. They will try to corrupt you. They find ways to reward obedient congressmen that aren't against the law. I remember hearing

---

4   Lana Bellamy, "Congressman Says Washington Committee Seats Come at a Price," *The Daily Independent*, Apr. 4, 2016. https://www.dailyindependent.com/news/congressman-says-washington-committee-seats-come-at-a-price/article_20db268a-faa8-11e5-9815-e79bf5457be0.html

5   Nancy Cook, "'One real mess': Trump aides face the prospect of giant legal bills," *Politico*, October 30, 2019. https://www.politico.com/news/2019/10/30/trump-aides-impeachment-fallout-061452

about different congressmen who were promised lobbyist jobs if they voted a certain way. That, or they were told their spouses would be put on some prominent board with a $100,000 salary if the congressmen agreed to play ball.

The Swamp can even behave like the mafia. I have had board members who have been contacted or threatened. They were told you better do what "we" want—or else.

Once I came home to find a manila envelope. Inside was a picture of me shopping for groceries. There was another photo of me pumping gas. Other pictures were of me walking around in familiar settings. This can shake you. It would shake anybody. But it's also when you know you're a threat. Those photos were obviously meant to threaten me. We have had threats at FreedomWorks's office. Some we recorded and gave to the police over the years.

But the most common threat we probably get is people who vow to go after our funding. That's why it's so important to work with people who aren't part of the corrupt status quo. If you look at FreedomWorks' board, it's all people who are outside of Washington. They are people who are committed to the overall principles that we fight for.

A lot of the behavior the Swamp engages in on a regular basis is either illegal or ought to be. Sometimes they will use loopholes and legal gymnastics to go after you or principled members of Congress. No matter how you cut it, all of it has a corrupting influence.

We have to work hard to elect courageous candidates. Once we elect this minority of principled people, we have to support them. That means not abandoning them after the election is over. We need to support them financially and through effective advocacy.

The Swamp has all the incentive. We just have *us*.

It's easy to get corrupted in Washington and just wade into the Swamp, because it will always take care of you. You are going to get your cushy job. It's safe. Everyone protects each other. It's an incredibly close fraternity. The only way to fight this is through the grassroots, by showing up to support the very small minority of elected officials who are in this game only to fight the status quo. Social media has been a breakthrough for FreedomWorks because we can now go around the media.

If we're going to save the country from these people, we have to go above and around them. We have to block them with the only tools at our disposal: We the People. That's never going to change. That's the only way to drain the Swamp.

The Only Way to Win is Through Grassroots

I've been in meetings with prospective donors who tell me that all we need is to publish a policy brief on a big issue of the day or get a white paper that they've read on the president's desk, and it'll change everything. That's not how Washington works.

This chapter was inspired by my mother-in-law, Patricia Beckvermit. During a family vacation, she expressed frustration that most politicians just don't listen. I understand her perspective, but the exact opposite is true. Politicians don't pay attention to white papers or great policy ideas. If an idea doesn't have mass demonstrable support, it's not going anywhere. A politician won't care unless there's muscle behind it.

Washington isn't about the best ideas. It's about what ideas have the most support. With all the talk about money in politics, all the money is trying to do is influence your vote. Why? Because there is power in your vote.

What is a politician's number one job? I begin speeches by asking this question all the time and everyone always has the right answer: to get re-elected. A politician believes a good idea is something that helps with re-election.

When some of us recall *Schoolhouse Rock!* during Saturday morning cartoons (remember those?) and think about the ideas we care about, many might think, "Well, the politician is supposed to care about certain ideas, have a debate and make the right decision." Nope. That's not how it works.

"Grassroots activists are the boots on the ground that gets the mission accomplished. They are the army behind the mission, the patriots in the trenches fighting for the very heart and soul of our country. Seasoned

*grassroots activists are especially valuable, they understand the game, know the players and the rules and are eager to mentor."—***Grassroots activist Ronda Vuillemont-Smith, Oklahoma**

Grassroots Activists Have More Power Over Politicians Than They Realize

Politicians in our current system, whether they are in the House or the Senate, are always thinking about carefully choosing whatever they do and say. Why? Because first and foremost, they care about how their actions might affect their chance at re-election.

Politicians are inconvenience minimizers. The less trouble they make for themselves by taking real stands, the better. So there is always little incentive to take a risk. There's lots of incentive to do nothing and to blame someone else for failures. Sound familiar?

Politicians will listen to voices back home. One of the most frequent responses we get from House offices when we warn them that activists are coming to town is, "Are they from the district?" If it's a Senate office, they'll make sure the activists are from their state. Staffers on the Hill can easily dismiss visitors who aren't from their home state or district. They don't have to meet with them, but they usually will if they know they're from home.

That is the greatness of the power of grassroots. Grassroots is also powerful because it's not partisan. It's family. It's a neighborhood. It's a community. It's real people who care about each other and their country.

"Just as the natural world allows a tiny grass seed to fall on fertile soil, take root, send out rhizomes and seeds to multiply itself into millions; so does a grassroots movement. A spark of outrage at injustice and the loss of freedom inspires a passionate response in many, and that passionate response ignites a fire in others. And so it multiplies.

*Grassroots is important because it's genuine and unbridled. It acts as a beacon to others to step up, speak up and be brave."—***Grassroots activist Carol Davis, Illinois**

When I was growing up, there would be that neighbor who would help you find your lost dog. Coming of age in Cleveland, you would sometimes get your car stuck in the snow when it slid off your driveway, but there would always be a neighbor who would come out with a shovel and help you push it out. You might not trust the media, you might not trust most politicians, but if that neighbor has a political view, it carries a lot of weight.

We often value the opinions and worldviews of those who are closest to us. The people we actually trust. During the COVID-19 pandemic, many of us rightly trusted what some of our family and friends were saying more than some of the "experts" on television. There was good reason for that.

When I go back to my earliest days, the reason I think the way I do is because a lot of people I grew up with were who I put my faith in. I knew they wouldn't let me down. That's why grassroots matters. They possess the ultimate power in our society: their votes and thus the ability to hire or fire a politician.

It's not just about merely showing up at that ballot box. It's about making sure you visit your representative in their office and making sure they know how you feel about an issue. Because it has a major effect on our leaders. That's why Democrats have moved so far to the Left. It was grassroots pushing them there.

I have observed firsthand at town halls where sometimes everyone comes primarily to tell a politician how great he or she is. Yet if the first two or three people at the microphone are asking strong questions, all of a sudden there could be a riot on your hands. The conversation begins to take the issues in new and challenging directions for the elected official.

I've seen politicians under fire who may be very principled people start to backpedal from their positions in a room full of opposition. These tense situations are a good test of who is worth supporting and who's not.

I'll ask activists sometimes how often they've visited their congressman or senators' office in the last six months. Maybe a third in the room will raise their hand. That should be *everyone*. I'm not talking about only your congressman or senators' office in

Washington. Every congressman has at least one office in his or her congressional district. Every senator has multiple offices spread out across his or her state. District and state congressional staff communicate with the main office in Washington.

If everyone made a point of doing this on a regular basis, we would have a different country. To have any fundamental change in Washington, we have to make politicians fear our voice. We have to put them on the spot to respond when they are taking away more of our liberties, expanding government, and being corrupt. We also have to be respectful and knowledgeable. You can come across fired up, but you never want to cross any lines to make politicians easily dismiss you.

If more of us approached our elected officials like this, they would respond differently.

Activism Doesn't Mean Just Watching Fox News

Consuming conservative media is not activism. Talking to people who agree with you is not activism. You've got to get out and participate. That's why I think the Left does such a good job at this. That is their strongest power and influence—being involved. Social media now magnifies this even more. The old excuse was conservatives or libertarians were too busy working and putting food on the table to go out and protest like the Left does incessantly.

But the Tea Party taught those on the Right how to play this game too. I believe some of the protests against the mass lockdowns during the Coronavirus pandemic also offer some important lessons for grassroots activism.

> *"I associate 'grassroots' with authenticity. Any group with enough funding can pay doorknockers, but exciting the grassroots means people care about more than a paycheck."*—**Grassroots activist Lynn Gibbs, Ohio**

Facebook, Twitter, and other social media platforms are invaluable for the grassroots. Make sure you always like or follow politicians' pages that appear in your newsfeed. Scroll through their recent posts and leave a reaction to them.

The power of the Tea Party movement was that it was real people getting involved; it was organic. Politicians and pundits tried to figure out who was behind the movement, but it was just people getting involved in the process. That's all it was. They were accused of being "AstroTurf"—after the artificial playing surface that was popularized in baseball and football stadiums in the 1960s and 1970s—and not being representative of the frustration in real America.

In September 2009, FreedomWorks organized the Taxpayer March on Washington. This was the brainchild of my then-colleague, Brendan Steinhauser. We shared an office at the time. He said, "There's so much of this Tea Party energy in America. We need to get it all together in one place at one time." And the Taxpayer March on Washington was born.

Speaker Nancy Pelosi tried to discredit the Taxpayer March on Washington. She said, "This initiative is funded by the high end; we call it AstroTurf, it's not really a grass-roots movement. It's AstroTurf by some of the wealthiest people in America to keep the focus on tax cuts for the rich instead of for the great middle class."[6]

While standing on stage in front of the US Capitol, Brendan looked at the crowd and said, "I heard that Nancy Pelosi wasn't in town, but if she's watching, we do have a message for her: Speaker Pelosi, if you noticed, we replaced the grass on the West Lawn [of the Capitol] with AstroTurf."[7]

It was frustration to bailouts, Obamacare, and increased spending that few in Washington at the time had seen.

Legislators frequently receive less than a hundred comments on each Facebook post. If you write a comment under one of their posts explaining why you support or oppose a policy, trust us—their staff will see it. Members may even see it. Back in 2014, the Congressional

---

6   Jennifer Bendery, "GOP Tax Protest is Astroturf, not Grass Roots," *Roll Call*, Apr. 15, 2009. https://www.rollcall.com/2009/04/15/pelosi-gop-tax-protest-is-astroturf-not-grass-roots/

7   "FreedomWorks Rally," C-SPAN, Sept. 12, 2009. https://www.c-span.org/video/?288868-1/freedomworks-rally

Management Foundation published the findings of a poll of Hill staff in which they found that social media is replacing email as the dominant form of communication to their offices.[8] A follow up survey in 2015 showed that thirty or fewer comments was enough to get an office's attention.[9]

Congressman David Schweikert of Arizona tells me that members often pull up Facebook or Twitter between votes or during debate on a bill to see what's being said on their social media pages. There's a well-known senator who checks Twitter and Facebook between meetings. His chief of staff gets frustrated because he can't brief the senator between meetings because he's reading his replies or comments.

Another very powerful tool for grassroots activists is letters to the editor. Some say, "No one reads this." Politicians do. Trust me. Every communications director or press secretary on Capitol Hill has a Google alert on his or her boss's name. Most politicians also have alerts on their name. They take notice when they see their names. It's one of the first things they look for on any given morning. When an average person praises them for something, that's a personal endorsement that they take to heart. It also signals to the politician that there are likely many others who believe this.

The Left has always understood this. In my early days at FreedomWorks, we studied the book *Rules for Radicals* by Saul Alinsky. Alinsky understood that if you play it right, you can dominate the process. Being a radical Leftist, what he stood for was atrocious and his goals were atrocious, but he understood the psychology behind how politics work.

Liberals pull at the heartstrings to get more of your taxpayer dollars to spend as they see fit. There's nothing wrong with our side

---

8   Chris Nehls, "Just a Handful of Social Media Comments Can Grab the Attention of Congress, Study Shows," *Congressional Quarterly*, Oct. 27, 2014. https://info.cq.com /resources/just-a-handful-of-social-media-comments-can-grab-attention-of-congress-study-shows/

9   "#SocialCongress 2015," Congressional Management Foundation, 2015. https:// www.congressfoundation.org/projects/communicating-with-congress/social-congress-2015

telling our own stories toward the goal of spending less. We have the moral high ground of individual liberty. It's our philosophy that has lifted billions of people out of poverty. The philosophy the Left is pushing has put people in poverty. Our message is freedom. I was in the room when Andrew Breitbart said, "If you can't sell freedom and liberty, you suck."[10] It's one of those axioms I've heard that still rings true.

Storytelling is such an important part of politics. I believe those of us on more of the conservative and libertarian side don't often do a good job of getting our message out through stories. The Left has done a great job for decades of giving personal tales demonstrating why more government in our lives is desirable. We need to tell stories that show why more liberty is desirable.

Politicians spend money because people show up asking for more money. If people show up saying "Don't spend money," then they will stop spending. Politicians are responding to what they think are the issues that will get them re-elected. Since most elected officials are unprincipled and just value power, activists making the right moves can have more influence than they would ever imagine.

Again, that's why grassroots matter, and in fact I think they matter more than ever before. The more we don't trust the media and politicians—and make no mistake, that distrust is deepening like never before—the more we rely on people we know and respect in our lives.

If you educate yourself on the issues, you can have a circle of influence amongst your friends and family. If you express them in a positive way—always be a happy warrior—your opinions on an issue will have an impact on how people behave and vote.

"Based on my experience, grassroots is non-partisan and issues oriented. Most times, a grassroots movement starts spontaneously . . . We've evolved and are having a major effect through education, etc.,

10 Kristina Ribali, "One Year Later: Remembering Andrew Breitbart," FreedomWorks.org, Mar. 1, 2013. https://www.freedomworks.org/content/one-year-later-remembering-andrew-breitbart

in empowering grassroots activists. The strength, in my opinion, of our current wave is there is no centralized formal leadership."—**Grassroots activist Jack Adkins, Oregon**

Grassroots Power Has Been an Influential Force Since the Country Began

If you go back to America's founding, it was a grassroots effort. The Committees of Correspondence that began to take shape in the 1760s were a grassroots movement. The Sons of Liberty that arose during that same time was also a bottom-up group.

Grassroots activism is in our country's DNA. I love living that important inheritance every day. It's beautiful to watch a new activist come to FreedomWorks for our many fly-in events. They show up to find a hundred other people from across the country, of all ethnicities, ages, and backgrounds, and everyone is in love with the concept of liberty. For many activists, it's like they are back in school.

These passionate people don't identify as "Republicans" but "constitutionalists" or "patriots" or whatever label they believe best defines them. They get to powwow with so many others who feel the same way. That fellowship is so important. It's the glue that binds and propels the grassroots.

One of the most important parts of grassroots activism is that it reminds you that you aren't alone. It's good for the individual. In today's world there are fewer places than ever where actual social interaction occurs, so it's healthy to be able to join with others and speak your mind around people who tend to agree with you. It fires you up. That's important for keeping these ideas alive.

Most importantly, you get to have fun. Especially when everyone gets together and forces a politician to engage in a dialogue that they'd rather avoid. What's more fun than that?

Benjamin Franklin said, "It's a republic, if you can keep it". Grassroots activism is the only way that we will keep it. When people gather to work on politics together, they can point to a lineage going back almost two and a half centuries to the beer halls in Boston where people came together to discuss liberty and why it's worth defending. It's an important inheritance.

> *"To me, grassroots is local governance. Perhaps you like where you live and want to keep it that way. Get involved because it may not stay that way if the rule is voter apathy. Perhaps you like where you live and you see that taxes keep going up, while quality of services, quality of education, etc., things are not working out the way they should. Get involved. Change it. Find people who share your values and support them. Or run!"*—**Grassroots activist Debbie Wall, Texas**

A big threat to freedom today is cynicism. When people believe that a system can't change, they naturally become cynical. When you begin to believe that the status quo can never change, you start to feel like nothing more than a cog in the machine. Don't be cynical.

Not too long ago, I had a friendly discussion with a relative, who basically said activism didn't matter because it didn't matter who we elected. Nothing would ever change, regardless. I understand why this person said this. Many people have the same opinion and for good reason, although one would have to believe even cynics saw the power in popular protest during the coronavirus pandemic and even the peaceful police brutality protests that preceded the grotesque looting and violence.

But believing activism doesn't matter is still a gross misunderstanding of how politics and the world work. Or to combine them—it's a flawed assessment of a politician's world. Their world—their every thought and move—is dominated by re-election and what their voters think. Believe me, they care what the people who vote for them think. Everything a politician does is viewed through the lens of how this will play back in their district. People believe they're little, but in our system, people are big.

Politicians are actually very responsive to voters. We get the politicians that people show up to vote for. This is why I do grassroots. Owning the politicians' fear is the only way to change anything. Congress is hyper-responsive to its voters. At the end of the day, that's where power is. Washington listens to those who show up. The Left is who has, historically, tended to show up in congressional offices. Conservatives listen to talk radio or watch Fox News.

Accountability is the responsibility of the citizen. Showing up at your congressman or senators' offices is the most powerful tool for accountability, and few do it. It all doesn't have to be political either. Grassroots work can do a lot of good for communities. Supporting veterans. Helping educate kids. Saving animals. Aiding neighbors in need. There are all sorts of things you can do.

But if you lose grassroots, you will lose that vibrant part of our democracy that is so important to keep us engaged. It drives me nuts when I see progressives and the Left getting together, but I deeply respect the fact that they are out there fighting for the ideas they believe in. In fact, I'm all for them doing this. I just want to make sure I get my people together and that we're doing it even more.

Over the years, I've met and talked to center-right leaders from Europe and Japan. One of them wanted to start a "green tea movement" in Japan. They are amazed by how active Americans are in the political process. That doesn't happen in these countries. The people in these countries may be involved in the parties, but that's where their activism ends. If you're going to be a conservative activist in the United Kingdom, you work in the party. You don't go to Westminster to lobby members of Parliament.

It's not just about pushing for change and preserving what we want to preserve. It's the heartbeat of the country. If we ever lose that, we'll lose what makes our system so unique.

"Grassroots means taking back our country from the ground up.

It is joining arms, like roots, to nourish a new tree of conservatism that returns decisions and power back to the citizens and will eventually grow to provide the fruits of freedom to the next generation."
—**Grassroots activist Michelle Morrow, North Carolina**

Grassroots Work Doesn't Always Go as Planned—But It Doesn't Matter

What's tough sometimes is when you participate in grassroots activity and work really hard, but then no one shows up. Maybe you work really hard to put an event together, and then a cataclysmic snowstorm hits and no one can make it the day before the rally. Hey, let's face it, shit happens.

FreedomWorks once organized a rally to oppose Obamacare that took place in twenty-degree weather. It snowed in the DC area overnight. FreedomWorks staffers were shoveling snow in the park adjacent to the Russell Senate Office Building so we could set up a stage and create a safer place for people to walk. Most of our buses north of DC got stuck in an ice storm, but we still had more than one thousand activists show up. National radio host Andrew Wilkow broadcast his radio show live. I think he's still thawing out. HBO even showed up to film the event.

We still had the event, but it was high risk. This happens. Sometimes things just go horribly wrong. But it's fun when things go fantastically right. It can be an adventure. You can't take anything personally when you work in grassroots. Sometimes people love what you're doing, sometimes they don't. Sometimes people get involved and become the best activist, but then they move on. They get married. They got a different job. Their lives lead them elsewhere.

That's actually one of the fun parts of grassroots, in that you're always meeting new people. I've learned that there is an endless reservoir of Americans who for whatever reason get involved, get engaged, but often feel defeated in some way. That's a shame because setbacks here and there never constitute actual defeat. But there's always a new wave of activists ready to go to battle again.

"Grassroots = the people."—**Grassroots activist Maggie Sandrock, North Carolina**

An Active Citizenry is the DNA of Being an American

For the American system to work as founded and intended, we must have an active citizenry. That's what grassroots is. If you go back to the original idea behind the Second Amendment and the part about a well-regulated militia, the whole concept was that we come together in communities to solve our problems. This is the DNA of being an American.

Voting is not where your civic duty begins and ends. If just voting is all you think is necessary, politicians are simply going to figure out how much free stuff they need to give you in order to get your vote.

That wasn't the intention of the Founders. Through the great traditions established in early New England town halls and similar events throughout the colonies, the idea is to vote, but then to stay extremely engaged with elected officials. If after some time, that politician didn't do their job, citizens can vote for them to stay or leave.

Grassroots is important because if you only pay attention to elections, you have given up all your power and influence. If you only care around election time, it incentivizes you to become a bad citizen.

"Grassroots = getting off the sidelines and participating in one or more of the following:

1. *Volunteering to canvass and/or call on behalf of a candidate.*
2. *Going to your precinct meetings and signing up to be a delegate at your county, District and State Conventions.*
3. *Attending and bringing your friends to political events and gatherings, including but not limited to… club meetings and educational events about policy, legislation and process, topics that are handled by politicians and legislation, meet the candidate events, fundraisers (more than just writing a check, but also volunteer at and to organize and host fundraisers). Volunteer at the polls.*
4. *Organize large assemblies, rallies, events that either support/push for a particular policy or protest against/stop a particular policy. Create enough buzz, attention and momentum to attend media attention and*

spread the word. This includes social media networks."—**Grassroots activist Elizabeth Fohey, Michigan**

Everyone knows President John F. Kennedy's famous quote, "Ask not what your country can do for you, but what you can do for your country." That line is actually a call for grassroots activism. Because if you seriously stay involved in the process, it means being involved at all levels. Not just national elections—your community.

> *"We grassroots activists (The Common People) are the majority of our country who believe in "GOVT STAY OUT OF OUR WAY" and as such suffer from the decisions created by politicians who very rarely are impacted by their own terrible decisions. The Tea Parties in this country are the Loyalists, Proud, Strong, and as True Patriots will always fight for and love their country."*—**Grassroots activist Mel Grossman, Florida**

You don't like what your kids are learning in school?

How many times have you gone to the school board meeting? You don't like that you don't have proper storm drainage in your neighborhood?

How are you getting involved in your local council meetings to make sure change happens?

That's why grassroots is so fundamentally important. I often think that because many citizens have focused so much on just elections, this is what allows the Swamp to grow. The only way you bleed the Swamp out is through active grassroots organization on the streets to make sure our leaders continuously feel the pressure.

I always remember former Republican presidential candidate and liberty advocate Steve Forbes saying that if you want change, you have to make politicians feel the "white heat" of public opinion. He's right. If you truly care about something and enough others do as well, politicians will react. (As an aside, the first vote I cast after registering to vote was for Steve Forbes in the 1996 Ohio presidential primary.)

The beauty of our system is you can have two people on opposite sides of an issue who are very fired up. Who gets more fired up can determine the direction of the country. Do we want more government or less? Do we want more centralized control or less? Do we want more individual responsibility or less? Do we want more freedom or less freedom?

We fight for more freedom. Always. The other side will always fight for more security in the form of free stuff and less liberty. The grassroots are the frontline of that battle. Through grassroots is the way to get their attention. Politicians will meet with you because they are terrified of you, and they should be. That's healthy in any constitutional republic.

Chapter 7
How Did We Lose Control?

W e keep an optimistic atmosphere at FreedomWorks, but one of my staffers, Jason Pye, is frequently overheard saying, "Everything is terrible." Jason is in charge of our policy department and leads congressional outreach. He sees what Congress is doing on a day-to-day basis. He reads the reports from the Congressional Budget Office on America's fiscal problems, and the budgetary outlook is alarming. It's a constant reminder of why I got into this business—to cut federal spending.

Not only is the budgetary outlook alarming, but much of what Congress does these days is focused on nothing more than political messaging, ignoring real problems like the budget. Much of the legislation passed out of the House is what we call "messaging bills." These are bills that appeal to the grassroots base of the party in power but have no real chance of becoming law. Democrats and Republicans are both guilty of this, but they continue to focus on messaging bills at the expense of the actual problems that face America.

It may be trite, but the old saying goes, "Those who cannot remember the past are condemned to repeat it." And we are repeating history because we haven't learned from the lessons of the past.

When Jimmy Carter took office in January 1977, America was facing a period of economic stagnation and inflation, known as "stagflation," and a high unemployment rate. These were problems that Carter inherited from Richard Nixon and Gerald Ford, who assumed the presidency after Nixon resigned in disgrace in August 1974.

Nixon had taken a series of steps in response to rising unemployment and inflation, known as the "Nixon shock." In August 1971, he ended the convertibility of the US Dollar to gold,[1] essentially ending the gold standard and all but ending the post-World War II Bretton Woods Agreement, which was a currency exchange system indexed to the gold-backed US Dollar, and established wage and price controls for a ninety-day period.

In a televised address to the nation, Nixon acknowledged the economic uncertainty and outlined the steps he was taking to address them. But he appealed to Americans, urging them to "raise our spirits" and "contribute all we can to this great and good country that has contributed so much to the progress of mankind."[2]

From a raw political perspective, the steps that Nixon took were a success. Americans seemed to buy into the actions. The *New York Times* Editorial Board praised Nixon, writing, "[W]e unhesitatingly applaud the boldness with which the President has moved on all economic fronts."[3]

But the political success of Nixon's actions didn't translate into economic success. Lewis E. Lehrman wrote, "The 'Nixon Shock' was followed by a decade of some of the worst inflation in American history and the most stagnant economy since the Great Depression."[4]

---

1   Sandra Kollen Ghizoni, "Nixon Ends Convertibility of US Dollars to Gold and Announces Wage/Price Controls," FederalReserveHistory.org, Nov. 22, 2013. https://www.federalreservehistory.org/essays/gold_convertibility_ends

2   Richard Nixon, "Address to the Nation Outlining a New Economic Policy: 'The Challenge of Peace,'" Aug. 15, 1971. Hosted online by The American Presidency Project at UC Santa Barbara, https://www.presidency.ucsb.edu/documents/address-the-nation-outlining-new-economic-policy-the-challenge-peace

3   "Call to Economic Revival," *The New York Times*, Aug. 16, 1971. https://www.nytimes.com/1971/08/16/archives/call-to-economic-revival.html

4   Lewis E. Lehrman, "The Nixon Shock Heard 'Round the World," *The Wall Street Journal*, Aug. 15, 2011. https://www.wsj.com/articles/SB10001424053111904007304576494073418802358

Inflation continued to rise, reaching 8.7 percent in 1973 and 12.3 percent by the end of 1974, only months after Nixon resigned from office, and the unemployment rate began ticking upward. Between January 1973 and December 1974, the Dow Jones Industrial Average declined by 46 percent. Exacerbating an already struggling economy was the Organization of Arab Petroleum Exporting Countries' oil embargo against countries, including the United States, supporting Israel in the 1973 Yom Kippur War.

In the midst of these economic problems, America was winding down its involvement in an unpopular and bloody conflict in Vietnam, racial tensions were still high, and crime was rising.

Vietnam had become a flashpoint in American politics, causing President Lyndon Johnson not to seek re-election in 1968. Protests against our involvement in Vietnam and the military draft, as well as the dramatic increase in the number of American service members who were killed in the conflict, had taken their toll and damaged Americans' confidence in Washington. By 1971, as Nixon was gradually winding down our involvement in the conflict, fully 60 percent of Americans viewed sending troops to Vietnam as a mistake.[5]

Although Nixon was elected on a platform of "law and order," violent crime and property crime began to rise in the late 1960s and 1970s, a trend that would continue through to the early 1990s.[6] Major cities like New York deteriorated as crime ran rampant.[7] Prior to the 1970s, many residents of these major cities left and moved into the suburbs. Even though their tax bases were dwindling as the exodus to the suburbs remained steady throughout the 1970s, cities continued to increase public services, creating financial strains.

---

5   "CBS News Poll: US Involvement in Vietnam," Jan. 28, 2018. https://www.cbsnews.com/news/cbs-news-poll-u-s-involvement-in-vietnam/

6   "Sourcebook of criminal justice statistics online," University at Albany, 2012. https://www.albany.edu/sourcebook/pdf/t31062012.pdf

7   Edmund White, "Why Can't We Stop Talking About New York in the Late 1970s?" *The New York Times*, Sept. 10, 2015. https://www.nytimes.com/2015/09/10/t-magazine/1970s-new-york-history.html

My home city, Cleveland, saw a nearly 24 percent decline in population in the 1970s.[8] The decline of the steel industry hastened the economic issues facing my hometown. Once an economic powerhouse of the Midwest, Cleveland defaulted on its debt obligations in 1978 during the administration of a leftist mayor, Dennis Kucinich,[9] who is more known for his time in the House of Representatives, making two unsuccessful bids for president, and chasing rainbows in his search for the Leprechaun's pot of gold.

The economic conditions that President Carter faced when he took office weren't his fault. Inflation continued to rise until the Federal Reserve, led by Paul Volcker, increased interest rates. Carter's undoing has been well-documented; another oil crisis caused by tensions in the Middle East, rising unemployment and another recession in 1980, and the Iranian hostage crisis.

Carter acknowledged the "erosion of confidence" that he saw in Americans in a July 1979 address to the nation, saying, "[A]fter listening to the American people I have been reminded again that all the legislation in the world can't fix what's wrong with America... Our people are losing that faith, not only in government itself but in the ability as citizens to serve as the ultimate rulers and shapers of our democracy."[10] This became known as the "malaise speech," although Carter never used the word.

The feeling was that America had seen its best days. Does this sound familiar? Does history repeat itself?

---

8   Jordan Rappaport, "US Urban Decline and Growth, 1950 to 2000," Federal Reserve Bank of Kansas City, 2013. https://www.kansascityfed.org/NKocZ/Publicat/ECONREV/PDF/3q03rapp.pdf

9   Reginald Stuart, "City of Cleveland Defaults on Loans," *The New York Times*, Dec. 16, 1978. https://www.nytimes.com/1978/12/16/archives/city-of-cleveland-defaults-on-loans-council-adjourns-without-action.html

10   Jimmy Carter, "The 'Malaise' Speech," July 15, 1979. Transcript hosted by Prentice Hall Publishing, https://wps.prenhall.com/wps/media/objects/108/111235/ch29_a5_d2.pdf

The Shining City on a Hill

President Ronald Reagan seized on this sentiment during his 1980 campaign for president. During a debate with Carter, Reagan pointedly asked Americans, "Are you better off than you were four years ago? Is it easier for you to go and buy things in the store than it was four years ago? Is there more or less unemployment in the country than there was four years ago? Is America as respected throughout the world as it was?"[11]

Reagan didn't simply posture.

"The Great Communicator" was focused on addressing the problems that faced Americans in 1980 and the sense that our best days were behind us. Reagan said, "This country doesn't have to be in the shape that it is in. We do not have to go on sharing in scarcity with the country getting worse off, with unemployment growing. We talk about the unemployment lines. If all of the unemployed today were in a single line allowing two feet for each of them, that line would reach from New York City to Los Angeles, California. All of this can be cured and all of it can be solved."[12]

On the eve of the presidential election in 1980, Reagan delivered a televised speech in which he focused on restoring a sense of optimism in America after a period of stagflation.[13] He framed America as a "shining city on a hill," and his optimistic outlook won Americans over.

The first couple of years of Reagan's presidency were not without economic problems. When Reagan took office in January 1981, the unemployment rate was 7.5 percent. By the end of the year, the unemployment rate was 8.5 percent. A deep recession, caused by efforts to fight inflation and the lingering effects of the oil crisis,

---

11   Ronald Reagan, Presidential debate vs. President Jimmy Carter, Oct. 28, 1980, transcript hosted by The Commission on Presidential Debates. https://www.debates .org/voter-education/debate-transcripts/october-28-1980-debate-transcript/

12   Ibid

13   Ronald Reagan, "Election Eve Address, 'A Vision for America,'" Nov. 3, 1980. Speech transcript hosted by the American Presidency Project at the UC Santa Barbara, https://www.presidency.ucsb.edu/documents/election-eve-address-vision-for-america

pushed the unemployment rate even higher, peaking at 10.8 percent in November 1982.

Reagan had long made cutting taxes a top priority. When his son, Michael Reagan, asked for an increase in his allowance, Reagan replied, "When I get a tax cut, I'll raise your allowance." Between 1936 and 1980, the top tax statutory tax bracket hadn't fallen below 70 percent,[14] and it went as high as 94 percent in 1944 and 1945.

In April 1942, Franklin D. Roosevelt asked Congress for a top income tax bracket of 100 percent.[15] Congress didn't act on the proposal. Several months later, he signed an executive order capping after-tax income at $25,000,[16] or about $392,000 in today's dollars.

Between 1950 and 1963, the top tax bracket exceeded 90 percent. Of course, these were the rates on the books; in reality, many who fell into the top income bracket found creative ways not available today to lower their overall tax liability.[17] Scott Greenberg of the Tax Foundation notes that "the top 1 percent of taxpayers in the 1950s only paid about 42 percent of their income in taxes."[18]

The Left tries to paint a picture of a strong economy when the United States had high income tax rates. It's true that the economy grew, but the economy also experienced a recession in 1949, two in the 1950s, and another in 1960. As historian Brian Domitrovic explains, "[T]here wasn't significant economic growth in the 1950s.

---

14 Joint Committee on Taxation, "Overview of Present Law and Economic Analysis Relating to Marginal Tax Rates and the President's Individual Income Tax Rate Proposals," Mar. 6, 2001. http://www.jct.gov/x-6-01.pdf (Table 1)

15 Franklin Delano Roosevelt, "President Franklin D. Roosevelt's Message to Congress," Apr. 27, 1942. Speech transcript hosted by iBiblio.org, Sept. 16, 1997. http://www.ibiblio.org/pha/policy/1942/1942-04-27b.html

16 Franklin Delano Roosevelt, "Executive Order 9250: Establishing the Office of Economic Stabilization," Oct. 3, 1942. Hosted by the American Presidency Project at UC Santa Barbara, https://www.presidency.ucsb.edu/documents/executive-order-9250-establishing-the-office-economic-stabilization

17 Laura Saunders, "How Wealthy Americans Like Jack Benny Avoided Paying a 70% Tax Rate," Wall Street Journal, Jan. 18, 2019. https://www.wsj.com/articles/how-wealthy-americans-like-jack-benny-avoided-paying-a-70-tax-rate-11547807401

18 Scott Greenberg, "Taxes on the Rich Were Not That Much Higher in the 1950s," The Tax Foundation, Aug. 4, 2017. https://taxfoundation.org/taxes-on-the-rich-1950s-not-high/

It only averaged 2.5 percent during the presidency of Dwight D. Eisenhower, and the tax code spawned inequality that is even unheard of today."[19] The inequality Domitrovic mentions was that the wealthy and politically connected either got creative with their accounting to avoid taxes or used their influence to get carve-outs in the tax code.

Putting average economic growth into perspective, between 2010 and 2017, annual economic growth averaged 2.2 percent. We would hardly call this strong or robust economic growth. Fans of the television show *The West Wing* may remember the fictional president, Jed Bartlet, telling his chief of staff, "Historically, 2 to 2.5 percent GDP expansion is classified as lackluster—even anemic—economic growth. Four and a half to 5 percent is needed just to be considered robust and not even spectacular."

Reagan ultimately honed the view of John F. Kennedy, the first supply-side president in the modern era. In his final State of the Union address, Kennedy explained that high tax rates were slowing economic growth. "Designed to check inflation in earlier years, it now checks growth instead," Kennedy told Congress. "It discourages extra effort and risk. It distorts the use of resources. It invites recurrent recessions, depresses our Federal revenues, and causes chronic budget deficits."

Kennedy was tragically assassinated in November 1963, but the tax cut he proposed was passed by Congress in 1964 and the top statutory tax rate was lowered from 91 percent to 70 percent.[20] The economy entered an impressive period of growth as a result.

In 1981, Reagan managed to get the largest tax cut in American history at the time passed through a Democrat-controlled House and

19 Brian Domitrovic, "How Taxing the Rich Paradoxically Resulted in More Inequality for All," *Learn Liberty*, Aug. 24, 2017. https://www. learnliberty.org/speakers/https://www.learnliberty.org/blog/how-taxing-the-rich-paradoxically-resulted-in-more-inequality-for-all//

20 Richard Morrison, "Happy Birthday to the Kennedy Tax Cuts," The Tax Foundation, Feb. 26, 2013. https://taxfoundation.org/happy-birthday-kennedy-tax-cuts

a Republican-controlled Senate.[21] This was back when Democrats understood that economic growth and private investment were good things. Passed with broad bipartisan support, the Economic Recovery Tax Act reduced taxes by 23 percent across the board, lowered the top income tax bracket down to 50 percent, and reformed the tax code.

The economy still stayed mired in a recession and the budget deficit grew. The following year, Congress passed the Tax Equity and Fiscal Responsibility Act, which partially rolled back the 1982 tax cut. Reagan reluctantly signed the bill into law. He also signed a gas tax increase into law in 1982 and payroll tax increase in 1983. He was re-elected in a landslide in 1984 and, in 1986, Reagan signed a historic tax reform bill into law, creating a three-tier income tax system, with the highest rate lowered to 28 percent.

Reagan is unfairly maligned by the Left because he pursued tax cuts while also increasing defense spending. Of course, he viewed the Soviet Union as the "Evil Empire" and pursued a policy of "peace through strength." Not long after he left office, the Soviet Union collapsed. Reagan also had to contend with a Democrat-controlled House and many moderate Republicans throughout his entire presidency, and his requests for spending cuts were rebuffed.[22] He made deals, and although not all of those deals were good ones, he left the nation far better off than he found it.

The economy began a boom period in 1983, real household income began to rise, and unemployment began to decline. Reagan restored the sense of optimism in Americans that had seemingly been lost in the decade before him. As Reagan said in his farewell speech to the nation:

---

21 "Is President Trump's Tax Cut the Largest in History yet?" Committee for a Responsible Federal Budget, Oct. 25, 2017. http://www.crfb.org/blogs /president-trumps-tax-cut-largest-history-yet

22 John Samples, "Limiting Government, 1980-2010," *Cato Foundation Policy Report*, March/April 2010. https://www.cato.org/policy-report/marchapril-2010 /limiting-government-1980-2010

We've done our part. And as I walk off into the city streets, a final word to the men and women of the Reagan revolution, the men and women across America who for eight years did the work that brought America back. My friends: We did it. We weren't just marking time. We made a difference. We made the city stronger, we made the city freer, and we left her in good hands. All in all, not bad, not bad at all.[23]

Although there was a brief recession in 1990 and early 1991, tax rates remained relatively low until 1993 when the newly elected president, Bill Clinton, signed a major tax increase into law. The tax increase that Clinton signed was one of the largest in American history. The top statutory rate was raised to 39.6 percent and the corporate tax rate to 35 percent.

Even Clinton acknowledged that he went too far. During a 1995 fundraiser, Clinton told supporters, "Probably there are people in this room still mad at me at that budget because you think I raised your taxes too much. It might surprise you to know that I think I raised them too much, too."[24] The economy grew, but it was held back because of the 1993 tax increase.[25]

The Republican Revolution of 1994 brought American politics into a new era. Clinton, who had Democratic majorities in both chambers of Congress during the first two years of his first term, learned how to conduct business with Newt Gingrich and a Republican-controlled Congress. Although he vetoed two previous welfare reform bills, Clinton signed the Republican-led Personal Responsibility and Work Opportunity Act into law in 1996. He also signed a capital gains tax into law in 1997.

---

23   Ronald Reagan, "Farewell Address to the Nation," Jan.11, 1989. Transcript hosted by the Ronald Reagan Presidential Foundation, https://www.reaganfoundation.org/media/128652/farewell.pdf

24   Todd S. Purdum, "Clinton Angers Friend and Foe in Tax Remark," *The New York Times*, Oct.19,1995. https://www.nytimes.com/1995/10/19/us/clinton-angers-friend-and-foe-in-tax-remark.html

25   Charles Kadlec, "The Dangerous Myth About the Bill Clinton Tax Increase," Forbes.com, July 16, 2012. https://www.forbes.com/sites/charleskadlec/2012/07/16/the-dangerous-myth-about-the-bill-clinton-tax-increase/#695f88006e8a

People say that the economy was good under Clinton. Sure. He benefited from the growth that came from the recovery from recession that ended in early 1991. Republicans also stopped some of the bad parts of Clinton's legislative agenda, including his failed health care plan. He also benefited from the technology boom of the 1990s.

This technology boom came from research in the 1970s matched with capital investment in the 1980s. If Reagan hadn't come around and pushed aggressively for tax cuts, we wouldn't have had the technology boom that we saw in the 1990s.

In his 1996 State of the Union address, Clinton tried to steal some thunder from Republicans by declaring that "the era of big government is over." Clinton and a Republican Congress produced four years of balanced budgets and the share of the national debt held by the public declined. Federal spending as a share of the economy decreased from 20 percent in 1995 to 17.7 percent in 2000.

This era of divided government saw less spending, increased investment, significant economic growth, and leaps in innovation. The dignity of work was restored, trade was liberalized, and investment was encouraged. Between 1997 and 2000, the economy grew at an annual average of 4.5 percent. The period of prosperity made Alan Greenspan quip that Clinton was "the best Republican president we've had in a while."[26]

Not everything was perfect in the 1990s and there was plenty of bitterness and political messaging, but the system worked, and it worked well.

Bush, Obama, and the Great Recession

The September 11, 2001 terrorist attacks shocked the system. President George W. Bush had only been in office for a short time. He ran as a "compassionate conservative," but he also wanted to

---

26   Mark Felsenthal, "Greenspan Faults Democrats on Trade," *USA Today*, Sept. 23, 2007. https://usatoday30.usatoday.com/money/economy/2007-09-23-greenspan-globalization_N.htm

aggressively cut taxes. Bush was successful, pushing through historic tax cuts in 2001 and 2003.

Bush became a wartime president on September 11, 2001. Standing on the rubble at Ground Zero in New York City with a bullhorn in his hand, Bush declared that "the people who knocked these buildings down will hear all of us soon."[27] He was cheered when he threw out the first pitch at Yankee Stadium before game three of the 2001 World Series. His approval rating in the aftermath of September 11 peaked at 90 percent.[28]

Unfortunately, Bush's brand of conservatism led to a frustrating growth of the size and scope of the federal government, angering fiscal conservatives. Adding insult to injury, Republicans had complete control of Congress during Bush's first term and for the first two years of his second. Congressional Republicans, who reduced federal spending under Clinton, became complicit in this growth in government under Bush.

Bush's apologists have defended his record on spending, pointing to the horrible September 11 terrorist attacks and the wars in Afghanistan and Iraq as the reason. It's true that defense spending did dramatically increase, but so did nondefense spending. He created a new entitlement program, the prescription drug benefit, adding trillions of unfunded liabilities to Medicare.[29] He also created a brand new cabinet-level federal bureaucracy, the Department of Homeland Security. Chris Edwards of the Cato Institute explained that the spending explosion under Bush made him "the biggest domestic spender since Nixon."[30]

---

27 Kenneth T. Walsh, "George W. Bush's 'Bullhorn' Moment," *US News*, April 25, 2013. https://www.usnews.com/news/blogs/ken-walshs-washington/2013/04/25/george-w-bushs-bullhorn-moment

28 "Presidential Approval Ratings - George W. Bush," Gallup, https://news.gallup.com/poll/116500/presidential-approval-ratings-george-bush.aspx Accessed Sept. 5, 2020.

29 John C. Goodman, "The Worst Entitlement Program in Our History," *Forbes*, July 6, 2016. https://www.forbes.com/sites/johngoodman/2016/07/06/the-worst-entitlement-program-in-our-history/

30 Chris Edwards, "George W. Bush: The Biggest Spender Since LBJ," *Cato at Liberty*, Dec. 19, 2009. https://www.cato.org/blog/george-w-bush-biggest-spender-lbj

Bush made Senator Ted Kennedy of Massachusetts the quarterback on No Child Left Behind,[31] the failed 2001 education reform law that was scuttled in 2015. Kennedy's former education staffer, Danica Petroshius, said, "[Bush's team] looked around and said, 'You can't do an education bill without Ted Kennedy. Why isn't he here?' Days later, the newly-elected, soon-to-be-sworn in president called. It was really nice. The senator was not upset . . .The president said, 'I can't do this without you. Will you help me?' And the senator said, 'Yes, of course I will. I want to do this too.'"[32] *Time Magazine* would later note that No Child Left Behind "may not have been passed without Senator Kennedy's strong support."[33] Relying on the so-called "liberal lion" to produce an education bill wasn't the best idea.

Bush also monumentally failed to deliver on his plan to allow young people to put some of their own money into personal accounts for Social Security. He didn't simply pay the issue lip-service. "Younger workers," Bush said in his 2004 State of the Union address, "should have the opportunity to build a nest egg by saving part of their Social Security taxes in a personal retirement account."[34] He even campaigned on personal accounts for Social Security.[35]

In his first press conference after winning re-election in November 2004, Bush said, "[T]his is a tough issue. Look, I fully understand how hard it is. Social Security—people are generally risk-averse when it comes time to Social Security. My problem with that is, is that the longer you wait, the more difficult the issue is going to become.

---

31 Darren Samuelsohn and Daniel Vinik, "No Child Left Behind: The Oral History," *Politico*, Sept. 23, 2015. https://www.politico.com/agenda/story/2015/09 /no-child-left-behind-education-law-history-000241/

32 Ibid.

33 "Kennedy's Top 10 Legislative Battles: No Child Left Behind," *Time* slideshow, accessed Oct. 8, 2020. http://content.time.com/time/specials/packages /article/0,28804,1918873_1918869_1918857,00.html

34 George W. Bush, "State of the Union Address, 2004," Jan. 20, 2004. Transcript hosted by *The Washington Post*. https://www.washingtonpost.com/wp-srv/politics /transcripts/bushtext_012004.html

35 George W. Bush, "President's Remarks at 'Focus on Health with President Bush' Event," Sept. 16, 2004. Transcript hosted by the White House archives, https:// georgewbush-whitehouse.archives.gov/news/releases/2004/09/text/20040916-15.html

And some will keep pushing it. And hopefully we can get something done."[36]

The message was clear: "I earned capital in this campaign, political capital, and now I intend to spend it."[37] Personal accounts for Social Security was a top domestic priority.

By June 2005, the effort on personal accounts for Social Security was falling apart. Bush hadn't properly courted Congress, particularly gettable Democrats. Congressional Democrats lined up against the proposal, even holding rallies to speak out against the plan.[38] The AARP came out hard against Bush and launched a massive campaign against his proposal.[39]

By September 2005, with the aftermath of Hurricane Katrina dominating the news cycle, the plan was on life support, The following month, as *The New York Times* put it, private accounts for Social Security had "almost completely disappeared from the Washington stage after being the central policy debate earlier this year."[40]

Bush squandered the political goodwill that followed September 11. The war in Afghanistan was entirely justified and righteous, but the war in Iraq was a mistake. Americans' confidence was shaken as thousands of American service members were killed in action. It was even further shaken in 2007 as the economy began to enter the worst downturn since the Great Depression, caused by the burst of the housing bubble.

---

36 George W. Bush, "Press Conference by the President," Nov. 8, 2006. Hosted by the White House archive, https://georgewbush-whitehouse.archives.gov/news/releases/2006/11/20061108-2.html

37 Andrew Glass, "President George W. Bush Pursues Social Security Reform, May 2, 2001," *Politico*, May 2, 2018. https://www.politico.com/story/2018/05/02/president-george-w-bush-pursues-social-security-reform-may-2-2001-559632

38 "Dems Rally Against Social Security Reform," CNN.com, Feb. 3, 2005. https://www.cnn.com/2005/ALLPOLITICS/02/03/dems.ss/index.html

39 Jessie Calmes, "On Social Security, It's Bush vs. AARP," *The Wall Street Journal*, Jan. 21, 2005. https://www.wsj.com/articles/SB110626566327732055

40 Vikas Bajaj, "Bush's Challenges Not Unusual for a Second-Term President," *The New York Times*, Oct. 28, 2005. https://www.nytimes.com/2005/10/28/politics/bushs-challenges-not-unusual-for-a-second-term-president.html

Home ownership is a good thing, but mismanagement of housing policy and over-involvement of federal forces is not. For example, my wife and I recently bought our first home, and we take pride in what we were able to accomplish together. But for too long, administrations and Congress promoted the idea that everyone should own a home.[41] The Federal Reserve was also complicit through its loose monetary policy. A housing bubble was created, as lenders began handing out loans to risky borrowers.

John Allison, who was the CEO of BB&T when the Great Recession began in 2008, said that the cause of the crash "was a combination of government housing policy, Fannie Mae and Freddie Mac in particular, which had $5 trillion in liabilities and $2 trillion in subprime mortgages when they failed, and the Federal Reserve, which held interest rates below inflation, that contributed to the bubble in the housing market, along with bubbles in other markets."[42]

The response was a massive bailout of Wall Street through the Emergency Economic Stabilization Act, which created the Troubled Asset Relief Program. In November 2008, Bush said, "I've abandoned free-market principles to save the free-market system."[43] The system was not a free market at the time, though, because of the manipulation of the financial atmosphere by Congress and the Federal Reserve. Regardless, Americans began to distrust capitalism.

The Tea Party movement began not long after Congress passed the Emergency Economic Stabilization Act. The frustration with bailouts, wasteful spending, the growth of government, and a massive increase in the national debt reached a tipping point. Most pundits don't realize that the Tea Party movement had its roots in the

---

41 Jo Becker, Sheryl Gay Stolberg, and Stephen Labaton, "Bush Drive for Home Ownership Fueled Housing Bubble," *The New York Times,* Dec. 21, 2008. https://www.nytimes.com/2008/12/21/business/worldbusiness/21iht-admin.4.18853088.html

42 John Maxfield, "A Conversation with John Allison, the CEO Who Led BB&T Through the Financial Crisis," *The Motley Fool,* Aug. 4, 2017. https://www.fool.com/investing/2017/08/04/a-conversation-with-john-allison-bbt-ceo.aspx

43 Conn Carroll, "Bush's Betrayal of Free-Market Principles is now Complete," *The Daily Signal,* Dec. 30, 2008. https://www.dailysignal.com/2008/12/30/bushs-betrayal-of-free-market-principles-now-complete/

Porkbusters movement, an effort led by fiscally conservative bloggers that began in 2005 in response to congressional earmarks.

Porkbusters cheered on the efforts of Senator Tom Coburn of Oklahoma and Congressman Jeff Flake of Arizona, who sponsored amendments to spending bills to strip out pork barrel spending like the "bridge to nowhere." Coburn wrote that "Porkbusters represent what is arguably the only grassroots *movement* since 1994 to gain traction and build momentum on the core American principle of limited government."[44]

After the 2008 bailout, Porkbusters evolved into the Tea Party. Local activists organized, staging rallies wherever they could. These activists were maligned by the media, talking heads derided them, and Democrats, as well as some Republicans, wanted them to disappear. Ultimately, the Tea Party shifted the narrative in American politics, a bottom-up that Washington couldn't simply ignore.

Most Republicans won't admit this, but George W. Bush made Barack Obama possible. He played Carter to Obama's Reagan. With Americans' confidence shaken by an unpopular war and a financial crisis, the message of "hope" and "change" resonated with voters. Of course, apart from a shared skill for oratory, Reagan and Obama had little in common. One wanted to cut taxes and limit the size of government; the other wanted to raise taxes and have a much larger and active government.

Obama came into office under the notion of "fundamentally transforming the United States of America."[45] He used the financial crisis to his advantage, almost immediately pushing an $840 billion stimulus package[46] through Congress in February 2009. He would later turn his attention to health care, pushing Obamacare, the

---

44 Tom Coburn, "There's No Defending Pork," *National Review*, May 17, 2007. https://www.nationalreview.com/2007/05/theres-no-defending-pork-tom-coburn/

45 Barack Obama, Transcript of campaign speech in Columbia, Missouri on Oct. 30, 2008, posted by RealClearPolitics. https://www.realclearpolitics.com/articles/2008/10/obama_rallies_columbia_missour.html#ixzz2sNoV8MER

46 "Estimated Impact of the American Recovery and Reinvestment Act on Employment and Economic Output in 2014," Congressional Budget Office, Feb., 2015. https://www.cbo.gov/sites/default/files/114th-congress-2015-2016/reports/49958-ARRA.pdf

so-called "Affordable Care Act," through Congress in late 2009 and early 2010, and the Dodd-Frank Wall Street Reform and Consumer Protection Act in July 2010. Obama also had an aggressive regulatory agenda.

Another era of divided government that began after Republicans won back the House in the 2010 midterm election did slow the growth of federal spending, but Obama's aggressive legislative and regulatory agenda hurt the recovery from the Great Recession. Economist Peter Ferrara writes, "The 2008–09 recession was so bad, the economy should have come roaring back with a booming recovery—even stronger than Reagan's boom in the 1980s. But Mr. Obama carefully, studiously pursued the opposite of every pro-growth policy Reagan had followed. What he got was the worst recovery from a recession since the Great Depression."[47]

America Is Broke

Until the COVID-19 pandemic and the government-exacerbated economic slowdown that accompanied it, the economic situation had steadily improved since Obama left office. Small business confidence saw a twelve-year high.[48] Americans' confidence in the economy had reached a post-recession high.[49] The unemployment rate had hit a fifty-year low. Americans and businesses both saw a long-overdue tax cut, and in 2018 Americans saw the largest annual economic growth rate since 2005, following an aggressive wave of deregulation.

---

47   Peter J. Ferrara, "Why the 'Obama Recovery' Took So Long," *The Wall Street Journal*, Sept. 10, 2018. https://www.wsj.com/articles/why-the-obama-recovery-took-so-long-1536619545

48   Reuters, "Trump Bump: Small-Business Confidence Reaches a 12-Year High," *Fortune*, Jan. 10, 2017. https://fortune.com/2017/01/10/small-business-confidence-trump/

49   Justin McCarthy, "US Economic Confidence Index at Post-Recession High," *Gallup*, Jan. 24, 2017. https://news.gallup.com/poll/202823/economic-confidence-index-post-recession-high.aspx

Still, as Congress continued to increase spending and allow federal entitlement programs to remain on autopilot, budget deficits were already growing—and that was before the trillions in coronavirus relief spending.

The vast majority of Americans don't understand how the federal budget works. In recent years, there has been fear over government shutdowns. Most people would be surprised to know that these government shutdowns have happened because of disagreements in Congress over what amounts to roughly 30 percent of federal spending.[50] We call this "discretionary" spending, which is essentially defense spending and domestic spending. Theoretically, Congress passes a budget that sets the spending levels and appropriates from there.

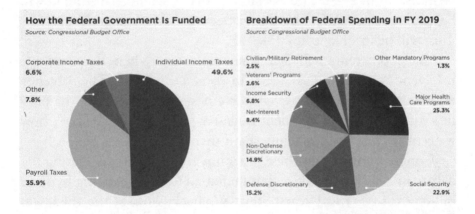

How the Federal Government Is Funded
Source: Congressional Budget Office

Corporate Income Taxes 6.6%
Individual Income Taxes 49.6%
Other 7.8%
Payroll Taxes 35.9%

Breakdown of Federal Spending in FY 2019
Source: Congressional Budget Office

Civilian/Military Retirement 2.5%
Other Mandatory Programs 1.3%
Veterans' Programs 2.6%
Income Security 6.8%
Major Health Care Programs 25.3%
Net-Interest 8.4%
Non-Defense Discretionary 14.9%
Defense Discretionary 15.2%
Social Security 22.9%

Congress is supposed to pass 12 appropriations bills each year to fund the federal government before the end of fiscal year, which ends on September 30. The last time Congress passed all of these appropriations bills on time was in 1997.[51] Congress has routinely consolidated the bills into at least one big package to fund the federal government. If an agreement on these appropriations bills can't be reached before the end of the fiscal year, Congress often passes a

---

50 Using Congressional Budget Office figures for FY 2019.

51 Drew DeSilver, "Congress Has Long Struggled to Pass Spending Bills on Time," Pew Research Center, Jan. 16, 2018. https://www.pewresearch.org/fact-tank/2018/01/16/congress-has-long-struggled-to-pass-spending-bills-on-time/

continuing resolution to fund the government at existing discretionary levels, either temporarily until an agreement can be reached, or for an entire fiscal year.

Nearly 70 percent of federal spending isn't subject to congressional appropriation. The largest part of this is called "mandatory" spending, which includes programs like Medicare, Medicaid, Social Security, food stamps, federal employee and military retirement programs, and more. The smaller portion is interest payments on the share of the national debt held by the public.

Here are some facts. Including the Hospital Insurance program, Medicare faces unfunded liabilities of $45.7 trillion.[52] Social Security has unfunded obligations of $16.8 trillion.[53] These were pre-pandemic estimates. The Medicare Hospital Insurance Trust Fund will be insolvent in 2024. The Social Security Disability Trust Fund will be insolvent by 2026. The Social Security Old-Age and Survivors Trust will be insolvent in 2031.[54]

These programs will face immediate cuts when they become insolvent unless Congress acts. This isn't a small feat. The solvency of these programs may be even worse now. As I write this, the public's share of the national debt is nearly $20.7 trillion.[55] That's how we get the $83.2 trillion figure that I mentioned before.

Congress knows that these programs are going broke. During the debate in 2019 on a budget that increased federal spending by $320 billion over two fiscal years, Steve Womack, who, at the time, was the highest-ranking Republican on the House Budget Committee, defended an increase in discretionary spending by pointing out that mandatory spending is what is driving budget deficits. "I think we

---

52   Patricia A. Davis, "Medicare Financial Status: In Brief," *Congressional Research Service*, updated June 9, 2020. https://fas.org/sgp/crs/misc/R43122.pdf

53   Barry F. Huston, "Social Security: The Trust Funds," *Congressional Research Service*, updated May 15, 2020. https://fas.org/sgp/crs/misc/RL33028.pdf

54   "The Outlook for Major Federal Trust Funds: 2020 to 2030," *Congressional Budget Office*, Sept. 2020. https://www.cbo.gov/system/files/2020-09/56523-Trust-Funds.pdf

55   US Department of the Treasury, "The Debt to the Penny and Who Holds It," *Treasury Direct*, last updated Aug. 15, 2020. https://www.treasurydirect.gov/govt/reports/pd/pd_debttothepenny.htm

have to fix that. I don't know what the answer is, but I do know this," Womack said.[56]

It would be funny if it weren't so frustrating. Womack is literally charged with developing these solutions. This is the best and brightest that House Republicans have? I know for a fact that there are a lot of smart fiscal conservatives in the House, but Womack is the guy House Republican leadership put in control of the committee.

Even before the spending Congress passed in response to the pandemic, America was in financial trouble. For the first time in American history, we have an age demographic problem.

We have an aging population. Never in our history have we been an old nation. We have always been a young nation. We aren't having enough children, and fewer immigrants are coming to America. In 1945, there were roughly 42 workers for every beneficiary of Social Security.[57] Today, there are almost three workers for every beneficiary. By 2040, there will be a little more than two workers for every beneficiary.

In 2019, the natural increase in population dropped below 1 million.[58] "This is the lowest annual growth rate since 1918, and caps off a decade that should show the slowest 10-year population growth since the first census was taken in 1790," writes William H. Frey of the Brookings Institution.[59]

Conservative critics of Obama used to point to the labor force participation rate as an economic indicator that showed the weak recovery from the Great Recession. Certainly, the recovery was weak, but the labor force participation rate—the percentage of Americans

56 US House of Representatives, "Bipartisan Budget Act of 2019," *Congressional Record*, Vol. 165, No. 126, July 25, 2019. https://www.congress.gov /congressional-record/2019/7/25/house-section/article/h7398-2

57 "2020 OASDI Trustees Report," *SSA.gov*, Apr. 22, 2020. https://www.ssa.gov /oact/TR/2020/IV_B_LRest.html#493869

58 US Census Bureau, "2019 US Population Estimates Continue to Show the Nation's Growth is Slowing," *Census.gov*, Dec. 30, 2019. https://www.census.gov /newsroom/press-releases/2019/popest-nation.html

59 William H. Frey, "The 2010s May Have Seen the Slowest Population Growth in US History," Brookings Institute, Jan. 2, 2020. https://www.brookings.edu/research /population-change-and-the-projected-change-in-congressional-representation/

between the ages of sixteen and sixty-four who are working or looking for work—peaked in 2000 and has been slowly declining since,
with only occasional blips of improvement.[60]

At the height of the pre-pandemic economic boom, there were 1
million more job openings than unemployed workers.[61] Because we
are getting older as a society, we don't have enough workers to fill
these jobs when we desperately need more workers to not only have
a productive economy but also to pay into programs like Medicare
and Social Security, the insolvency of which has become inevitable.

An aging workforce and the lack of workers to fill the jobs
our economy needs to grow should be considered a crisis by every
American. This is a devastating future that we face. Fewer workers
mean lower productivity. Lower productivity means less economic
output. Less economic output means a nation in decline.

Our power as a nation is directly linked to the American economy. Full stop. If our economic engine goes into decline, our global
influence and our ability to protect our way of life also go into
decline. This is the problem with many defense hawks. They're
so concerned about our foreign interventions in countries that we
don't have any real business being involved in that they don't realize that they're mortgaging the entire future in exchange for short-
term gains. Defense hawks don't understand that until we get the age
demographic and budget situations straightened out, we're not going
to be able to have the military that we want.

The "New Normal"

Everyone is talking about the "new normal" in a post-COVID-19
world. Wearing a mask when going to the supermarket or on an

---

60 "Labor Force Participation Rate," Federal Reserve Bank of St. Louis, updated
Sept. 4, 2020. https://fred.stlouisfed.org/series/CIVPART

61 "The US Has 1 Million More Job Openings than Unemployed Workers," *CBS
News*, Mar. 15, 2019. https://www.cbsnews.com/news/the-u-s-has-1-million-more-job-
openings-than-unemployed-workers/

airplane is part of this new normal. We are staying at home more than we used to. We are spending less.

Big businesses like JCPenney, Neiman Marcus, Tailored Brands, and J.Crew have filed for bankruptcy.[62] Tens of thousands of small businesses have shuttered their doors, never to reopen.[63] This is also causing significant problems in the commercial real estate market.[64] Many of the jobs lost during the pandemic won't be coming back.[65] The nature of work is changing, with more and more companies allowing employees to work from home.

After the death of George Floyd, racial unrest of an intensity not seen in decades has gripped major cities around the country. Of course, no one points the finger at peaceful protesters, but the situation has been exacerbated by agitators who have sought to capitalize on the sentiment through rioting and looting. Confidence in law enforcement has plummeted,[66] and major cities have seen an increase in violent crime.[67]

We're entering an era where many Americans want a return to normalcy. Well, what is "normal"? We're entering a period of

---

62   Lee Clifford, Phil Wahba, and Fortune Editors, "A running list of companies that have filed for bankruptcy during the coronavirus pandemic," *Fortune*, last updated Spet. 22, 2020. https://fortune.com/2020/08/04/companies-filing-bankruptcy-2020-due-to-covid-list-filed-chapter-11-coronavirus-pandemic/

63   Madeleine Ngo, "Small Businesses Are Dying by the Thousands—and No One is Tracking the Carnage," *The Washington Post*, Aug. 11, 2020. https://www.washingtonpost.com/business/on-small-business/small-businesses-are-dying-by-the-thousands--and-no-one-is-tracking-the-carnage/2020/08/11/660f9f52-dbda-11ea-b4f1-25b762cdbbf4_story.html?arc404=true

64   Paul R. LaMonica, "Commercial real estate flounders as housing market booms," *CNN Business*, Sept. 22, 2020. https://www.cnn.com/2020/09/22/investing/commercial-real-estate-recession/index.html

65   Christopher Rugaber, "Gone for Good? Evidence Signals Many Jobs Aren't Coming Back," *AP News*, Aug. 5, 2020. https://apnews.com/89992979ca3c3ba72eb2cd31a9ca0e5d

66   Megan Brenan, "Amid Pandemic, Confidence in Key US Institutions Surges," Aug. 12, 2020. https://news.gallup.com/poll/317135/amid-pandemic-confidence-key-institutions-surges.aspx

67   Josh Campbell, "Violent Crime Rises During Pandemic as Confidence in Police Takes a Hit," *CNN.com*, Aug. 16, 2020. https://www.cnn.com/2020/08/16/us/violent-crime-soars-confidence-in-police-takes-hit/index.html

uncertainty. Because deficits have to be financed through sale of securities, which have a guaranteed interest rate, this can leave fewer loanable dollars for private investors. As deficits continue to rise, those who may have been willing to buy government securities may be less willing to do so if they begin questioning our ability to meet our obligations.

This is America under the status quo. Ultimately, this means a less prosperous America.

Regardless of which party has the White House and control of Congress, the response from the political class will be "stimulus." More government spending to "prime the pump" to spur economic growth, much like what Obama did after entering office to counter the effects of the Great Recession. We know our experiment with Keynesian economics hasn't worked out so well, but we aren't the only ones who have tried.

In the 1990s, Japan experienced a decade of lagging growth caused by an asset bubble. The fiscal and monetary policy responses led to what is known as the "lost decade." Businesses were not attracted by low interest rates. Investment in the economy declined. Japan tried a fiscal policy response.

Amity Shlaes writes, "Between 1992 and 2000, the Japanese launched ten stimulus packages that included public works. The Land of the Rising Sun became the Construction State. Other worthy issues, such as consistent tax reform, lagged. In fact, fiscal reform overall was postponed."[68]

Economist Dan Mitchell adds, "[H]ow they mishandled their approach to the bubble is very similar to the way we're mishandling approaches with bailouts today. But what Japan did in the 1990s to try to help their economy is they had one Keynesian stimulus program after another. And they focused a lot on infrastructure. I'm surprised that all the Japanese islands aren't covered in concrete now. But what happened? There was no positive effect on the economy."

---

[68] Amity Shlaes, "From Japan, Lessons for Obama's Infrastructure Plans," *The Washington Post*, Dec. 10, 2008. https://www.washingtonpost.com/wp-dyn/content/article/2008/12/09/AR2008120902785.html

Bloomberg recently noted that the effects of Japan's lost decade are still felt today.[69] "Faced with limited job prospects, many ended up single and childless," writes Yoshiaki Nohara. "Japan's 2015 census revealed there were 3.4 million people in their forties and fifties who had not married and lived with their parents."

This is already happening in America. Millennials and Generation Z are staying at home longer or putting off buying a home or building their retirement nest egg.[70] When young people graduate, they're finding a tough job market.[71] The situation is even worse since COVID-19 hit America and could take years for recent graduates to recover from the recession caused by the pandemic.[72]

Like in Japan, this epidemic of "failure to launch" among young adults is fueling the shift in demographics that we've already discussed. Young adults are getting married later (if at all) and having fewer kids (if at all). A poll conducted on behalf of *The New York Times* found that four of the top five reasons cited by young adults for having fewer children even though they wanted kids were concerns about their finances and the economy.[73]

It appears that America has entered its own lost decade in which economic growth will slow to a near grinding halt and prosperity and opportunity will be difficult for many to find. Few are taking the challenges that face our nation seriously.

---

69 Yoshiaki Nohara, "Japan's Lost Generation is Still Jobless and Living with Their Parents," *Bloomberg Businessweek*, Oct. 1, 2020. https://www.bloomberg.com/features/2020-japan-lost-generation/

70 Zack Friedman, "50 Percent of Millennials are Moving Back Home with Their Parents After College," Forbes.com, June 16, 2019. https://www.forbes.com/sites/zackfriedman/2019/06/06/millennials-move-back-home-college/?sh=5b8a11c6638a

71 John Crudele, "College grads can't find work despite strong jobs report," *The New York Post*, Aug. 6, 2018. https://nypost.com/2018/08/06/college-grads-cant-find-work-despite-strong-jobs-report/

72 Joe Pinsker, "The Misfortune of Graduating in 2020," *The Atlantic*, May 22, 2020. https://www.theatlantic.com/family/archive/2020/05/class-of-2020-graduate-jobs/611917/

73 Clair Cain Miller, "Americans are having fewer babies. They told us why." *The New York Times*, July 5, 2018. https://www.nytimes.com/2018/07/05/upshot/americans-are-having-fewer-babies-they-told-us-why.html

CHAPTER 8

Our Economy Must Continue to Evolve

A merica faces serious long-term challenges, and our prosperity is
at risk if they go unaddressed. How do we address the solvency
of our unsustainable entitlement programs? How do we begin to pay
down the national debt? Will we devalue our currency? Will we discourage investment and economic growth by raising taxes?

America's long-term challenges existed before the COVID-19
pandemic, but the pandemic, and the government's response to it,
certainly didn't help. Before the pandemic, America had seen its
best economy in more than a decade. But even in this period of sustained job growth, the Congressional Budget Office forecasted that
annual real economic growth would dip below 2 percent in 2029.[1]
That's not too far away.

We are getting older as a society. Entitlement programs like
Medicare and Social Security are insolvent. Democrats and
Republicans alike continue to largely ignore these severe problems,
steadily increasing discretionary spending while doing nothing about
mandatory spending programs that are driving budget deficits. The

---

1   "The Budget and Economic Outlook: 2020 to 2030," Congressional Budget Office,
January 2020. https://www.cbo.gov/publication/56073#_idTextAnchor147

end result is $1 trillion annual budget deficits as far as the eye can see.

Congressman Tom McClintock of California explains that "a deficit is simply a future tax."[2] Before COVID-19 hit the United States, the budget deficit for FY 2020 was projected to be in excess of $1 trillion, rising to $1.74 trillion in 2030.[3] Then, Congress spent another $2.4 trillion in response to COVID-19, dramatically increasing the budget deficit for the year.[4] Some of the spending that has been passed in response to COVID-19 is almost certainly here to stay.

The short of it is, Congress has placed a tremendous burden on the next few generations of Americans, who will be faced with fewer opportunities and less prosperity because of the looming fiscal crisis in which their predecessors have left the country. Former House Speaker Paul Ryan once called this fiscal crisis that America faces "the most predictable economic crisis we've ever had in this country."[5] It's a generational disaster.

Democrats are planning an expansion of the federal government of a magnitude not seen since the Great Depression. Joe Biden plans to raise taxes by $3.6 trillion.[6] He has proposed $11 trillion in new federal spending, including a so-called "public option" health care plan that will undercut private health insurance companies and, eventually, lead to a single-payer, "Medicare for All" system.[7] Section 107 of the Medicare for All Act makes it "unlawful" for a

---

2   Tom McClintock, "Debt Crisis," *Washington Times*, July 28, 2011. https://mcclintock.house.gov/newsroom/columns/debt-crisis

3   See footnote 218.

4   "The Budgetary Effects of Laws Enacted in Response to the 2020 Coronavirus Pandemic, March and April 2020," Congressional Budget Office, June 2020. https://www.cbo.gov/system/files/2020-06/56403-CBO-covid-legislation.pdf

5   Paul Ryan, "Congressman Paul Ryan discusses budget plan in Milwaukee," *FOX 6 Now Milwaukee*, April 9, 2012. https://www.fox6now.com/news/congressman-paul-ryan-discusses-budget-plan-in-milwaukee

6   Ibid.

7   Brian Riedl, "Joe Biden has an $11 trillion spending plan. Can he enact it?" *The Dispatch*, Sept. 2, 2020. https://thedispatch.com/p/joe-biden-has-an-11-trillion-spending

private insurer to compete with the services provided by the federal government.[8] A completely government-run health care system, which is the Left's eventual goal, would force more people into a broken system.

Far-left Democrats who don't shy away from socialism are pushing a radical economic theory—"modern monetary theory"—which Warren Coats of the Cato Institute describes as "an unsuccessful and empty attempt to convince us that we can finance the Green New Deal and a federal job guarantee program painlessly by printing money."[9]

Modern monetary theory (MMT) is, in a literal sense, voodoo economics. Those pushing this snake oil believe that there's nothing too expensive for the government because the Federal Reserve can simply print money.

Subscribers to MMT seem to believe that government has a monopoly on money. Tell that to the Weimar Republic in the early 1920s and Zimbabwe beginning in 2007. They also had a monopoly on money, and people had money that was virtually worthless. Those who follow MMT don't understand that money is backed by a society's future productivity. If we don't have productivity, we don't have anything.

According to those who believe MMT, large long-term structural deficits don't matter, and inflation can be managed through fiscal policy set by Congress rather than monetary policy set by the Federal Reserve.

From a practical standpoint, this won't work. Those who believe in MMT are saying that the two chambers of Congress, party control of which has often been divided, should be in charge of keeping inflation in check through a mix of spending and tax policy. Politicians will always agree to spend more money, but there are very different

---

8   US Congress, Senate. *Medicare for All Act of 2019*, S. 1129, 116th Congress, introduced in the Senate April 10, 2019. https://www.congress.gov/bill/116th-congress/senate-bill/1129/text#toc-ide37941c014034d0b92c46663a00be99d

9   Warren Coats, "Modern Monetary Theory: A Critique," *Cato Journal*, Vol. 39 No. 3, Fall 2019. https://www.cato.org/publications/cato-journal/modern-monetary-theory-critique

views on taxation. The end result will be price instability brought on by inflation, potentially hyperinflation.

We've also used taxation as a method of controlling inflation. It didn't work. As I mentioned in the previous chapter, John F. Kennedy noted that high tax rates were "[d]esigned to check inflation in earlier years...but check[ed]growth instead."[10] I also mentioned in the 1980s that lower tax rates, along with monetary policy moves, coincided with a significant period of economic growth and declining inflation. That shatters the MMT narrative, but the socialists aren't listening to facts.

Talk show host Neal Boortz frequently said that Democrats believe government is what makes America great. However, expanding entitlement programs like Medicare and Social Security, drowning Americans in taxes, and modern monetary theory only dig us further in a hole.

Unfortunately, Republicans haven't exactly been leading on restraining spending recently either.

In 1994, House Republicans produced a bold and aggressive vision for the country, the Contract with America.[11] While not perfect, the Contract with America told voters what Republicans were for, offering specific legislative remedies that appealed to Americans. They won control of both the House and Senate as a result.

Gone are the days of big ideas. Like him or not, former Speaker Ryan offered solutions when he chaired the House Budget Committee, producing budgets that reformed Medicare and overhauled the tax code. Democrats spent much of their time demagoguing Ryan's "Path to Prosperity" budget blueprint. Today, the Republican Party seems adrift when it comes to advancing policy ideas. There is, perhaps,

---

10   John F. Kennedy, "State of the Union Address," John F. Kennedy Presidential Library and Museum, January 14, 1963. https://www.jfklibrary.org/asset-viewer/archives/JFKPOF/042/JFKPOF-042-021

11   "The Republican 'Contract with America' (1994)," Oxford University Press. https://global.oup.com/us/companion.websites/9780195385168/resources/chapter6/contract/america.pdf (accessed Sept. 23, 2020)

no better example of this than Republicans not bothering to write or adopt a platform at the 2020 Republican National Convention.[12]

We can't manage the economy through the problems that America faces. Managing the economy through these problems is only managing our decline. We should be getting government out of the way, keeping taxes low, and reducing regulation. There is a role for government to help those who are unable to work and need help. That doesn't change the fact that a freer market leads to freer people. A more active government only manages our decline. As I learned when I was five years old, don't kill the goose that lays the golden egg.

The good news is that there is a way forward. We don't have to go down the road of European welfare states that suffer from anemic economic growth and sovereign debt crises. It's not simply Congress creating good tax policy through low rates and federal agencies focusing on deregulation or producing fewer, less economically impactful regulations.

Pro-growth tax and regulatory policies are vitally important and essential for economic growth, but Congress also has to address federal spending by reforming entitlement programs and developing an immigration system that meets the needs of America's economy. Before we can do any of this, we need to fervently defend how America became the economic powerhouse that it is.

Defend Free-Market Capitalism

I know I've already touched on this, but it needs to be repeated. It amazes me that far-left Democrats have claimed the mantle of "progressivism." It's one of the greatest marketing schemes that the world has ever seen. It's impossible to look at Democrats' agenda and call it

---

12   Reid J. Epstein, "The G.O.P. Delivers Its 2020 Platform. It's From 2016," *The New York Times*, August 25, 2020. https://www.nytimes.com/2020/08/25/us/politics/republicans-platform.html

"progressive." Words have meaning. "Progressivism," as we know it in the United States, is really shamefaced socialism.

Socialism has a record of failure and societal breakdown. It suppresses individualism and discourages achievement, spreading shared suffering across every citizen. Today's "progressivism" is really "regressivism." The advancements that helped America become an economic powerhouse are frowned upon, and these so-called "progressives" are intent on taking America back decades in time.

Free-market capitalism has lifted billions of people out of extreme poverty across the globe. We have done this, as economist Deirdre McCloskey writes, through "a mere idea, which the philosopher and economist Adam Smith called 'the liberal plan of equality, liberty and justice.'"[13] This classical notion of liberalism is based in free-market capitalism.

The attacks on free-market capitalism aren't limited to the far-left of the political spectrum. Some on the political right are embracing state-based economic nationalism and a skepticism of big business that's similar to France.

To some degree, a skepticism of big business is understandable considering the strength of special interests on K Street, who often lobby for anti-competitive laws and regulatory schemes. It's true that what is good for big business may not always be good for taxpayers like you and me. Still, this growing nationalist sentiment coming from some conservatives is dangerous.

Free-market capitalism has not failed. Free marketers have failed to communicate. Iain Murray of the Competitive Enterprise Institute explains, "For decades, capitalists have failed to present their arguments in the language of traditional conservatism."[14] We have failed to explain that normalized relations with other nations is as beneficial to Americans as it is to the countries with which we freely trade.

---

13   Deirdre N. McCloskey, "The Formula for a Richer World? Equality, Liberty, Justice," *The New York Times*, September 2, 2016. https://www.nytimes.com/2016/09/04/upshot/the-formula-for-a-richer-world-equality-liberty-justice.html

14   Iain Murray, "Free-Marketeers Have Taken Social Conservatives for Granted," *Wall Street Journal*, August 19, 2019. https://www.wsj.com/articles/free-marketeers-have-taken-social-conservatives-for-granted-11566255556

We have failed to communicate how the changes in the economy are beneficial to the middle class.

Look at 2019. The story of 2019 is just so important. The Left and the media didn't like to talk about a growing economy because it showed that lower taxes and less regulation that conservatives and libertarians advanced in 2017 worked the way we said it would. The evidence is there. In 2019, America saw:

- Median household income jump by 6.8 percent[15]
- The lowest poverty rate on record at 10.5 percent[16]
- Black unemployment drop to 5.5 percent, a record low[17]
- Hispanic unemployment fell to 4.1 percent, also a record low[18]

Critics of free-market capitalism focus on the middle class, often claiming that the middle class is "shrinking." There's some truth to that, but it's not because people have become worse off. Robert Samuelson of the *Washington Post* notes that although the middle-class has been shrinking, the upper-middle-class has risen steadily. He writes, "The shrinkage of the traditional middle class will be mourned by some, but the reality is that most of those who have left the middle class have moved up, not down."[19]

Samuelson highlights a paper from Stephen Rose of the Brookings Institution. The August 2020 paper reviews data collected from the

---

15 Paul Davidson, "Median US household income rises 6.8% to $68,700 in 2019, poverty rate falls for fifth year," *USA Today*, Sept. 15, 2020. https://www.usatoday.com/story/money/2020/09/15/u-s-median-household-income-2019-income-rises-6-8-t-o-68-700-2019/5800117002/

16 US Census Bureau, "Income, Poverty and Health Insurance Coverage in the United States: 2019," Census.gov, Sept. 15, 2020. https://www.census.gov/newsroom/press-releases/2020/income-poverty.html

17 Maggie Fitzgerald, "Black and Hispanic unemployment is at a record low," CNBC, Oct. 4, 2019. https://www.cnbc.com/2019/10/04/black-and-hispanic-unemployment-is-at-a-record-low.html

18 Ibid.

19 Robert J. Samuelson, "The Rise of the Upper Middle Class," *Washington Post*, August 16, 2020. https://www.washingtonpost.com/opinions/the-rise-of-the-upper-middle-class/2020/08/16/3aa1aea4-de60-11ea-b205-ff838e15a9a6_story.html

Panel Study on Income Dynamics.[20] What Rose discovered is incredibly profound.

Using income thresholds to determine where respondents fit, the data show that those considered "poor and near-poor" (incomes under $32,500) fell from 16 percent in 1967 to 13 percent in 2016. Those considered "lower middle class" (incomes between $32,500 and $54,500) declined from 31 percent in 1967 to 16 percent. That's extraordinary.

The data from the Panel Study on Income Dynamics show that the "middle class" (incomes between $54,000 and $108,500) has shrunk from 47 percent in 1967 to 36 percent in 2016. Anyone who seizes on that one data point while ignoring the rest is doing so disingenuously. Why? Because they're moving up. What Rose defines as the "upper middle class" (incomes between $108,500 and $380,500) has grown from only 6 percent in 1967 to 33 percent in 2016. The "rich" (incomes of $380,500 and up) grew from 0 percent in 1967 to 2 percent in 2016.

Americans' incomes

Share of population in each category.

	1967	1981	2002	2016
Poor and near poor Less than $32,500 income	16%	11%	14%	13%
Lower middle-class $32,500 to $54,500	31%	20%	17%	16%
Middle-class $54,000 to $108,500	47%	50%	39%	36%
Upper middle-class $108,500 to $380,500	6%	18%	29%	33%
Rich $380,500 and up	0%	0%	1%	2%

Source: Stephen Rose; PSID   THE WASHINGTON POST

---

20 Stephen Rose, "Squeezing the middle class: Income trajectories from 1967 to 2016," Brookings Institution, August 2020. https://www.brookings.edu/wp-content/uploads/2020/08/Squeezing-the-middle-class_Report-1.pdf

This is a phenomenal achievement. This growth in the upper-middle-class has come at a time when old institutions have become obsolete as developments and technology and innovation have dominated the economy.

Critics of capitalism on both the political Right and Left will say that wages aren't rising and that workers aren't benefiting from a friendlier tax and regulatory climate, but this view is simplistic because it focuses on one data point. A wage isn't the only form of compensation that workers receive. Other compensation includes health insurance, retirement programs that include an employer contribution, bonuses, and paid vacations.[21]

Some view free-market capitalism as a zero-sum game. This notion is ridiculous. Money doesn't come from the printing presses at the Federal Reserve or government spending and a misallocation of resources. The immense wealth that America has produced comes from a productive society. Politicians and talking heads are fixated on jobs, but they miss the larger point: Jobs are the means but not the end. Businesses creating products consumers want is what drives investment and job growth.

One of the most basic, important aspects of free-market capitalism is that it forces constant change. This has been true throughout history.[22] The automobile put the horse and carriage out to pasture. Increased air travel lessened the need for trains and ocean liners. The telephone rendered the telegraph useless. Email has made communication easier than the days of mailing a letter.

Twenty years ago, a high school student might have owned a clunky desktop, a CD player, a portable DVD player, a digital camera, and dreamed of owning a cell phone like the one Zach Morris had in *Saved by the Bell*. In 2007, Apple released its first iPhone, which allowed users to store their favorite music and movies, take

---

21 Binyamin Appelbaum, "One Reason for Slow Wage Growth? More Benefits," *The New York Times*, September 25, 2018. https://www.nytimes.com/2018/09/25/us/politics/wage-growth-benefits.html

22 Richard Alm and W. Michael Cox, "Creative Destruction," The Library of Economics and Liberty, accessed Sept. 23, 2020. https://www.econlib.org/library/Enc/CreativeDestruction.html

photos and videos, send text messages and emails, browse the internet, and make phone calls. Sales have grown from 1.4 million in 2007 to a peak of 231.2 million in 2015.[23]

Capitalism requires change. A business model that worked in the 1970s and 1980s may not work in the twenty-first century because of innovation and emerging technologies. Even governmental entities like the US Postal Service, while hemorrhaging money, are learning that business models that may have worked decades ago don't work today. Competition benefits consumers, and it weeds out businesses that fail to adapt.

I mentioned this before, but my favorite quote about economics comes from Joseph Schumpeter, who wrote about the evolutionary nature of capitalism:

> *The fundamental impulse that sets and keeps the capitalist engine in motion comes from the new consumers' goods, the new methods of production or transportation, the new markets, the new forms of industrial organization that capitalist enterprise creates.*
>
> *[...]*
>
> *The opening up of new markets, foreign or domestic, and the organizational development from the craft shop and factory to such concerns as US Steel illustrate the same process of industrial mutation—if I may use that biological term—that incessantly revolutionizes the economic structure from within, incessantly destroying the old one, incessantly creating a new one. This process of Creative Destruction is the essential fact about capitalism. It is what capitalism consists in and what every capitalist concern has got to live in.*[24]

There are, of course, tradeoffs that come with this evolutionary nature of capitalism. Workers in some industries may be displaced and need training to adapt and hone skills in another industry. Politicians will

---

23 H. Tankovska, "Unit sales of the Apple iPhone worldwide from 2007 to 2018," *Statista*,   September 21, 2020. https://www.statista.com/statistics/276306 /global-apple-iphone-sales-since-fiscal-year-2007/

24 Joseph A. Schumpeter, *Capitalism, Socialism, and Democracy*, Harper & Bros, 1942.

undoubtedly try to protect some favored industries, shielding them from competition caused by a new and emerging technology or foreign competition.

Coming from Cleveland, the main thing that hurt our economy so badly was the loss of steel manufacturing jobs.[25] The city's economy was largely based on this industry. At its peak, the main mill in Cleveland had some thirty thousand steel industry jobs.[26] Today, the largest steel company in the city is Cleveland-Cliffs, formerly ArcelorMittal Cleveland, which only employs about 1,900 workers.[27]

Politicians often like to solely blame competition from overseas for hurting American manufacturing, but the reality is that most of these jobs went away because of increased productivity, including automation.

A 2015 study by Michael J. Hicks and Srikant Devaraj estimated that "[a]lmost 88 percent of job losses in manufacturing in recent years can be attributable to productivity growth, and the long-term changes to manufacturing employment are mostly linked to the productivity of American factories."[28] Some studies give a higher percentage. Some say at least half of the job losses are attributable to gains in productivity.

Bringing it back to Cleveland, it's true that foreign competition impacted the American steel industry. But gains in productivity in the steel industry were a huge factor. In 1980, it took 10.1-man

---

25 "Cleveland hit hard by factory closing since 1960," *The Toledo Blade*, July 3, 2016. https://www.toledoblade.com/business/2016/07/03/Cleveland-hard-hit-by-factory-closings-since-1960/stories/20160703168

26 "History of Steel in Cleveland," Arcelor Mittal, accessed Oct. 8, 2020. https://usa.arcelormittal.com/~/media/Files/A/Arcelormittal-USA-V2/our-operations/Fact%20sheets/history-of-steel-in-cleveland.pdf

27 "Cleveland," Arcelor Mittal website, accessed Oct. 8, 2020. https://usa.arcelormittal.com/our-operations/steelmaking/cleveland

28 Michael J. Hicks and Srikant Devaraj, "The Myth and Reality of Manufacturing in America," Ball State University Center for Business and Economic Research, June, 2015. https://projects.cberdata.org/reports/MfgReality.pdf

hours to produce a ton of steel. In 2017, it took only 1.5-man hours.[29]

Real manufacturing output in the United States, by the way, was trending upward until the Great Recession.[30] Real output was still rising even though fewer Americans have manufacturing jobs. After a significant drop because of the recession, real manufacturing output began to rise again until the end of 2018.

We also have to remember that businesses respond to consumer demand. The iPhone became popular because it put the power of a computer in the palm of a user's hand. Uber and Lyft have enjoyed success because they make short-distance travel easier for riders. There may be some sentiment for older technologies. For example, vinyl records have enjoyed a comeback in recent years, but a music fan can't listen to his or her favorite vinyl record in a car.[31] Streaming services like Apple Music and Spotify have filled that void.

The creative destruction of capitalism allows America's economy to continue to grow. This doesn't mean that we should abandon those who are displaced by the evolution of the economy. Government does have a role to help those displaced, but it's more than simply providing "trade adjustment assistance." We should be looking at this from the ground up, starting with our education system, which can help train people to be prepared for disruptions by teaching them more than one skillset. But holding onto old institutions prevents us from growing.

W. Michael Cox and Richard Alm wrote, "Instead of going out of business, inefficient producers hang on, at a high cost to consumers or taxpayers. The tinkering short-circuits market signals that shift

---

29   Mark J. Perry, "The main reason for the loss of US steel jobs is a huge increase in worker productivity, not imports, and the jobs aren't coming back," American Enterprise Institute blog, *AEIdeas*, Mar. 7, 2018. https://www.aei.org/carpe-diem /the-main-reason-for-the-loss-of-us-steel-jobs-is-productivity-and-technology-not-imports-and-theyre-not-coming-back/

30   "Manufacturing Sector: Real Output," FRED Economic Data, Federal Reserve Bank of St. Louis, accessed Oct. 8, 2020. https://fred.stlouisfed.org/series/OUTMS

31   Elias Leight, "Vinyl Is Poised to Outsell CDs For the First Time Since 1986," *Rolling Stone*, September 6, 2019. https://www.rollingstone.com/pro/news /vinyl-cds-revenue-growth-riaa-880959/

resources to emerging industries. It saps the incentives to introduce new products and production methods, leading to stagnation, layoffs, and bankruptcies. The ironic point of Schumpeter's iconic phrase is this: societies that try to reap the gain of creative destruction without the pain find themselves enduring the pain but not the gain."[32]

Ultimately, consumers are responsible for the creative destruction that we see in the economy. There will always be those who are triggered by the development of a new product that disrupts the status quo, but this is the very innovation that allows our economy to grow.

Wealth and Profit Are Not Dirty Words

There's a cacophony of cries from far-left Democrats like Bernie Sanders, Elizabeth Warren, and Alexandria Ocasio-Cortez that "the rich" don't pay their "fair share" of taxes. They already pay their "fair share." They shoulder the income tax burden. They also invest in the economy and provide capital to businesses to develop new products and services.

According to data from the Internal Revenue Service (IRS), the top 1 percent of income earners paid 38.5 percent of all income taxes in tax year 2017,[33] the last year of data before the Tax Cuts and Jobs Act went into effect. Although the Tax Cuts and Jobs Act was maligned as a "tax cut for the rich," the top 1 percent paid 40 percent of all income taxes in tax year 2018,[34] which reflects the first year of tax returns under the individual tax cuts and reforms. The share of income taxes paid by the bottom 50 percent of income

---

32 Richard Alm and W. Michael Cox, "Creative Destruction," The Library of Economics and Liberty, accessed Sept. 23, 2020. https://www.econlib.org/library/Enc /CreativeDestruction.html

33 Jason Pye, "Biden's Tax Plans Would Make America Less Prosperous," FreedomWorks, Sept. 29, 2020. https://www.freedomworks.org/content/bidens-tax-plan-would-make-america-less-prosperous

34 Demian Brady, "Who Pays Income Taxes: Tax Year 2018," National Taxpayers Union Foundation, Dec. 7, 2020. https://www.ntu.org/library/doclib/2020/12/2018-who-pays-1-.pdf

earners declined from 3.1 percent in tax year 2017 to 2.9 percent in tax year 2018.

Congresswoman Ocasio-Cortez and others who repeat the "fair share" and "income inequality" lines also never seem to take wealth transfers into account. Phil Gramm and John F. Early note that the Census Bureau doesn't include wealth transfers when determining household income.

"The Census Bureau...fails to count $1.9 trillion in annual public transfer payments to American households. The bureau ignores transfer payments from some 95 federal programs such as Medicare, Medicaid and food stamps, which make up more than 40 percent of federal spending, along with dozens of state and local programs," Gramm and Early write. "Government transfers provide 89 percent of all resources available to the bottom income quintile of households and more than half of the total resources available to the second quintile."[35]

Let's go over that one more time: programmatic transfers from government provide nearly 90 percent of all resources available to lower-income households. Wealth makes these transfers possible.

My friend and colleague John Tamny is one of the biggest promoters of free-market capitalism who I have ever met. He's unapologetic about wealth, and rightly so. He explains it this way:

> *As individuals we all have endless wants and needs that those eager to attain wealth are working feverishly to get to us so that they may become rich. The richer these individuals become, the more our living standards rise.*
>
> *These innovators need capital to get us things at prices that continue to fall. Taxation, whether coerced by government, or handed to the government by the dim, is a cost we all bear. Better yet, it's a cost we all*

35 Phil Gramm, and John F. Early, "The Truth About Income Inequality," *Wall Street Journal*, Nov. 3, 2019. https://www.wsj.com/articles/the-truth-about-income-inequality-11572813786

suffer simply because money that flows to Washington is money that's not reaching those who aim to mass produce former luxuries.[36]

Every one of us has aspirations. To a substantial extent, the prosperity that has turned America into an economic powerhouse has also made us lazy. We have a sense of entitlement, and that sense of entitlement is particularly strong in younger generations.

Without the wealth that has been created in America, the innovation that we have seen may not have come to market. It's humorous to listen to self-proclaimed socialists complain about the rich and corporate profits before pulling out their iPhone. The irony is thick.

People get rich in America because they solve people's problems. Look at the biggest companies that call the United States home. Amazon, Apple, Facebook, Google, and Microsoft. I could go on and on, but they all produce products or services that make people's lives easier.

Consumers have decided that they want convenience, and those companies have to continue to develop new products or services to keep consumers interested. The companies turn a profit, incentivizing them to continue to innovate and create more jobs. Shareholders receive a return on their investment and use the return on their investment to continue to invest.

We also are hearing the phrase "corporate social responsibility" more and more often. Milton Friedman writes, "[T]here is one and only one social responsibility of business—to use its resources and engage in activities designed to increase its profits so long as it stays within the rules of the game, which is to say, engages in open and free competition without deception or fraud."[37]

---

36 John Tamny, "To the Rich and Left Wing, Please Don't Pay Your 'Fair Share'," *RealClearMarkets*, April 15, 2019. https://www.realclearmarkets.com /articles/2019/04/15/to_the_rich_and_left_wing_please_dont_pay_your_fair_ share__103696.html

37 Milton Freedman, "The Social Responsibility of Business is to Increase its Profits," *New York Times Magazine*, September 13, 1970. http://umich.edu/~thecore/doc /Friedman.pdf

None of this is to say that businesses shouldn't be good stewards of the environment or shouldn't ensure that they are taking care of employees by providing them with a competitive wage and benefits. Businesses that cause environmental damage or fail to compensate employees may not be around long.

Some will point to the bad apples in business. These are the businesses that seek bailouts and subsidies. Cronyism will always be a concern because Democrats and Republicans alike incentivize some of this rent-seeking behavior. Free-market capitalism is about profit and loss. If a business can't survive on its own, it needs to die. The government shouldn't pick winners and losers in the marketplace.

After all, a cornerstone of what makes America great is that we have the world's most competitive economy.

We Need Workers, and We Need Them Now

America can't sustain the $83.2 trillion in unfunded liabilities and national debt that we have accumulated. Birth rates in the United States have dropped to a thirty-five-year low. According to the Census Bureau, 17 percent of the population in the United States in 2020 are aged sixty-five and older.[38] By 2050, nearly 22 percent of the population will be sixty-five and older. [39]

In only twenty years, the labor force participation rate is projected to decline to under 60 percent, a level not seen since the 1960s. [40] The weight of the fiscal commitment that America has made in the form of debt obligations, Medicare, and Social Security will break us. The simplistic approach is to raise taxes, but that comes with an

38 Jonathan Vespa, Lauren Medina, and David Armstrong, "Demographic Turning Points for the United States: Population Projections for 2020 to 2060," US Census Bureau, revised February 2020. https://www.census.gov/content/dam/Census/library /publications/2020/demo/p25-1144.pdf

39 Janet Adamy, "US Birthrates Fall to Record Low," *Wall Street Journal*, May 20, 2020. https://www.wsj.com/articles/u-s-birthrates-fall-to-record-low-11589947260

40 "Labor Force Participation Rate," Federal Reserve Bank of St. Louis, updated Sept. 4, 2020. https://fred.stlouisfed.org/series/CIVPART

unacceptable trade off of lower economic growth, investment, and productivity.

We aren't having enough children to ensure that America remains prosperous. By 2048, the Congressional Budget Office projects that Americans will be having just enough children to keep up with those passing away.[41] Our population growth may come, unless something changes, solely from immigration. A conservative Republican representative from Arizona, David Schweikert, often speaks on the House floor about the long-term fiscal predicament in which America finds itself.

> *We are getting older very fast as a society, and our birth rates as a society have collapsed. We don't have enough children right now, over the last decade, to even be at replacement rates. We are basically following the trend of the rest of the industrialized world.*
>
> *You have to think that through. What does that mean for our ability to promise Americans, as they move into their senior years, that retirement security? That, I think, both Republicans and Democrats all agree we must have, but, yet, then we do everything we can to avoid the actual math.*[42]

One of the solutions to this problem is merit-based immigration. I'm not talking about opening our borders to everyone. Border security and enforcement should remain a top priority. At the same time, we need an immigration system that fills the critical labor shortages across our economy.

Our current immigration laws were largely written decades ago for an America and an American economy that no longer exists. The economy has evolved from one heavily focused on manufacturing, as it was decades ago, into a service-based economy.

---

41 Long-Term Budget Projections," Congressional Budget Office, September 2020. https://www.cbo.gov/data/budget-economic-data#1

42 David Schweikert, "Our Greatest Difficulty as a Society is Demographics," *Congressional Record*, Vol. 165, No. 5, January 10, 2019. https://www.congress.gov/congressional-record/2019/1/10/house-section/article/H454-2

Previous presidents, such as George W. Bush and Barack Obama, failed to put together an immigration reform plan that could attract wide bipartisan support. Part of the reason these plans failed was because neither administration was serious about passing immigration reform. These administrations were more interested in scoring political points. The handling of immigration reform by these administrations turned the issue into a political football.

Congress needs to fundamentally rethink immigration to respond to the needs of the American economy, with an eye toward tomorrow. This means moving our immigration system to one based on merit, rather than the predominantly humanitarian and familial-based system that we have today. In FY 2017, only 12 percent of immigrants gaining lawful permanent status were employment-based.[43] Some of the legislative proposals for a merit-based immigration system have other motives, such as reducing immigration levels. This shouldn't be the goal of moving in this direction.

This is one of those rare instances in which we should be seeking to emulate Australia or Canada. Both countries have tests to determine whether or not someone seeking to immigrate is a public health or safety threat, but both systems emphasize job skills and the ability to contribute.[44]

As the labor force shrinks in America because our population grows older, businesses will need more workers to fill gaps. The private sector and the existing American labor force should passively determine the level of legal migrant workers who come to America, instead of central planners actively and inaccurately imposing quotas.

An immigration system focused on merit would help bring the best and the brightest to the United States. Immigrants would be considered on their ability to contribute, education level, proficiency in English, and work experience. But a merit-based immigration

---

43   "Table 6. Persons Obtaining Lawful Permanent Resident Status by Type and Major Class of Admission: Fiscal Years 2015 to 2017," Department of Homeland Security, October 2, 2018. https://www.dhs.gov/immigration-statistics/yearbook/2017/table6

44   Adam Donald, "Immigration points-based systems compared," BBC, June 1, 2016. https://www.bbc.com/news/uk-politics-29594642

system shouldn't pick industry winners and losers. For example, the agriculture industry will still need low-skilled immigrant workers, as will some other industries, such as construction. These are jobs, particularly in agriculture, native-born workers tend to not seek.

A merit-based system will bring immigrants who want to contribute to our economy, and these immigrants will help us grow our economy, creating better jobs. There is already evidence showing this correlation. A 2018 policy brief from the National Foundation for American Policy shows 5 to 7.5 jobs are created in the same industry for every high-skilled immigrant hired.[45]

An influx of high-skilled workers contributing to our economy by paying into Medicare and Social Security will help extend the solvency of these programs. As economist Dan Griswold explains, "A steady or increased inflow of immigrant workers helps to spread the cost of funding old-age pension payments across a larger pool of workers, reducing the need to raise payroll taxes, cut benefits, or both."[46]

Our budgetary choices are clear. We either grow the economy by bringing in high-skilled workers, which will lead to more jobs created and more people paying into the system, or face dramatic cuts in Medicare and Social Security.

Growth Will Help Us Solve the Big Problems We Face

Moving towards an immigration system that will encourage the best and the brightest from around the world to come to America to prosper is one piece of the puzzle. We also have to address federal spending. We can't spend our way into prosperity. We need economic growth. Federal spending and deficits caused by federal spending

---

45   "H-1B Visas and Job Creation," National Foundation for American Policy, March 2008. http://www.nfap.com/pdf/080311h1b.pdf

46   Daniel Griswold, "Reforming the US Immigration System to Promote Growth," Mercatus Center, October 2017. https://www.mercatus.org/system/files/griswold-immigration-reform-mercatus-research-v1.pdf

will drown us in red ink, reduce investment, and eventually lead to higher taxes.

Congress has to address entitlement programs in a way that encourages economic growth. This means allowing Americans more freedom to make decisions for themselves in their retirement, such as giving them a voucher to purchase health insurance coverage and allowing them to take some of their payroll tax to invest in a private retirement account.

There is an idea from Europe that we could also adopt to control federal spending. Yes, there is occasionally a good idea from Europe. In December 2001, voters in Switzerland adopted the *Schuldenbremse*, or debt brake.[47] The debt brake, adopted as a constitutional amendment, is designed to prevent structural budget deficits and increased national debt by capping spending to anticipated revenues while also considering economic circumstances. Deficits can happen, but they must be made up for in future years when there is a surplus.

Seeking to emulate the success of the Swiss model, Congressman Kevin Brady of Texas and Senator Mike Braun of Indiana have proposed the Maximizing America's Prosperity Act, or the MAP Act, to cap non-interest spending, including entitlement spending, as a percentage of potential gross domestic product (GDP).[48] Potential GDP is the estimate of GDP at full employment and would ensure stability during a time of economic downturns. During times of strong economic growth, this cap on federal spending would prevent Congress from spending at unsustainable levels.

Much like trendline revenue in Switzerland, potential GDP is a stable metric that ensures economic certainty and fiscal restraint. Under the MAP Act, increases in spending would slowly decrease as it did in Switzerland. When it was implemented, Swiss spending increases totaled 4.3 percent of GDP. Afterward, they shrank to

---

47 "Debt brake," Swiss Federal Finance Administration, accessed Sept. 23, 2020.　　　　https://www.efv.admin.ch/efv/en/home/themen/finanzpolitik_grundlagen /schuldenbremse.html

48 US Congress, *Maximizing America's Prosperity Act.* HR 3930 and S 2245. 116th Congress, 1st Session.

2.6 percent.[49] Spending continued to decrease even throughout the 2008 recession. This is the restraint the US needs in order to get its fiscal ship under control.

If we get spending in check and lure more high-skilled workers who want to contribute to our economy, America will grow.

We also need to continue to pursue tax reform further. The Tax Cuts and Jobs Act lowered individual income and corporate tax rates, providing a shot in the arm of the economy. The individual income tax cuts, which included provisions to provide fairer treatment for pass-through businesses, will expire at the end of 2025. On the business side, the full and immediate expensing of capital expenditures is a growth driver that will soon begin to phase out.[50] These tax cuts must be made permanent. Providing certainty to taxpayers and pass-through entities will mean higher economic growth in the long run and more opportunities for all Americans.

Moving our tax system to a flat tax is an even better idea. When Donald Trump's tax returns came out, there was outrage that he paid only $750 in 2016.[51] If we had a flat tax system, the deductions and loopholes that some use to avoid taxes would go away.

Steve Forbes popularized the concept during his two runs for the Republican presidential nomination. His plan would have provided a personal exemption of $13,000 and $5,000 for each child and subjected the adjusted gross income to a 17 percent flat tax.[52] This would encourage growth through investment and savings, as well as discourage creative accounting to get around the tax code.

49 Daniel J. Mitchell, "How the Swiss 'Debt Brake' Tamed Government," *Wall Street Journal*, April 26, 2012. https://www.cato.org/publications/commentary/how-swiss-debt-brake-tamed-government

50 Anna Tyger, "New Evidence on the Benefits of Full Expensing," Tax Foundation, August 15, 2019. https://taxfoundation.org/benefits-of-full-expensing/

51 Russ Buettner, Susanne Craig, and Mike McIntire, "The President's Taxes: Long-Concealed Records Show Trump's Chronic Losses and Years of Tax Avoidance," *The New York Times*, Sept. 27, 2020. https://www.nytimes.com/interactive/2020/09/27/us/donald-trump-taxes.html

52 "Steve Forbes for President 2000 Campaign Brochures: 'A new birth of freedom,'" 4President.org, accessed Oct. 8, 2020. http://www.4president.org/brochures/steveforbes2000brochure.htm

We have to remember that government doesn't create jobs. It only takes resources out of the economy that could be better used in the private sector. Government misallocates resources. We can solve the big problems that America faces through economic growth and prosperity through private investment and attracting the best and brightest from around the world, but it will only happen if politicians in Washington can see it.

CHAPTER 9

Words Matter

M y background is in communications. I joined FreedomWorks in 2004 as a press secretary and moved up the ranks to president of the organization in 2015. Messaging on political issues has been a part of my job for the better part of two decades. Messaging focused on free markets and individual liberty can win big policy battles and elections, but we need to find what works in today's political climate.

A little more than a third of the country is conservative. Another quarter is liberal. Everyone else is in the middle.[1] If you're going to win the suburbs and win elections, you have to talk to your base and the middle. Your principles can't change, but how you present them to different audiences matters. You have to understand your audience.

We are losing control of the words "freedom" and "capitalism." My wife and I have a very good neighbor who has decided not to put up an American flag at their home because they were worried it

---

1   Lydia Saad, "The US Remained Center-Right, Ideologically, in 2019. Gallup, Jan. 9, 2020   https://news.gallup.com/poll/275792/remained-center-right-ideologically-2019. aspx

would be viewed as a political statement. That's the country we're living in right now.

We have to learn how to make the moral case for capitalism and freedom to a wider audience who believe in these core values. We have to make an argument that the American experiment is worth fighting for. This will help us not only win elections but also to win major policy battles in Congress.

There's no real way to get around it. Conservatives and the Republican Party have serious challenges. Some conservatives, like progressives, tend to live in an echo chamber. They watch cable news programs and listen to talk shows that only confirm their biases. Conservative politicians aren't speaking beyond the base of the Republican Party. The opportunity is that so-called "progressives" aren't speaking beyond the base of the Democratic Party. The only difference is that the Left has the media backing them up.

Republicans, driven by their consultant class, constantly strive for short-term political victories while ignoring long-term demographic trends. These demographics are our next audience. Our message can't be confined to one or two demographics. We have to talk to all demographics. Republicans' attempts to reach out to new voters come across as insincere or laughable. We show up in an election year, and that's it. We need to have a sustained, long-term conversation. We have to be there all the time, not every two or four years.

Back in 2014, for example, the Republican National Committee rolled out a series of ads aimed at millennials. The ads were mocked in the media[2] and parodied on television.[3] The fact that they were mocked isn't a surprise, but, in this instance, the ads were that laughably bad and showed a disconnect between Republicans and younger voters, one that has progressed over the past few decades. The ads came across like how campaign consultants thought Millennials

---

2   Jessica Roy, "The GOP Attempts to Court Millennials with Hilariously Awkward Hipster Ads," *Time*, March 19, 2014. https://time.com/30185/the-gop-attempts-to-court-millennials-with-hilariously-awkward-hipster-ads/

3   "GOP - Whatevs: Last Week Tonight with John Oliver (HBO)," *Last Week Tonight*, March 20, 2014. https://www.youtube.com/watch?v=8q7esuODnQI

talked or what mattered to this age demographic, but it didn't reflect reality.

In 1984, *The New York Times*[4] and *The Washington Post*[5] ran stories about Ronald Reagan's youth movement. In 1994, Republicans held a five-point advantage over voters between the ages of 18 and 29, or Generation X, and a two-point advantage over voters between the ages of 30 and 48,[6] or Baby Boomers. Democrats held advantages of five points and seven points with the Silent Generation and the Greatest Generation. George W. Bush actually ran even with Al Gore with voters between the ages of 18 and 24 in the 2000 presidential election and trailed Gore by only three points with voters between the ages of 25 to 29.[7]

The exit polls in the 2016 presidential election showed Hillary Clinton winning voters between the ages of 18 and 24 by 22 points, ages 25 and 29 by 16 points, and ages 30 and 39 by 12 points.[8] The good news for Trump and Republicans was that these three age demographics were only 36 percent of the electorate. He also won every other age demographic.

Generation Z, people born after 1996, are different from their counterpart generations. They're more racially and ethnically diverse.[9] They're more highly educated. Fully 70 percent of them

4   Steven V. Roberts, "Younger Voters Tending to Give Reagan Support," *The New York Times*, October 16, 1984. https://www.nytimes.com/1984/10/16/us/younger-voters-tending-to-give-reagan-support.html

5   Bill Peterson, "Reagan's Youth Movement," *Washington Post*, August 24, 1984. https://www.washingtonpost.com/archive/politics/1984/08/24/reagans-youth-movement/2fa6fde2-14da-4ace-8dfe-b4721c1e41d6/

6   "A Different Look at Generations and Partisanship," Pew Research Center, April 30, 2015. https://www.pewresearch.org/politics/2015/04/30/a-different-look-at-generations-and-partisanship/

7   "How Groups Voted in 2000," Roper Center for Public Opinion Research, accessed Sept. 23, 2020. https://ropercenter.cornell.edu/how-groups-voted-2000

8   "exit polls," CNN, November 23, 2016. https://www.cnn.com/election/2016/results/exit-polls

9   Richard Fry and Kim Parker, "Early Benchmarks Show 'Post-Millennials' on Track to Be Most Diverse, Best-Educated Generation Yet," Pew Research Center, November 15, 2018. https://www.pewsocialtrends.org/2018/11/15/early-benchmarks-show-post-millennials-on-track-to-be-most-diverse-best-educated-generation-yet/

believe the government should do more to solve problems and are more socially accepting.[10]

The problem for Republicans and conservatives is that the voters on whom they have relied for electoral victories are getting older. In 2018, there were more Generation X, Millennial, and Generation Z voters than Baby Boomer and Silent Generation voters.[11]

Another problem is that Millennials and Generation Z view Republicans as anti-everything—immigrant, environment, gay, black, and women. It's hard to win new audiences when you begin in the hole and are so completely pre-defined.

The pro-growth economic message that conservatives promote is ignored. The irony shouldn't be lost on us. Conservatives promote an economic message that is focused on opportunity. Younger voters are concerned about job opportunities when they graduate from college, the economy, and housing costs. A pro-growth agenda should be an easy sell to young voters, but conservatives find it difficult to even have these conversations with young voters.

Many are still puzzled by the rise of Bernie Sanders. Although he was unsuccessful in his two bids for the White House, he gained a dedicated following of young voters.[12] He didn't present a stereotypical Democratic Party message. A self-described "democratic socialist" who popularized "Medicare for All" inside the Democratic Party, Sanders wanted to move the political debate inside the party to the left. He was successful.

---

10 Kim Parker, Nikki Graf and Ruth Igielnik, "Generation Z Looks a Lot Like Millennials on Key Social and Political Issues," Pew Research Center, January 17, 2019. https://www.pewsocialtrends.org/2019/01/17/generation-z-looks-a-lot-like-millennials-on-key-social-and-political-issues/

11 Anthony Cilluffo and Richard Fry, "Gen Z, Millennials and Gen X outvoted older generations in 2018 midterms," Pew Research Center, May 29, 2019. https://www.pewresearch.org/fact-tank/2019/05/29/gen-z-millennials-and-gen-x-outvoted-older-generations-in-2018-midterms/

12 Melissa Gomez and Melanie Mason, "Just what is it about Bernie Sanders that young voters love?," *Los Angeles Times*, February 27, 2020. https://www.latimes.com/politics/story/2020-02-27/bernie-sanders-young-voters-2020

But before there was Bernie Sanders, there was Ron Paul, who also had a dedicated following of young voters.[13] In New Hampshire during the 2012 campaign, for example, Paul carried 46 percent of voters under the age of thirty. Paul believed very strongly in free markets, opposed more foreign intervention and government surveillance, and blasted the Federal Reserve. The message was new and different. Paul may not have won Republican nomination in 2008 and 2012, but it's undeniable that he shifted the debate inside the Republican Party.

Perhaps the most puzzling aspect of this is that both Sanders and Paul were in their seventies when they ran for president, but they still performed so well with young voters. Yet, when you listen to their core message, they share a focus on many common problems—a mutual distrust of a political system that seems to work for entrenched, powerful interests and not for ordinary people. Playing up this frustration with a corrupt political establishment was also a key part of Trump's appeal, once again promising a very different set of solutions.

Most Americans, and particularly younger generations, agree that the status quo sucks. These people also realize, even if only subconsciously, that they're the ones who are going to get stuck with the tab of the massive debt that Congress is irresponsibly racking up. I believe that limited-government conservatives can show them that the way to a brighter future is more freedom, but we need to stop talking like we're just trying to convince ourselves.

Understand What People Mean

We tend to talk like if we just bombard people with enough statistics, everyone will suddenly understand how freedom and markets work. More importantly, the Left has long been far more savvy in

---

13 Beth Fouhy, "Young Voters Propelling Ron Paul's Campaign," American Association of Retired Persons, January 13, 2012. https://www.aarp.org/politics-society/government-elections/news-01-2012/young-voters-ron-paul.html

understanding that semantics—not just the words we use, but how people hear them—matter. Much more savvy.

The topic of race has always been a source of news coverage, but justice has increasingly been paired with it over the past several years. The rhetoric around the issue is meant to divide us. The media are focusing on race and justice because they want better ratings to beat their competitors. Politicians are focusing on these issues to win elections. Many Democrats are not-so subtly accusing Republicans of being racists. Many Republicans claim Democrats are encouraging the violence we have seen in many cities across the country.

In September 2020, a poll conducted by Scott Rasmussen found that 48 percent of voters believed America was a racist nation.[14] Only 41 percent disagreed. Conservatives may respond harshly to this and blame public schools and universities or the media. Some may believe that many Americans are buying the revisionist history of *The New York Times Magazine's* 1619 Project, which clearly has a political agenda.

The 1619 Project initially claimed that preserving slavery was a central issue in the American Revolution. Slavery has been an issue since the founding, but history is complex. Even while the Second Continental Congress debated the Declaration of Independence, the topic of slavery loomed large and was fiercely debated. Thomas Jefferson's draft of the document included a condemnation of King George III for furthering the slave trade, as well as a condemnation of slavery itself.

> *He has waged cruel war against human nature itself, violating its most sacred rights of life and liberty in the persons of a distant people who never offended him, captivating & carrying them into slavery in another hemisphere or to incur miserable death in their transportation thither. This piratical warfare, the opprobrium of infidel powers, is the warfare of the Christian King of Great Britain. Determined to keep open a market*

---

14 Daniel Payne, "Poll: Three-quarters of Democrats believe America is a racist nation," justthenews.com, September 4, 2020. https://justthenews.com/politics-policy/polling/poll-three-quarters-democrats-believe-america-racist-nation

where Men should be bought & sold, he has prostituted his negative for
suppressing every legislative attempt to prohibit or restrain this execrable
commerce.[15]

Jefferson, himself a slave owner, was as complex as our history. He
was a man who recognized the evils of slavery but failed to live up
to his principles. Ultimately, the passage was struck from the draft
primarily because of the objections of South Carolina and Georgia.[16]
Still, states began to gradually prohibit slavery as early as 1777.

One of the historians who was consulted on the 1619 Project,
Leslie M. Harris, pushed back on the assertion made by its founder,
Nikole Hannah-Jones. "Despite my advice, the *Times* published the
incorrect statement about the American Revolution anyway, in
Hannah-Jones's introductory essay," Harris wrote. "In addition, the
paper's characterizations of slavery in early America reflected laws
and practices more common in the antebellum era than in Colonial
times and did not accurately illustrate the varied experiences of the
first generation of enslaved people that arrived in Virginia in 1619."[17]

Harris also noted, "Far from being fought to preserve slavery,
the Revolutionary War became a primary *disrupter* of slavery in the
North American Colonies."

The New York Times Magazine was forced to somewhat walk back
the assertion.[18] But the goal of the 1619 Project is clear: They want
to discredit the Founders. If you discredit the Founders on slavery,

---

15   Thomas Jefferson, "A Declaration by the Representatives of the United States of
America, in General Congress Assembled," in *Thomas Jefferson: Writings*, The Library
of America, 1984, pg. 22.

16   Thomas Jefferson, "Extract from Thomas Jefferson's Notes of Proceedings in the
Continental Congress," July 2, 1776. Hosted by the Thomas Jefferson Foundation,
http://tjrs.monticello.org/letter/54

17   Leslie M. Harris, "I Helped Fact-Check the 1619 Project. The Times Ignored Me,"
Politico, March 6, 2020. https://www.politico.com/news/magazine/2020/03/06/1619-
project-new-york-times-mistake-122248

18   Jake Silverstein, "An Update to The 1619 Project," *New York Times*, March 11,
2020. https://www.nytimes.com/2020/03/11/magazine/an-update-to-the-1619-project
.html

you also discredit the Constitution. If you discredit the Constitution, you can begin to move America to a direct democracy and mob rule.

I appreciate the fact that we are talking more about the immorality and horrors of slavery, as well as its troubling legacy. The solution isn't to burn everything down. I want to move more people into our economic system because I believe the Constitution, limited government, and free markets benefit everyone. I want to tear down the barriers of generational poverty that prevent people from taking part in our economic system because it's inherently good and leads to prosperity.

To push back on these notions that America isn't a racist country, some may point to the words of Nikki Haley, an accomplished second generation Indian-American, who declared that "'America is not a racist country."[19] Others may cite the words of the only African-American Republican in the Senate, Tim Scott of South Carolina, who said, "[W]e are not a racist country."[20] This is enough for many conservatives.

It has only been in the last several years that conservatives have started fully realizing that the Left has used the focus on racial tensions to actually change what the word "racism" means—literally. The old definition of the word of "racism" in Merriam Webster's online dictionary as of 2015 was probably what most people think of:

1. A belief that race is the primary determinant of human traits and capacities and that racial differences produce an inherent superiority of a particular race.
2. Racial prejudice or discrimination.[21]

---

19 Orion Rummler, "Nikki Haley: 'America is not a racist country,'" *Axios*, August 25, 2020. https://www.axios.com/nikki-haley-republican-national-convention-d99153b0-1199-443a-b868-e1377e1fd056.html

20 Mairead McArdle, "Sen. Tim Scott Declares 'We Are Not a Racist Country,' Argues Dems' Focus on Race Obstructs Police Reform," *National Review*, June 17, 2020. https://www.nationalreview.com/news/sen-tim-scott-declares-we-are-not-a-racist-country-argues-dems-focus-on-race-obstructs-police-reform/

21 "racism," Merriam Webster, 2015. https://web.archive.org/web/20150102094334/https://www.merriam-webster.com/dictionary/racism

That definition expanded at some point in 2016 to include "a political or social system founded on racism,"[22] which makes perfect sense when you think about Jim Crow or apartheid laws. However, in 2020, at the request of an activist, the definition expanded to include "the systemic oppression of a racial group to the social, economic, and political advantage of another," with examples following that included "institutional racism."[23]

This concept of "institutional racism" is closely tied to Marxist ideas of critical race theory that have been popular in academia since the 1960s.[24] Under this understanding of the term, conscious racism of the sort that ignorant people direct towards others of a different skin color is not necessary for one to be a culpable member of a racist system. It's an absurd notion, but this is what is being taught in colleges and other places around the country.

As I've already mentioned, it's important to understand our history and acknowledge that racism exists. We should be learning about our past and each other, but the notion behind critical race theory is ridiculous. Still, the most important conversation that we can have with people in America today is about what it's like to walk a mile in their shoes.

The insidiousness of revisionist historical projects like the 1619 Project is the way they attempt to attach this idea of institutional racism to the very structure of American government and society—to both the Constitution and free-market capitalism. These ideas have gained mainstream currency in academia and the media, and it's a real danger, because no decent person wants to be a racist. Attach racism to capitalism in people's minds, no matter how thin the factual connection, and it becomes anathema. Words matter.

---

22 "racism," Merriam Webster, 2016. https://web.archive.org/web/20161113014118/https://www.merriam-webster.com/dictionary/racism

23 "racism," Merriam Webster, 2020. https://www.merriam-webster.com/dictionary/racism

24 John Murawski, "To Find The Origins Of Today's Race Rage, Start In 1960s Academia," The Federalist, September 3, 2020. https://thefederalist.com/2020/09/03/to-find-the-origins-of-todays-race-rage-start-in-1960s-academia/

Fortunately, although many of the media elites have succumbed to this sad, pessimistic view of America, much of the populace has not. An August 2020 survey found that just 11 percent of voters believed the United States was founded on racism and slavery while 79 percent believe it was founded on noble ideals, while acknowledging that we have failed to live up to them.[25]

Across the board, large majorities of subgroups believe that America was founded on noble ideas, with the exception of one demographic. Only 51 percent of those between the ages of eighteen and twenty-four believe that America was founded on noble ideals while 33 percent believe that the nation was founded as a racist society.

Other surveys show an understanding that, while our history of slavery and legalized racism through Jim Crow laws played a role in our nation's history, the founding ideals played a bigger role. This is why 63 percent view the Founding Fathers as heroes while 15 percent view them as villains.[26] Looking ahead, voters overwhelmingly expect the founding ideals to gain in importance.[27]

One of the ways the Left bypasses this reverence for America's founding is by appealing to the closely related concepts of "social justice" and "equality." To the Left, the concept of social justice is similar to that of the Jacobins during the French Revolution. Social justice means eliminating inequality through government action, such as the redistribution of wealth. One of Congresswoman Alexandria Ocasio-Cortez's staffers, Dan Riffle, puts the concept of

---

25 Daniel Payne, "Eight out of 10 American voters believe the US was founded on ideals of freedom and equality," justthenews.com, August 7, 2020. https://justthenews.com/politics-policy/polling/eight-out-10-american-voters-believe-us-was-founded-ideals-freedom-and

26 Dana Blanton, "Fox News Poll: 63 percent see country's Founders as heroes, 15 percent say villains," *Fox News*, July 19, 2020. https://www.foxnews.com/politics/fox-news-poll-63-percent-see-countrys-founders-as-heroes-15-percent-say-villains

27 Deseret News Editorial Board, "In our opinion: In polarized America, the country still believes in its founding ideals," *Deseret News*, August 25, 2020. https://www.deseret.com/opinion/2020/8/25/21399816/polarized-america-founding-ideals-scott-rasmussen-poll-leaders-work-together

social justice in one simple phrase, "Every billionaire is a policy failure."[28]

Equality, also similar to the Jacobins, is more about equality of outcome than equality of opportunity. Democratic vice presidential nominee Kamala Harris frames it this way: "[T]here's a big difference between equality and equity. Equality suggests, 'Oh, everyone should get the same amount.' The problem with that, not everybody's starting in the same place. So if we're all getting the same amount, but you started out back there and I started out over here, we could get the same amount, but you're going to be that far back behind me. It's about giving people the resources and the support they need, so that everyone can be on equal footing and then compete on equal footing. Equitable treatment means we all end up at the same place."[29]

We have much progress to make towards equality of opportunity. This is a continuing challenge for everyone, regardless of their political ideology. We all want to achieve our own vision of the American Dream, and we want others to have the same chance to achieve their dreams. But we are never going to agree on equality of outcome.

What did people mean when they said America is racist? This is a difficult question to answer. What is clear is that believing America is in some sense racist doesn't mean accepting the worldview of the Left. It doesn't mean that they believe America is evil. We know this because 78 percent of voters are proud to be an American and 62 percent are proud of America's history, even with its flaws.[30]

America was founded on "self-evident [truths], that all men are created equal, that they are endowed by their Creator with certain unalienable Rights, that among these are Life, Liberty and the

---

28   Taylor Nicole Rogers, "The AOC adviser behind the 'Every billionaire is a policy failure' slogan says there's a critical issue with depending on the richest people to fix the world's biggest problems," *Business Insider*, July 16, 2019. https://www.businessinsider.com/aoc-adviser-dan-riffle-every-billionaire-policy-failure-billionaires-philanthropy-2019-7

29   Robby Soave, "Kamala Harris Says Equal Outcomes Should Be the Goal of Public Policy," Reason, Nov. 2, 2020. https://reason.com/2020/11/02/kamala-harris-equality-equity-outcomes/

30   John Solomon and Scott Rasmussen, "62% of voters are proud of America's history," justthenews.com, accessed Sept. 23, 2020. https://justthenews.com/podcasts/scott-rasmussens-number-day/62-voters-are-proud-americas-history

pursuit of Happiness." We haven't always lived up to these ideals, but Americans tend to agree with them. Because we don't think about what voters might really mean when they say America is racist, freedom lovers often push people away and into the other camp.

We also make mistakes when we think people agree with us. A poll released in July 2020 found that 62 percent of voters believe it's very important to place limits on the power of governments and 28 percent say that is somewhat important.[31] We see that and make an assumption that these voters are with us in opposing big government. The same poll, however, also found that 60 percent also say it's very important to place limits on the power of big corporations. Another 28 percent consider it somewhat important to do so.

The point is that words matter, but we need to recognize that words don't always mean what we, as believers in free markets and limited government, think they mean. We need to understand the way terms are used and understood in popular culture if we want to engage with the culture.

A great example of this is socialism. Yes, 39 percent or so of Americans have a positive opinion of socialism.[32] But what they like is nothing like the historical definition of socialism, which is government ownership of the means of production and the abolition of private property. Socialism is the transition from a capitalist economic system to communism. As perplexing as it may be, according to polling conducted by Scott Rasmussen, fully 80 percent of those who like socialism also like free markets. Only a third think it means more power and money going to Washington.

If we attack these voters' interest in socialism by saying free markets are better, they won't have a clue what we are talking about. If we attack their interest by saying centralized power is bad, they will agree and say that is why they don't like socialism.

31 Scott Rasmussen, "Scott Rasmussen's Number of the Day for July 31, 2020," Ballotpedia, July 31, 2020. https://ballotpedia.org/Scott_Rasmussen%27s_Number_of_the_Day_for_July_31,_2020

32 Jeffrey M. Jones and Lydia Saad, "US Support for More Government Inches Up, but Not for Socialism," Gallup, November 18, 2019. https://news.gallup.com/poll/268295/support-government-inches-not-socialism.aspx

We would also have an angle to talk to these voters by agreeing with them that rewarding powerful corporations is bad. Most Democrats and Republicans in Congress love crony capitalism—bailouts, subsidies, and picking winners and losers in the marketplace—and many on K Street thrive on it. Outside the Beltway, Americans, regardless of their political beliefs, hate crony capitalism.

The Challenges Before Us

Politics is a communications war. Grassroots is the largest form of communication. We've got to find our message, hone it, and sell it. In today's political climate, we have our work cut out for us. We have two huge challenges, one of which is long-term while the other is short-term and ongoing.

The long-term goal is to define what freedom, equality, and other key words mean in the popular culture. We start with a solid foundation. That foundation is that 94 percent of voters believe every American has the right to live their life as they see fit as long as they respect the rights of others to do the same.[33]

This is essentially an encapsulation of John Stuart Mill's "harm principle." Mill wrote:

> *That the only purpose for which power can be rightfully exercised over any member of a civilised community, against his will, is to prevent harm to others. His own good, either physical or moral, is not a sufficient warrant . . .The only part of the conduct of any one, for which he is amenable to society, is that which concerns others. In the part which merely concerns himself, his independence is, of right, absolute. Over himself, over his own body and mind, the individual is sovereign.*[34]

---

33 Scott Rasmussen, "Scott Rasmussen's Number of the Day for June 28, 2019," Ballotpedia, June 28, 2019. https://ballotpedia.org/Scott_Rasmussen%27s_Number_of_the_Day_for_June_28,_2019

34 John Stuart Mill, "On Liberty," Project Gutenberg, January 10, 2011. https://www.gutenberg.org/files/34901/34901-h/34901-h.htm

We need to define our terms when it comes to key words. This is vitally important because there is enormous power in how we define our terms. Drawing from something he saw decades ago, Rasmussen explains how terms can be defined in ways that may produce worthless data.

> *Some company decided to rate the best jobs in the world and concluded that being an actuary was the ideal job. What made it funny is that being a Major League Baseball player didn't even make the top 200. Obviously, that was a silly conclusion. Millions of young boys dream of growing up to play professional sports but I don't remember any of my friends dreaming of a career as an actuary.*
>
> *So, how did the absurd result come about? It wasn't a mistake in the calculations. Instead, it was all about the definitions. Jobs where people worked outdoors were defined as less desirable. So were jobs in a competitive environment. And, all salary levels above $50,000 or $75,000 were deemed to have the same value.*
>
> *So, Gerrit Cole's $36 million a year job is defined as less desirable because he works outdoors in a competitive environment. Oh, and did I mention that he sometimes has to work at night and put up with the adulation of countless fans and ballplayers across the nation. Uh huh, right! Being an actuary may be an ideal job for some, but the results had no value because the standards didn't reflect reality.*[35]

Freedom means decentralizing power from Washington and letting people live their lives how they see fit. Equality means a level playing field where everyone has an equal opportunity to succeed. Justice is punishing someone when actual harm is done against another person. These are the definitions of key words that we absolutely need to sell to voters. Americans cherish freedom and equality. Right now, the Left is redefining those terms. If we let them get away with it, we will lose. We need an ongoing effort to influence the culture and define those terms.

---

35 Scott Rasmussen, "How a Babe Ruth home run illustrates the importance of good data calculation," *Deseret News*, August 31, 2020. https://www.deseret.com/opinion/2020/8/31/21408755/covid-19-testing-data-babe-ruth-data-collection-numbers

Another ongoing challenge is that we must be a translator of real America to Washington's political class. Unfortunately, when people in Washington hear that people like "socialism," they believe people agree with Bernie Sanders and Alexandria Ocasio-Cortez. When they hear that 48 percent of voters believe America is a racist country, they think people agree on defunding the police. The reality is, neither of those things are close to true.

One of our goals at FreedomWorks is to actively explain to officials what voters are really thinking. We share what our activists are thinking with our allies on Capitol Hill, but we are also providing more information on the pulse of America, breaking down polling data into consumable information that our allies in Congress can understand and use to shape their own messaging. We may be politically divided, but we all speak a common language. It's simply a matter of getting outside of our comfort zones to speak to voters who share our beliefs but may not know it.

Ultimately, we need to listen to what voters are really saying and build bridges to them. The best messaging begins with careful listening and a sincere attempt to understand. We need to learn that there is a difference between listening and hearing. If we just let someone who we are trying to convince talk and don't hear and address what they are saying, instead going into our pitch, we will lose them.

We can't simply explain to those we are trying to win that just because something is in the Constitution—whether we are talking about the concept of limited government, the separation of powers, the right to free speech, the protections against illegal searches and seizures, the right to due process—is never good enough. We need to explain why it is relevant today. Only then can we draw wisdom from the Founding Fathers and the Framers of the Constitution.

Finally, we should always remember that most people love our country. They want to celebrate it. They want to make it better. We should tap into those positive vibes. We can't be an angry mob. We want to be the people promoting the ideal of liberty and justice for all. We can admit we aren't there yet, but we can tap into the shared interest in striving to make it so.

CHAPTER 10
The Battle for the Suburbs Isn't Over

⸻

I grew up in the suburbs between Cleveland and Akron, Ohio. People who live in the suburbs care about good and well-paying jobs, a quality education for their kids, and political and economic stability. Much has been made about the suburban revolt against Republicans. It's not an acceptance of Democrats or their policy priorities as much as it is venting frustration at what they perceive as the status quo.

The fight for the heart and soul of America will be won or lost in the suburbs. It's impossible for either party to have control of the White House or Congress without winning many of these voters. With the Electoral College in danger, any presidential candidate needs to win the popular vote.

Democrats, driven by the far left of their party, believe that the suburbs are trending in their direction, but they're misreading their recent electoral victories.

Unnoticed because of the pandemic and a narrative counter to what the media would like you to know, voters in California rejected 64 percent of the local tax and bond measures on their ballots in

March 2020.[1] This was the first school bond measure to fail in California in more than two decades.[2]

One of the more noticeable ballot measures that failed was the proposed extension of the quarter-cent sales tax for the Sonoma–Marin Area Rail Transit (SMART), a commuter rail service that operates in the northern San Francisco Bay area.[3] This is one of the most reliably Democratic areas in the country, but when directly asked, voters rejected the extension of a tax.

California is one of the most taxed states in the country. The Golden State has the highest income tax rate at 13.3 percent.[4] Even individual tax filers who earn as little as $57,824 or joint filers who earn at least $115,648 get hit with a 9.3 percent income tax. The median household income in the state is roughly $70,500.[5] The combined state and local tax rate is 8.68 percent.[6] Considering the high cost of living in California, this isn't exactly a lot of income.[7]

Although there have been times voters have elected a Republican to serve as governor, Democrats have dominated California politics

1   Edward Ring, "Primary Election: Californians Reject New Taxes and Borrowing," *California Globe*, March 10, 2020. https://californiaglobe.com/section-2/primary-election-californians-reject-new-taxes-and-borrowing/

2   Ricardo Cano, "California's Prop. 13 school bond is officially defeated," Cal Matters, March 11, 2020. https://calmatters.org/education/2020/03/california-prop-13-school-bond-defeated/

3   "North Bay Voters Put Brakes On Sales Tax Extension To Fund SMART Train Service," KPIX CBS San Francisco, March 4, 2020. https://sanfrancisco.cbslocal.com/2020/03/04/north-bay-voters-put-brakes-on-sales-tax-extension-to-fund-smart-train-service/

4   Katherine Loughead, "State Individual Income Tax Rates and Brackets for 2020," Tax Foundation, February 4, 2020. https://taxfoundation.org/state-individual-income-tax-rates-and-brackets-for-2020/

5   "Median Household Income in California," Federal Reserve Bank of St. Louis. https://fred.stlouisfed.org/series/MEHOINUSCAA646N (accessed Sept. 24, 2020)

6   Janelle Cammenga, "State and Local Sales Tax Rates, Midyear 2020," Tax Foundation, July 8, 2020. https://taxfoundation.org/state-and-local-sales-tax-rates-2020/

7   Erika Rawes, "7 most expensive states to live in the US," *USA Today*, September 13, 2014. https://www.usatoday.com/story/money/personalfinance/2014/09/13/cheat-sheet-most-expensive-states/15455129/

for decades. The very people Democrats claim to want to help are the ones leaving the state. Most of the people leaving California have incomes below $100,000.[8] In 2019, more than seven hundred thousand people left California, with Arizona and Texas being the primary destinations.[9] Some are also flocking to Idaho.[10] The only reason California has been saved is because of the number of people earning $100,000 or more coming to the state.

Some wealthier Californians are also pursuing a freer political and economic atmosphere. Elon Musk has threatened to pull Tesla's headquarters out of California to either Texas or Nevada.[11] His threat was in response to Tesla being prevented from continuing manufacturing during the pandemic. Musk called it "the final straw."

New York has fared even worse. Since 2010, the Empire State has lost a net 124,000 residents.[12] The cost of living, which is higher than in California, is a concern. Income taxes and state and local taxes are high. Among other states, New Yorkers are flocking to Florida, North Carolina, and Texas.[13]

8   Kate Cimini, "'Not the Golden State anymore': Middle- and low-income people leaving California," *Cal Matters*, January 8, 2020. https://calmatters.org/california-divide/2020/01/not-the-golden-state-anymore-middle-and-low-income-people-leaving-california/

9   Steve Brown, "Almost 700,000 Californians moved out last year, and many ended up in Texas," *Dallas Morning News*, December 10, 2019. https://www.dallasnews.com/business/real-estate/2019/12/10/almost-700000-californians-moved-out-of-state-last-year/

10   Dion Lim, "Californians are leaving the state at a rapid pace... and going to Idaho?," ABC News 7 San Francisco, January 3, 2020. https://abc7news.com/moving-out-of-california-residents-leaving-to-idaho-people/5809250/

11   Hannah Jones, "Elon Musk Says Tesla Will Move to Texas or Nevada, Dallas Officials Respond," NBC News 5 Dallas-Fort Worth, May 11, 2020. https://www.nbcdfw.com/news/local/elon-musk-says-tesla-will-move-to-texas-or-nevada-dallas-officials-respond/2367353/

12   Carl Campanile, "New York is losing residents at an alarming rate," *New York Post*, December 30, 2019. https://nypost.com/2019/12/30/new-york-is-losing-residents-at-an-alarming-rate-report/

13   E.J. McMahon, "Where Are New Yorkers Headed?" Empire Center for Public Policy, Jan. 1, 2020.   https://www.empirecenter.org/publications/wherearenewyorkersgoing/

Let's Take a Look at the Numbers

Going into the 2020 presidential election, the media made Americans seem divided along different lines, but the results of the election showed that Democrats' focus on identity politics appears to have backfired. Although Donald Trump may have lost the election, he won 26 percent of non-white voters, which was the largest percentage of the non-white vote that a Republican has received since 1960 when Richard Nixon lost to John F. Kennedy.[14]

The results of the election may have surprised many political observers, but Americans had seen the benefits of a strong economy. The economy certainly took a hit because of the pandemic. No one questions that, and that's why we were focusing so hard on re-opening the economy to get people back to work. After all, we want to see all Americans thrive and succeed.

Before the pandemic hit America, the economy was humming. Americans saw a 6.8 percent increase in household income, the lowest poverty rate on record, the lowest unemployment rate in decades, the lowest black unemployment rate on record, and the lowest Hispanic unemployment rate ever. Voters responded.

Democrats lost Miami-Dade County, Florida because Cuban-American voters, who either have experienced socialism firsthand or have family members who have experienced socialism, rejected the so-called "progressivism" they're seeing in America that so closely resembles what they fled.

Democrats appear to have taken the Hispanic vote for granted. Writing at the *Wall Street Journal*, Mike Gonzalez explains, "Identity politics lost in South Texas: Zapata County, 95% Mexican-American, went for Hillary Clinton by 33 points in 2016—but Mr. Trump won with 52.5% this time. Throughout the Rio Grande Valley, President Trump did better in 2020 than in 2016: In Starr County he lost by only five points (47% to Mr. Biden's 52%), compared with a 60-point

---

14 Zachary Evans, "Trump Won One-Quarter of Non-White Voters, Improving on 2016 Numbers: Exit Poll," National Review, Nov. 4, 2020. https://www.nationalreview .com/news/trump-won-highest-share-of-non-white-vote-of-any-republican-since-1960-exit-polls-show/

spread in Mrs. Clinton's favor four years ago. In Jim Hogg County, Mr. Trump lost by 18 points, down from more than 50 in 2016. In Webb County, Mr. Trump won 36.6% of the vote, up from 22.8% in 2016."[15]

Identity politics and promises of "free" things may be good for raising money, but it doesn't translate into electoral victories. Just ask the Democratic nominees in the 2020 Senate races in Kentucky, Maine, North Carolina, and South Carolina. Republican incumbents in these races were wildly outspent.

In Kentucky, the Democratic nominee, Amy McGrath, raised $88 million[16] and was the beneficiary of $4.2 million from PACs backing her and another $11.8 million from PACs that attacked Mitch McConnell,[17] who has led Senate Republicans since 2007. McGrath lost by nearly 20 points. Asked if there was any voter fraud in his race, McConnell, replied, "I don't know. At risk of bragging, it wasn't very close."[18]

In South Carolina, Democrats thought they had a chance to beat Lindsey Graham. They were wrong. Graham's Democratic opponent, Jamie Harrison, raised more than $107 million.[19] He received another $16.8 million in support from PACs.[20] The end result? Graham won by 10 points.

---

15 Mike Gonzalez, "Tuesday's Big Loser: Identity Politics," *The Wall Street Journal*, Nov. 4, 2020. https://www.wsj.com/articles/tuesdays-big-loser-identity-politics-11604535714

16 "Kentucky Senate 2020 Race: Summary Data," OpenSecrets, accessed Nov. 10, 2020. https://www.opensecrets.org/races/summary?cycle=2020&id=KYS1

17 "Kentucky Senate 2020 Race: Outside Spending," OpenSecrets, accessed Nov. 10, 2020. https://www.opensecrets.org/races/outside-spending?cycle=2020&id=KYS1&spec=N

18 "Beastmode: McConnell: Haven't thought about vote fraud in my race because 'it wasn't very close,'" *The Washington Free Beacon*, Nov. 11, 2020. https://freebeacon.com/2020-election/beastmode-mcconnell-havent-thought-about-vote-fraud-in-my-race-because-it-wasnt-very-close/

19 South Carolina Senate 2020 Race: Summary Data," OpenSecrets, accessed Nov. 10, 2020. https://www.opensecrets.org/races/summary?cycle=2020&id=SCS2

20 "South Carolina Senate 2020 Race: Outside Spending," OpenSecrets, accessed Nov. 10, 2020. https://www.opensecrets.org/races/outside-spending?cycle=2020&id=SCS2&spec=N

Maine and North Carolina were thought to be two of Democrats' best pickup opportunities. Sarah Gideon, who challenged Collins in Maine, raised $68.5 million.[21] Gideon was aided by another $60.9 million in support from allied PACs.[22] Those PACs spent heavily to beat Collins, but Collins won by 9 points. In North Carolina, the Democratic nominee, Cal Cunningham, raised $46.7 million[23] and had another $115 million in support from PACs.[24] Tom Tillis squeaked out a close one, but he still beat Cunningham.

Republicans were expected to lose the Senate and see their minority in the House shrink. What actually happened was Republicans picked up seats in the House, substantially narrowing Democrats' majority in the chamber, and also held state legislatures targeted by Democrats.[25] This not only could cripple the agenda of Joe Biden, Kamala Harris, and Nancy Pelosi in the House but also sets the stage for redrawing of congressional districts ahead of the 2022 midterm election.

However, Republicans have also misread the tea leaves. According to Catalist, younger suburban voters cast their ballots for Democrats by wide margins in 2018,[26] giving Democrats 37-point and 27-point margins over Republicans with suburban voters between the ages of 18 and 29 and ages 30 and 44. Democrats also had a 2-point margin over Republicans with suburban voters between the ages of 45 and

---

21   "Maine Senate 2020 Race: Summary Data," OpenSecrets, accessed Nov. 10, 2020. https://www.opensecrets.org/races/summary?cycle=2020&id=MES2&spec=N

22   "Maine Senate 2020 Race: Outside Spending," OpenSecrets, accessed Nov. 10 2020 https://www.opensecrets.org/races/outside-spending?cycle=2020&id=MES2&spec=N

23   "North Carolina Senate 2020 Race: Summary Data," OpenSecrets, accessed Nov. 10, 2020. https://www.opensecrets.org/races/summary?cycle=2020&id=NCS1&spec=N

24   "North Carolina Senate 2020 Race: Outside Spending," OpenSecrets, accessed Nov. 10, 2020. https://www.opensecrets.org/races/outside-spending?cycle=2020&id=NCS1&spec=N

25   Ally Mutnick and Sabrina Rodriguez, "'A decade of power': statehouse wins position GOP to dominate redistricting," *Politico*, Nov. 4, 2020. https://www.politico.com/news/2020/11/04/statehouse-elections-2020-434108

26   Catalist, "What Happened Last Tuesday, Part 2 - Who Did They Vote For?" Data for Progress, Nov. 18, 2018. https://docs.google.com/spreadsheets/d/1UwC_GapbE3vF6-n1THVbwcXoU_zFvO8jJQL99ouX3Rw/edit?ts=5beae6d4#gid=433702266

64 while Republicans had a 4-point margin with suburban voters aged 65 and over.

In 2006, suburban white voters were 49 percent of the electorate. In 2018, they were 42 percent. Suburban non-white voters have grown to 13 percent of the electorate in 2018 from 10 percent in 2006. Democrats won suburban white voters by 8 points in 2018 and suburban non-white voters by 61 points. Republicans carried suburban white voters by 21 points in 2010 and lost suburban non-white voters by 48 points.

There's no question that the suburbs are becoming more racially diverse. In 2000, minorities represented 27 percent of suburban residents.[27] Today, that figure is at least 35 percent.[28] Republicans have gotten a late start in responding to these changing dynamics on the ground, but there have been improvements.

We've seen that people of color are willing to vote for Republicans. Exit polls from the 2020 presidential race show that Trump significantly increased his share of votes from black voters between the ages of 30 and 44, to 19 percent in 2020 from 7 percent in 2016. He also improved with Latino voters over the age of 45.

Exit polls show that Biden carried suburban voters with 50 percent of the vote. In 2016, Hillary Clinton received 45 percent of the vote from suburban voters.[29] Trump won 59 percent of suburban white voters in 2020 while Biden took 87 percent and 66 percent of African-American and Hispanic voters.[30]

27 William H. Frey, "Melting Pot Suburbs: A CEnsus 2000 Study of Urban Diversity," Brookings Institute, June 1, 2001. https://www.brookings.edu/research/melting-pot-suburbs-a-census-2000-study-of-suburban-diversity/

28 Richard Florida, "The Changing Demographics of America's Suburbs," *Bloomberg Citylab*, Nov. 7, 2019. https://www.bloomberg.com/news/articles/2019-11-07/the-changing-demographics-of-america-s-suburbs

29 "Exit polls 2016," CNN *Politics*, updated Nov. 23, 2016. https://www.cnn.com/election/2016/results/exit-polls

30 "Exit polls 2020," CNN *Politics*, accessed Nov. 10, 2020. https://www.cnn.com/election/2020/exit-polls/president/national-results/

The 2020 presidential election saw voters in suburban areas in Atlanta and Phoenix pull further away from Republicans,[31] handing Georgia and Arizona to a Democratic presidential candidate for the first time in decades.

Congresswoman Abigail Spanberger of Virginia, whose district is in suburban Richmond, blasted progressives in the House Democratic Caucus in a post-election call with her colleagues.[32] She said, "The number one concern in things that people brought to me in my [district] that I barely re-won, was defunding the police." She said, "[W]e need to not ever use the words 'socialist' or 'socialism' ever again."

"If we are classifying [the 2020 election] as a success from a congressional standpoint, we will get fucking torn apart in 2022," Spanberger also reportedly said.[33]

Democrats still haven't wrapped their heads around the fact that America is a fundamentally center-right nation. Congresswoman Rashida Tlaib of Michigan, a member of Alexandria Ocasio-Cortez's "Squad," lashed out at the few moderate Democrats left in the House after the election. Tlaib said that she "can't be silent" about Leftist causes.[34]

Please, Congresswoman Tlaib, keep talking. Please keep ignoring the rejection of socialism that we saw in the 2020 election. Identity politics is on its last legs. Voters aren't easily swayed by promises of "free" stuff. The 2020 election showed that.

Suburban voters don't typically concern themselves with issues that may appeal to the base of one political party or the other. These

---

31 Emily Badger and Quoctrung Bui, "How the Suburbs Moved Away from Trump," *The New York Times*, updated Nov. 9, 2020. https://www.nytimes.com /interactive/2020/11/06/upshot/suburbs-shifted-left-president.html

32 Chris Cillizza, "This Democratic Congresswoman just spoke some hard truth to her party," *CNN Politics*, Nov. 6, 2020. https://www.cnn.com/2020/11/06/politics /abigail-spanberger-house-democrats-2020-election/index.html

33 Tim Alberta, "Elissa Slotkin Braces for a Democratic Civil War," *Politico Magazine*, Nov. 13, 2020. https://www.politico.com/news/magazine/2020/11/13 /elissa-slotkin-braces-for-a-democratic-civil-war-436301

34 Laura Barròn Lòpez and Holly Otterbein, "Tlaib lashes out at centrist Dems over election debacle: 'I can't be silent,'" *Politico*, Nov. 11, 2020. https://www.politico.com /news/2020/11/11/rashida-tlaib-progressives-election-435877

voters are typically turned off by extremes on either side of the ideological spectrum. They care about meat and potatoes issues. They care about the economy and its job opportunities for themselves and their children, health care and its rising costs, and education. They also want a government that works. If you want to win, you have to address these issues.

One key voting bloc that should be on our minds is suburban women. In the 2020 presidential election, exit polls show that 56 percent of suburban women voted for Biden.[35] It's true that many of these voters cast their ballots for Biden because they often didn't like Trump's tone, but Trump's typical message on immigration and "law and order" didn't resonate with them. There was also an absolute failure to address health care in a meaningful way, and this issue is a big one in the suburbs.

Issues like climate change, abortion, and fringes of the immigration debate on both sides aren't the issues at the forefront of suburban voters' minds.[36] Few politicians are interested in meeting these voters where they are. The rest of the political class focuses on what divides us.

Voters Want Economic Opportunity

During the 1992 presidential race, then-candidate Bill Clinton's campaign honed in on a simple three-pronged message to appeal to voters: "Change vs. more of the same. The economy, stupid. Don't forget health care."[37]

---

35 "Exit polls 2020," CNN *Politics*, accessed Dec. 1, 2020. https://www.cnn.com /election/2020/exit-polls/president/national-results/

36 "Important Issues in the 2020 Election," Pew Research Center, Aug. 13, 2020.   https://www.pewresearch.org/politics/2020/08/13/important-issues-in-the-2020-election/

37 Michael Kelly, "The 1992 Campaign: The Democrats—Clinton and Bush Compete to Be Champions of Change, Democrat Fights Perceptions of Bush Gain," *The New York Times*, Oct. 31, 1992. https://www.nytimes.com/1992/10/31/us /1992-campaign-democrats-clinton-bush-compete-be-champion-change-democrat-fights.html

Bush had unequivocally said that he wouldn't raise taxes only four years before.[38] The growth of entitlement programs and a recession in 1990 left America with large budget deficits. This was when politicians still cared about deficits. Bush retreated on his pledge not to raise taxes in November 1990 when he signed the Omnibus Budget Reconciliation Act into law.

Clinton's campaign used Bush's pledge against him during the 1992 presidential campaign, running an ad that noted that "Bush signed the second biggest tax increase in American history" and "increased taxes on the middle class."[39] For good measure, the ad also criticized Bush for increasing the "beer tax" and gas tax.

Clinton's message on the economy was directed at the middle class. His record as an authentic centrist from a southern state gave him credibility with voters. Clinton made voters believe him when he said, "I feel your pain."[40] On the other hand, Bush embarrassingly didn't know the price of milk.[41] During a tour at the National Grocers Association, he was seemingly amazed by the checkout counter and technology that had existed for quite some time.[42] It painted the image of someone who was out of touch with average Americans.

Ultimately, Clinton's strategy worked.

Of course, Clinton and a Democratic Congress almost immediately raised taxes when he got into office. He also successfully

---

38   George H. W. Bush, "1988 Flashback, George H. W. Bush says, 'Read my lips, no new taxes,'" speech at Republican National Convention, Dec. 4, 2018. NBC News video clip posted Dec. 4, 2018. https://www.nbcnews.com/video/1988-flashback-george-h-w-bush-says-read-my-lips-no-new-taxes-1388261955924

39   Classic New Orleans TV, "Bill Clinton Campaign Ad, George Bush RML Taxes, Oct., 1992," Youtube video, Nov. 10, 2015. https://www.youtube.com/watch?v=8PsCBR0qLHs

40   Clinton's famous cry "I feel your pain" was in response to a heckler at a campaign event. "The 1992 Campaign: Verbatim; Heckler Stirs Clinton Anger: Excerpts from the Exchange," *The New York Times*, Mar. 28, 1992. https://www.nytimes.com/1992/03/28/us/1992-campaign-verbatim-heckler-stirs-clinton-anger-excerpts-exchange.html

41   Vanessa Barford, "Should Politicians Know the Price of a Pint of Milk?" BBC.com, Apr. 24, 2012. https://www.bbc.com/news/magazine-17826509

42   Andrew Rosenthal, "Bush Encounters the Supermarket, Amazed," *The New York Times*, Feb. 5, 1992. https://www.nytimes.com/1992/02/05/us/bush-encounters-the-supermarket-amazed.html

pushed an aggressive gun control agenda and tried to fundamentally alter America's health care system. Voters responded by giving Republicans control of Congress in the 1994 midterm elections. The Contract with America, in which House Republicans defined their agenda, was a suburban-focused document.

Although there was intense political bickering at times, culminating with Clinton's impeachment, the 1990s are looked at as a decade of prosperity. Divided government worked. It may not have been perfect, but the system that the framers of the Constitution gave us worked. Today, people look back on the late 1990s as a period of strong job growth, innovation, and opportunity.

Suburban voters, particularly suburban women, don't care about the latest political drama in Washington. They are skeptical of political extremes and radical agendas. They are desperate for straight talk, not chaos. What they want is an economy that creates good jobs for themselves and their children.

It's hard not to laugh when I hear someone on the House or Senate floor or in a committee hearing talk about what the American people want. These are the emptiest words uttered in Congress. In reality, what the American people want is a foreign concept to most in Washington.

Many view the 2010 midterm election as a referendum on Obamacare, but that wasn't the issue on the minds of voters. The *Washington Post* found that 63 percent of voters listed the economy as the most important issue facing the country.[43] The Great Recession had just ended, but Americans were still faced with high unemployment caused by a weak economic recovery.

As CBS News noted in its post-mortem of the election, "[V]oters had become disillusioned with Mr. Obama and the Democratic-controlled Congress with many thinking they are part of the problem rather than the solution. Nearly a quarter of voters (23 percent) now believe that Mr. Obama is more to blame for the current economic problems than former President George W. Bush or Wall

---

43 "Election 2010: Exit Polls," *The Washington Post*, Nov. 2, 2010. https://www .washingtonpost.com/wp-srv/special/politics/election-results-2010/exit-poll/

Street bankers. Nearly two-thirds of voters (65 percent) believe the economic stimulus package has hurt the economy or made no difference."[44]

A message of "hope" and "change" might have catapulted Barack Obama into the White House, but unicorns and fairy dust don't create jobs. Obama's legislative and regulatory agendas were hampering businesses. The Great Recession officially ended in June 2009, but private sector employment increased by only sixty-four thousand in October 2010,[45] the month before the midterm election, far below the 125,000 jobs needed to keep up with population growth.[46]

Ironically, what saved Obama's presidency was oil and gas. The Obama administration actively worked to restrict the very industry that led the economy as a percentage of GDP growth. Oil and gas development accounted for nearly half of GDP growth and the hydraulic fracking boom alone accounted for 9.3 million jobs,[47] nearly half of the jobs created during his entire presidency. States such as Texas contributed nearly 70 percent of all jobs created during the Obama administration. Wage growth for workers in the natural gas industry also skyrocketed, with workers in states such as North Dakota seeing their weekly wages increase up to 40 percent post-shale boom.[48]

---

44   Samuel Best, "Why Democrats Lost the House to Republicans," CBS News, Nov. 3, 2010. https://www.cbsnews.com/news/why-democrats-lost-the-house-to-republicans/

45   Ian Swanson, "Economy Loses 95,000 Job, Unemployment Rate Steady at 9.6 Percent," *The Hill*, Oct. 8, 2010. https://thehill.com/policy/finance/123333-economy-loses-95000-jobs-unemployment-rate-steady-at-96-percent

46   This figure varies depending on who you read. See: Mary Ann Milbourne, "US Loses 95,000 Jobs in September," *Orange County Register*, Oct. 18, 2010. https://www.ocregister.com/2010/10/08/us-loses-95000-jobs-in-september-2/

47   Isaac Orr, "Fracking Boom Masks Obama's Horrifying Economic Numbers," Heartland Institute, Oct. 17, 2016. https://www.heartland.org/news-opinion/news/fracking-boom-masks-obamas-horrifying-economic-numbers

48   Robert Bradley, Jr. "The American Oil & Gas Industry is Rescuing the Obama Economy," *Forbes*, Jun. 27, 2013. https://www.forbes.com/sites/robertbradley/2013/06/17/the-american-oil-gas-industry-is-rescuing-the-obama-economy/

Without oil and gas development, there would have been almost no economic or job growth during the Obama administration. Let that irony sink in.

Democrats wail and gnash their teeth about corporations, but in today's economy, small businesses are a driving force of the economy. According to the Small Business Administration, 47.3 percent of workers were employed by small businesses in 2019.[49] The number of corporations has been in steady decline since the 1990s.[50] The number of pass-through businesses—S corporations, partnerships, and sole proprietorships—have been on the rise. If Democrats do eventually succeed in increasing taxes or force the individual tax cuts to expire as scheduled, small businesses owners will be among the hardest hit.

The fact of the matter is that today's Democratic Party is anti-business. More government and less private sector is almost always their answer to any problem. Corporations may be an easy target for Democrats, but small businesses will be caught in the crossfire.

Democrats will undoubtedly deny that they are anti-business, but the agenda of higher taxes that Democrats are pushing can't be viewed on a static basis. It will negatively impact job creators in our economy, leading to fewer economic opportunities for all Americans, regardless of their race or background.

And the impact on jobs isn't limited to taxes. The Democrats' energy policy agenda will drive up the cost of gas and electricity, negatively impacting consumers and businesses. There will be fewer dollars available for businesses to expand and hire new workers. The cost of living will rise across the country. Households across the country will have to budget larger percentages of their income for electricity bills and gas to get to and from work.

---

49 "Small Businesses Drive Job Growth in United States; They Account for 1.8 Million New Jobs, Latest Data Show," US Small Business Association, Office of Advocacy, Apr. 24, 2019. https://advocacy.sba.gov/2019/04/24/small-businesses-drive-job-growth-in-united-states-they-account-for-1-8-million-net-new-jobs-latest-data-show/

50 Scott Eastman, "Corporate and Pass-Through Business Income and Returns Since 1980," Tax Foundation, Apr. 23, 2019. https://taxfoundation.org/pass-through-business-income-since-1980/

Restoring American Health Care

In 2017, I took a week-long trip to Havana, Cuba and got a firsthand look at what socialism does to its citizens. What I witnessed was Cubans being equally poor and struggling to make ends meet.

Leftists like to rave about the country's health care system and how socialism has successfully worked. Filmmaker Michael Moore even produced a movie, *Sicko*, in which he hailed the Cuban health care system.

On a walk through Old Havana, surrounded by what were once beautiful buildings, we approached a busy pharmacy. I was surprised to see that the shelves were nearly empty even as the line was extended down the sidewalk.

I paused in my footsteps as my jaw dropped. I thought, "How could this reality for millions of Cubans exist? Hell, they are only one hundred miles away from America. We are so lucky as Americans and we need to do better."

Unfortunately, the Affordable Care Act, what we know as Obamacare, set our great country on a path towards what I personally witnessed in Havana. Obamacare was a stepping stone. A "public option" is the next step. The government will undercut insurance companies and eventually lead to the collapse of the private health insurance system. It's Democrats' long-term goal.

Americans are concerned about the rising costs of health care. The Affordable Care Act hasn't lived up to its name. In May 2017, the Department of Health and Human Services released a report showing that individual market health insurance premiums rose by an average of 105 percent since 2013.[51] The health insurance plans available on the Marketplace exchange have consistently fallen far below projections.

After years of talking about repeal of Obamacare, Republicans had an opportunity in 2017 to finally repeal Obama's signature legislative

---

51 "ASPE Data Point: Individual Market Premium Changes, 2013-2017," US Department of Health and Human Services, May 23, 2017. https://aspe.hhs.gov /system/files/pdf/256751/IndividualMarketPremiumChanges.pdf

achievement. They blew it. Not only did they fail to pass a bill to fix the problems with Obamacare, but health care subsequently became a central issue in the 2018 midterm elections. Democrats focused on one in issue during the election: ensuring coverage for Americans with pre-existing conditions.

Democrats insisted Republicans would take health insurance coverage away from Americans with pre-existing conditions. The claim wasn't true, but Republicans didn't have a coherent message against the attack, and they were routed at the ballot box in 2018.

Today, a large number of Democrats are supporting "Medicare for All." Democrats claim that Americans are supportive of a government-run, single-payer health insurance system for all Americans, but when Americans learn that it would mean the elimination of private health insurance and higher taxes—both of which would be required under "Medicare for All"—Americans oppose it by a large margin.[52]

Democrats may not want to admit it, but Americans are happy with the private health insurance system that America has.[53] Even in Medicare itself, the only real private element of the program, Medicare Advantage, has proven quite popular. Medicare Advantage enrollment has grown to 36 percent of Medicare beneficiaries from 24 percent in 2010.

Unfortunately, after Republicans' failure to get health insurance reform across the finish line in 2017, the Affordable Care Act is sticking around, as are the concerns about rising health insurance premiums and health-care costs.

The Affordable Care Act and Republicans' alternative in 2017, the American Health Care Act, were more about rearranging who

---

52 "Public Opinion on Single-Payer, National Health Plans, and Expanding Access to Medicare Coverage," Kaiser Family Foundation, May 27, 2020. https://www.kff .org/slideshow/public-opinion-on-single-payer-national-health-plans-and-expanding-access-to-medicare-coverage/

53 Tami Luhby, "Americans Are Still Pretty Happy with Their Private Health Insurance," CNN.com, Dec. 9, 2019. https://www.cnn.com/2019/12/09/politics /gallup-private-health-insurance-satisfaction/index.html

pays what. Empowering Americans to take control over their health insurance and health care is the better approach.

How can we address the cost of health care? It's a tough question to answer. One of the reasons health-care costs have continued to rise is the design of our health-care system. In 2018, only 10.3 percent of national health expenditures came in the form of out-of-pocket costs compared to 23 percent in 1980, according to the Centers for Medicare and Medicaid Services.[54] Roughly 85 percent of national health expenditures were paid by a third-party such as private health insurance companies, Medicare, and Medicare compared to almost 70 percent in 1980.

I'm not suggesting that we blow up the health insurance system. Quite the opposite, I believe we need more health-care freedom and competition in our health insurance system to bend the cost curve and make health care more affordable.

Expanding health savings accounts (HSAs) and increasing contribution limits are part of the solution. Created in 2003 through the Medicare Prescription Drug, Improvement, and Modernization Act, HSAs have seen tremendous growth over the past several years. In 2019, there were 28.3 million HSAs, up 13 percent over the previous year.[55]

HSAs give patients direct control over their health-care dollars. You have the money taken out of your paycheck each pay period, tax free, and put in your HSA. You can use your HSA to pay for your doctor's visit and prescription drugs.

One catch with an HSA is that it has to be tied to a high-deductible health insurance plan. Another is that HSA funds cannot

---

54 The Centers for Medicare and Medicaid Services, "National health expenditures by type of services and source of funds, 1960-2018," https://www.cms.gov/Research-Statistics-Data-and-Systems/Statistics-Trends-and-Reports/NationalHealthExpendData/NationalHealthAccountsHistorical Accessed Sept. 23, 2020. (The data are available at the link. Figures for third-party payers include private health insurance, Medicare, Medicaid, other government programs, other third-party payers, and state and local health activity.)

55 "Health Savings Accounts Continue Strong Growth: HSA Assets Reach a Record $65.9 Billion," *Devenir Newsroom*, Mar. 3, 2020. https://www.devenir.com/health-savings-accounts-continue-strong-growth-hsa-assets-reach-a-record-65-9-billion/

be used to purchase regular health insurance plans, over-the-counter medications, or countless other health-related services. Those restrictions should be eliminated to maximize the ability of Americans to purchase health plans and services that are best for them.

I know price transparency is an important issue in the conservative movement. Price transparency only works if people have choice and more control over their health-care dollars. What that looks like is that we shift our health-care system to one in which everyone has a large HSA to pay for their basic health-care expenses. Health insurance returns to being used for major medical expenses. The goal here is to make buying health insurance as easy as buying car insurance.

As HSAs become more widespread, patients will demand to know more about the cost of services and foster competition. As health-care providers actually have to compete for your services, price transparency will increase as a side effect of a functioning market.

Among the innovative services that should be eligible for HSA funds are direct primary care (DPC) plans, a cost-effective option for covering basic health-care needs. Under a DPC arrangement, you pay a fee on a monthly or quarterly basis that is probably cheaper than what you pay for internet at home.

Think of direct primary care as Netflix for health care. The fee covers all typical primary care services such as diagnosis and preventive care. You visit when you need to within the agreement with the doctor. Insurance isn't necessary under direct primary care. There aren't any copayments or deductibles. You pay a fee. That's it.

Health reimbursement arrangements, through which an employer provides a contribution directly to the employee to purchase coverage, is another way to promote ownership of their health insurance and health care.

Increasing personal ownership of health benefits will reduce the persistent problem of "job lock," where people feel tethered to a job because they stand to lose their employer-provided health plan. Cost-conscious individuals are also more likely to buy health plans that are scaled to their actual needs, reducing the costly overconsumption of health care that employer-provided insurance plans often encourage.

Patients who want to leverage the bargaining power of group insurance without being locked into an employer-provided insurance plan should also be able to take advantage of Association Health Plans (AHPs). These plans allow any association of individuals and small businesses to band together in purchasing health benefits as if they were a single large company.

This can be a cost-effective option for people who might otherwise be relegated to Obamacare's expensive individual market, and also defeats the barriers to selling insurance across state lines, as membership in AHPs is not geographically limited (for Americans).

The government also needs to get out of the way of innovative technologies that can revolutionize the delivery of medical services— starting with telemedicine. The need for socially distanced services during the COVID-19 pandemic forced state and federal agencies to suspend existing barriers to virtual doctor visits, and within months nearly a third of Americans had reported taking advantage of online medical services.[56] Telemedicine has been held back by regulations, but has the potential to drastically decrease the cost of and increase access to routine health care, both in terms of time and money.

Of course, there is a role for government in health care. A working-class family of a five-year-old girl with leukemia may need help to ensure that they have health insurance. Government should have a role to make sure that five-year-old girl has a private health insurance plan.

Finally, we need to promote competition among hospitals to help bring down the costs associated with health care. This particular issue is too often overshadowed by the debate over insurance coverage. The lack of competition hospitals face is largely a

---

56 Ken Alltucker and Karen Weintraub, "Telehealth called a 'silver lining' of the COVID-19 pandemic. This time, it might stick," *USA Today*, updated July 6, 2020. https://www.usatoday.com/story/news/health/2020/07/02/telehealth-soars-covid-19-shutdown-limits-doctor-visits/5355739002/

government-generated problem that has to be addressed both at the state and federal levels.

An Innovative Approach to Education

Americans who live in the suburbs are very careful about education for their children. They tend to believe the schools in their communities provide a quality education. COVID-19 has increased parents' interest in homeschooling and other education options.[57]

Of course, school choice has always been a policy goal we've pushed at FreedomWorks. Many states already provide some options for families through school voucher programs, tax credit scholarships, and education savings accounts.[58] A frequently overlooked provision of the Tax Cuts and Jobs Act expanded 529 savings plans to be used for K-12 education expenses,[59] including tuition up to $10,000 per student. These avenues provide parents with options to educate their children.

But one of the unique approaches that we've seen since COVID-19 is "pod schools" or "learning pods."[60] A small group of students will gather at a home where a teacher will provide an individualized education. For many households in which both parents work, a pod school is a necessity because without the option, one of the parents may have to stay home to teach their child. For single-parent households, a pod school might be the only option.

---

57   Jeffrey M. Jones, "Fewer US Parents Want Full-Time, In-Person Fall Schooling," Gallup, Aug. 3, 2020.   https://news.gallup.com/poll/316412/fewer-parents-full-time-person-fall-schooling.aspx

58   "The ABC's of School Choice: 2020 Edition," EdChoice, Jan., 2020. https://www.edchoice.org/wp-content/uploads/2020/01/2020-ABCs-of-School-Choice-WEB-OPTIMIZED-REVISED.pdf

59   Bob Carlson, "Benefits of 529 Education Accounts Expanded Under 2017 Tax Reform," *Forbes*, June 16, 2018. https://www.forbes.com/sites/bobcarlson/2018/06/16/benefits-of-529-education-accounts-expanded-under-2017-tax-reform/

60   Laura Meckler and Hannah Natanson, "For parents who can afford, a new solution this Fall: Bring the teachers to them," *The Washington Post*, July 17, 2020. https://www.washingtonpost.com/education/fall-remote-private-teacher-pods/2020/07/17/9956ff28-c77f-11ea-8ffe-372be8d82298_story.html

Another interesting development during the pandemic is that some parents have developed their own curriculum because distance learning programs offered by school systems aren't engaging their children. Bureaucrats who put together curricula and teachers' unions that try to dictate when and where children can be educated have caused many parents to second-guess the system. One parent, Liz Self, an assistant professor of education at Vanderbilt University, told NPR, "Parents should remember that they know what's going on with their child better than anyone."[61]

Cost will still be a problem for many families.[62] This has been one of the most frustrating things about how state and local governments approached education during COVID-19. There were some school systems offering parents what can only be described as day care so parents could work.[63] These parents are already taxed to pay for public school, but they were being asked to pay more.

Senator Elizabeth Warren has railed against private schools and public-charter schools. She has also said, "We must stop the privatization of public schools."[64]During her failed presidential campaign in 2020, Warren was put on the spot during a campaign stop in Atlanta. Warren was asked by someone who attended her rally why she is anti-school choice since Warren had sent her own son to private school.

61 "Some Parents Develop School Curriculum for their Children," NPR.org, Apr. 15, 2020. https://www.npr.org/2020/04/15/834746349/some-parents-develop-school-curriculum-for-their-children

62 Neal McCluskey, "By the Numbers: If Public Schools Shared, the Poor Could Pod," *Cato at Liberty*, Aug. 11, 2020. https://www.cato.org/blog/numbers-public-schools-shared-poor-could-pod

63 Lindsey Burke, "Schools Use Empty Classes for Expensive Day Care, and Parents are Charged Twice. This Needs to End," *The Daily Signal*, Aug. 20, 2020. https://www.dailysignal.com/2020/08/20/districts-are-using-empty-schools-as-expensive-day-cares-and-taxpaying-parents-are-being-charged-twice-this-needs-to-end/

64 Elizabeth Warren (@ewarren), Twitter, Oct. 21, 2019, 9:00 AM. https://twitter.com/ewarren/status/1186266019016445953

Warren lied about her son's education, telling the woman who asked the question, "No, my children went to public schools."[65] Her campaign eventually admitted that her son "went to public school until 5th grade."[66] The hypocrisy is astounding.

The money should always follow the student. Always. Neal McClusky of the Cato Institute writes, "Were public schooling dollars to follow kids, it appears that pods would be within financial reach of almost everyone, often with funds left over. So instead of decrying inequality, public schooling groups should be saying, 'Here, have the money.'"[67]

But cost isn't only a challenge for parents wanting to homeschool their kids or send them to a private school. The costs of higher education are even more daunting. Since Congress essentially nationalized student loans in 2010 through the Health Care and Education Reconciliation Act, the cost of college has continued to rise.

There is a reason that the costs of college have grown faster than inflation.[68] Whenever the government subsidizes something, the costs associated with it will rise. Education is no different from health care. A report of the Federal Reserve Bank of New York found that for every dollar spent by the federal government on college, the cost rises by 40 cents to 60 cents.[69]

As a society, we have overemphasized the necessity of a college education and undervalued and even demeaned learning a trade. The result is that we are devaluing college degrees. Economist Bryan

---

65 Madison Dibble, "'No, my children went to public schools': Warren Accused of Lying about Her Children's Education," *The Washington Examiner*, Nov. 22, 2019. https://www.washingtonexaminer.com/news/no-my-children-went-to-public-schools-warren-accused-of-lying-about-her-childrens-education

66 D'Angelo Gore, "Warren Misleads on Her Kids' Schooling," FactCheck.org, Nov. 27, 2019. https://www.factcheck.org/2019/11/warren-misleads-on-her-kids-schooling/

67 McCluskey, "By the Numbers," https://www.cato.org/blog/numbers-public-schools-shared-poor-could-pod

68 "Tuition Inflation," Edvisors, accessed Sept. 23, 2020. https://www.edvisors.com/plan-for-college/saving-for-college/tuition-inflation/

69 David O. Lucca, Taylor Nadauld, and Karen Shen, "Credit Supply and the Rise in College Tuition: Evidence from the Expansion in Federal Student Aid Programs," Federal Reserve Bank of New York, Staff Report No. 733, July 2015, Revised Feb., 2017. https://www.newyorkfed.org/medialibrary/media/research/staff_reports/sr733.pdf

Caplan explains, "If everyone had a college degree, the result would be not great jobs for all, but runaway credential inflation. Trying to spread success with education spreads education but not success."[70]

Democrats have campaigned on forgiving student loans, but this is unfair to those who have earned college degrees and paid off their loans and especially unfair to those who chose to forego college due to the expense or any other reason. The worst thing Congress did for the costs of college was subsidize it.

We should be weighing credit risk while still maintaining programs for those who may not otherwise have the opportunity to go to college. Nick Gillespie of *Reason* magazine writes, "If college students have skin in their own game, they'll think more seriously about going to college in the first place and be more motivated to be serious and to finish."[71]

I had the opportunity to spend a year studying economics at the University of Oxford in 1998. One of the things that happened there was that many of the students would take a gap year between their secondary studies and university. During this gap year, these students would go and learn about the world. They would spend a year volunteering or learning a career.

Too often, people go right from high school to college. Too often, students go to college, rack up tens of thousands of dollars of student loan debt, get a degree, and later realize that this isn't what they want to do with their lives. There's a wasted opportunity here, especially when a student is about to enter college, to spend a year doing something else before going back to school.

We should be encouraging more students to take a year or two to go and learn about the world and find out who they are. They may decide during that year that adding all that debt may not be a good idea. I'm not encouraging anyone to live off their parents while making these decisions about the future, but many kids coming out

70 Bryan Caplan, "What's College Good For?" *The Atlantic*, Jan/Feb 2018. https://www.theatlantic.com/magazine/archive/2018/01/whats-college-good-for/546590/

71 Nick Gillespie, "The Immorality of Student Loan Forgiveness and Free College," *Reason*, Apr. 29, 2019. https://reason.com/2019/04/29/the-immorality-of-student-loan-forgiveness-and-free-college/

of high school can benefit from learning about themselves during a break from their education.

The topic is one that requires an honest conversation with Americans, one that hasn't really been broached apart from the overtures of "free" college, which is simply not realistic because Congress has already put the country so far in debt and the certainty of devaluing a college education.

Constitutional Norms Lead to Prosperity

We have more political freedom than anywhere else in the world, although we are slipping in economic freedom. The document that established our independence from Great Britain outlined the brilliance of the American mind. Inspired by the great thinkers of the Age of Reason, the Founding Fathers had a strong belief in the concept of self-government and prosperity.

The classical liberalism of the Declaration of Independence wasn't only a formal dissolution of political bonds between American colonists downtrodden by the abuses of a tyrannical king but also a treatise on human liberty. The Constitution that the framers left us clearly established three separate branches of government and a system of checks and balances. It enshrined the concept of limited government.

America is fundamentally a center-right nation. Most of us want the government to leave us alone. We want lower taxes and less regulatory interference. We also want a government that works. In the mid-to-late 1990s, we had a divided government, but it worked. There were major legislative accomplishments—welfare reform, a capital gains tax cut, less spending as a percentage of the economy, and four consecutive years of balanced budgets—in those years of divided government. We had prosperity even when there was strong disagreement and political drama.

Today, Congress has deferred too much of its power to the Executive Branch. The legislative process is almost entirely controlled by congressional leadership, regardless of which party is in power of the House or Senate. When the White House and Congress are controlled by the same party, the Congress views itself as subservient to the Executive Branch. The power of the Executive Branch only continues to grow at the expense of the Legislative Branch.

Conservatives have increasingly relied on federal courts to answer questions on too many policy issues that should be left to Congress to address or clarify, only to be let down when federal courts go against conservative thought. When judges let us down, it's not always a failure of the Judicial Branch; it's often a failure of Congress to legislate.

Regardless of what many may think, the constitutional system that the framers left us works quite well. The way Washington has functioned—or, more accurately, dysfunctioned—over the past twenty years isn't how the federal government is supposed to work. Republicans and Democrats have increasingly moved away from constitutional norms when it serves their interests in their quest for more political power. The Constitution, the separation of powers, and checks and balances have become inconveniences that can be easily disregarded when necessary to score political victories.

The only way to bring us back to constitutional norms is for rank-and-file members of the House and Senate to demand a return to regular order, not only for themselves but also for their constituents. This means restoring the committee process for legislation and allowing members to offer amendments to legislation from the floor.

As voters, we have a responsibility to demand a return to constitutional norms. We have to back lawmakers who demand a return to regular order and a restoration of the power that has been irresponsibly and wrongly ceded to the Executive Branch. We also have a responsibility to stop schemes pushed by Democrats. This includes stopping packing the Supreme Court with far-left justices and their plans to eliminate the legislative filibuster. We were never intended to be a direct democracy, but Democrats are moving America in that direction. It's up to us to stop them and reinforce our constitutional republican form of government.

We also have to understand that the government is, far more often than not, the wrong answer to address problems that Americans face. We want more job creation, but that has to be driven by lower taxes and less regulation. We want prosperity, but only the free market can create prosperity because of the government proclivity for misallocating resources. We want to preserve our political freedom, but the government wants us to be docile and distracted.

The reason the 1990s were so prosperous is because the system the Framers left us worked. I'm not implying that there wasn't drama. Obviously, there was. But a Democratic president and a Republican Congress were able to get some big things done.

The only way to restore a government that works is to restore the very constitutional norms that made America an economic powerhouse and the envy of the world. We have proven that our constitutional system works when we let it. We have to demand Congress let it work. But we have to keep in mind that the only way you're ever going to have a majority in Congress to accomplish these goals is to win the suburbs. Republicans have been routed with college-educated voters, particularly women. If Republicans don't learn to compete with these voters, they will never win the suburbs.

CHAPTER 11
Conclusion: The Case for Optimism

I've always considered myself, first and foremost, a principled fiscal conservative. I'm also an optimist. That's the tradition that I came from. I was heavily influenced by President Ronald Reagan. The Great Communicator was a figure who inspired so many people—conservatives, libertarians, and even some Democrats who became disaffected with the party as it moved to the Left.

Reagan was himself influenced by the free-market economic thought of thinkers such as economists Friedrich Hayek and Milton Friedman, both of whom he leaned on for advice before and during his time in the White House. They, in turn, were direct intellectual descendants of the founders of libertarian economic thought, such as Frédéric Bastiat, Ludwig von Mises, and Henry Hazlitt. He cut taxes, took on the Soviet Union, and his eight years in office set up one of the most prosperous times in American history.

Reagan once said:

Freedom is never more than one generation away from extinction. We didn't pass it to our children in the bloodstream. It must be fought for, protected, and handed on for them to do the same, or one day we will spend our sunset years telling our children and our children's children what it was once like in the United States where men were free.[1]

Those words resonate with me more today than the first time I heard them.

I was also very influenced by the Contract with America. Then-House Speaker Newt Gingrich had a vision that would appeal to suburban voters and led to the Republican Revolution of 1994, breaking the grip Democrats had on the House since 1955.

Not long after Republicans took control of the House in January 1995, Gingrich, who had recently taken the gavel to become speaker, discussed the first hundred days of Republican control of the chamber. Gingrich was at the forefront of recognizing the fiscal ticking time bomb on which America sits.

"This talk of burdening future generations is not just rhetoric; we're talking about hard, economic consequences that will limit our children's and grandchildren's standard of living. Yet that is what we are doing," Gingrich said. "For the children trapped in poverty, for the children whose futures are trapped by a government debt they're going to have to pay, we have an obligation . . .to talk about the legacy we're leaving our children and grandchildren, an obligation to talk about the deliberate remaking of our government...we must start by recognizing the moral and economic failure of the current methods of government."[2]

Although Republicans didn't keep all of their promises in the years after taking control of the House, Gingrich led the drive that kept spending down, produced four years of balanced budgets, cut taxes, reformed welfare programs, and helped keep the government out of the way during an economic boom period. These were historic

---

1   Ronald Reagan, "A Time for Choosing," speech delivered Oct. 27, 1964, in *The US Constitution: A Reader*, Hillsdale College, 2012 http://cdn.constitutionreader.com/files/pdf/constitution/ch123.pdf

2   Newt Gingrich, "House Speaker Address," speech delivered Apr. 7, 1995. Online video and transcript from C-SPAN, https://www.c-span.org/video/?64434-1/house-speaker-address

achievements that happened while a Democratic president was in office. Gingrich proved that divided government can work.

Reagan and the Contract with America are among the things that inspired me to get in this fight. I spent a lot of this book discussing the immediate problems that we face as a nation: our national debt is skyrocketing, our entitlement programs are going broke, and we face an age-demographic crisis.

One of my favorite congressmen is Warren Davidson of Ohio. This is a guy who is a former Army Ranger turned successful businessman. Davidson won a hard-fought primary battle in June 2016, filling the seat left vacant after John Boehner's resignation. He has established himself as a strong fiscal conservative and jealous defender of constitutional principles.

One thing Davidson has told me several times is: "Don't bankrupt America. That's why I'm here." That's why FreedomWorks continues to work so hard. America is heading down a perilous path, but I'm optimistic that we can address these problems and move America back in a direction of freedom and prosperity. I wouldn't still be involved if I didn't believe that we can right the ship.

Most of the problems that face America are solvable through the economic growth that only free market capitalism can bring us. I would go as far as to say that many of the societal tensions that we face can be addressed through the economic growth.

I fully understand that people reading this book may have different views on immigration, trade, or other issues. We're all different. We each have different backgrounds and views. Where we come together is that we all agree that this is a center-right nation and that our basic fundamental constitutional system of government should be preserved.

We Need Conservatives and Libertarians to Work Together

I believe in fusionism between conservatives and libertarians because America is a fundamentally center-right nation. In 2019, 37 percent of Americans identified as conservatives, according to Gallup. Only 24 percent identify themselves as liberals.[3] Those of us who subscribe to libertarianism are a small segment of Americans. Working with conservatives is a path forward to accomplish shared goals of reducing the size and scope of government.

The concept of fusionism has been around for decades, even before Reagan. But fusionism found a champion in Reagan. Reagan was a conservative who understood the close ties that conservatism has to libertarianism.

Back in 1975, Reagan gave an interview to *Reason*, in which he said, "If you analyze it, I believe the very heart and soul of conservatism is libertarianism. . . . The basis of conservatism is a desire for less government interference or less centralized authority or more individual freedom, and this is a pretty general description also of what libertarianism is."[4]

Some may say that fusionism was easy when there was a common enemy in the Soviet Union. Well, the Soviet Union may have been defeated, but collectivism is very much alive and well. It has moved from a slow pace into a steady march in America, and we're staring it down at this very moment in time. We either work together, conservatives and libertarians alike, or we watch America fall into the grips of wannabe despots who purport themselves to be "democratic socialists."

There are certainly some conservatives and libertarians who would rather go their separate ways and do their own thing. That's nuts. That's a guaranteed way to hand the government over to the socialist Left and gradually lose our freedoms. Some libertarians even believe that fusionism with the Left is preferable to working with conservatives.

There are opportunities to work with the Left, but these opportunities are limited and few and far between. The Left is also far

---

3   Lydia Saad, "The US Remained Center-right Ideologically in 2019," Gallup, Jan. 9, 2020. https://news.gallup.com/poll/275792/remained-center-right-ideologically-2019.aspx

4   Manuel Klausner, "Inside Ronald Reagan," *Reason Magazine* interview, July 1975. https://reason.com/1975/07/01/inside-ronald-reagan/

too caught up in identity politics, which are contrary to libertarians' belief in the individual. That's not to say that we shouldn't ensure protections for minority groups, but dividing us through identity politics only makes us a weaker country.

Some conservatives believe libertarians are too socially liberal, but conservatives need libertarians to work with them on fiscal issues, reining in the regulatory state, and, in recent years, a foreign policy of restraint. One of FreedomWorks staffers, Josh Withrow, has repeatedly said over the years, "I often remind people that libertarianism is a political, not a moral, philosophy. We don't have to agree on the social issues if we can all agree the government shouldn't be able to tell us what to believe."

In his 1962 book, *In Defense of Freedom: A Conservative Credo*, Frank Meyer wrote, "A free economy can no more bring about virtue than a state-controlled economy. A free economy is, however, necessary in the modern world for the preservation of freedom, which is the condition of a virtuous society." Meyer, who essentially created the concept of fusionism, had a tremendous influence on William F. Buckley, Jr., the founder of *National Review*.

Buckley's mission statement for *National Review* states: "It is the job of centralized government (in peacetime) to protect its citizens' lives, liberty and property. All other activities of government tend to diminish freedom and hamper progress. The growth of government (the dominant social feature of this century) must be fought relentlessly. In this great social conflict of the era, we are, without reservations, on the libertarian side."[5]

There are areas of disagreement, for sure. Buckley had his own disagreements with libertarian thinkers. Whatever our disagreements, we need to work together to get America on the right path. "We must all hang together, or we shall all hang separately," as Benjamin Franklin supposedly once said.

If you agree with me on 80 percent of the issues, I consider you a friend and ally. Let's work on the things we agree on first. Let's begin

---

5   William F. Buckley, Jr., "Our Mission Statement," *National Review*, Nov. 19, 2020. https://www.nationalreview.com/1955/11/our-mission-statement-william-f-buckley-jr

to get those problems solved. We have our work cut out for us. Let's get in the trenches together and fight for more economic freedom. After we put some of those problems behind us, then we'll see if we can come to an accommodation on all of these other issues.

I've quoted a lot from the Declaration of Independence. It's such an amazing treatise on human liberty. We need a revival of those principles in America. One line from the Declaration of Independence that rings true right now is: "[F]or the support of this Declaration, with a firm reliance on the protection of divine Providence, we mutually pledge to each other our Lives, our Fortunes and our sacred Honor."

Each founding father had to put their lives and fortunes on the line. Although he isn't as well-known as George Washington, Benjamin Franklin, or Thomas Jefferson, Robert Morris financed the war for independence from Great Britain.

When Washington asked Morris for $10,000, Morris provided the money.[6] Without that, the American Revolution would have ended with a whimper. Washington subsequently crossed the Delaware River on Christmas Day and attacked at Trenton, New Jersey the following morning, leading a victory for the Continental Army. Morris continued to loan money to the nascent American government to finance the war and donated a ship that became the first in the new American Navy.[7]

Several Founding Fathers saw their homes and property destroyed or taken by the British. Some lost sons who fought for American independence. Some died in poverty because of the personal sacrifices they made they made for the cause of independence.

The revival of these principles, as well as the principles of limited government that are laid out so clearly in the Constitution, will take personal sacrifice and unity. We are going to have to work together to achieve these goals. The differences between conservatives and

---

6   "Signers of the Declaration of Independence: Robert Morris," USHistory.org, accessed Oct. 10, 2020. https://www.ushistory.org/declaration/signers/morris_r.html

7   Robert Begley, "Robert Morris: America's Financial Atlas," *The Objective Standard*, Jan. 26, 2019. https://theobjectivestandard.com/2019/01/robert-morris-americas-financial-atlas/

libertarians aren't going to mean much if we continue to slide into the grips of socialism and direct democracy where rights are subject to the whims of the Leftist mob.

My main goal in writing in this book is that we get people in our movement more involved. Listening to talk radio or cable news isn't activism. Voting isn't activism. Government does go to those who voluntarily show up, but we have to be active in the off years to put pressure on the White House and Congress. If we're going to defeat the so-called "progressive" Democratic Party, we need to be active in grassroots. We have to invest in grassroots more than we ever have.

I hope that this book has inspired you to visit your congressman and senator's offices. Drop in and tell them the issues that you believe in. Recruit your friends and family to get involved in the fight to restore free markets and constitutionally limited government.

Another goal is that we take our core values and get them beyond the base and begin reaching new audiences. One of my great fears is that FreedomWorks is talking to only 40 percent of America. I don't want to keep preaching only to the choir. I need the choir, but I need to be talking to at least another 15 percent more routinely to build a community large enough to meet our legislative goals. My goal isn't to talk to all Americans. That's unrealistic. But to meet our goals, we need to be talking to 55 percent of the country.

There are so many voters who are tired of the status quo. They want a return to a government that works but also one that leaves them alone to pursue their version of the American dream. I believe that there's 55 percent of the country who wants that.

This battle is going to be won or lost in the suburbs. We'll never sacrifice our principles. Those principles are what define us. We may have to look at our messaging to gain broader appeal to disaffected suburban voters. If we focus on the 80 percent of the issues we agree on, we can save America.

Senator Mike Lee's former chief of staff, Boyd Matheson, always told me that we need to have two visions. He explains it through the lens of the founding generation. We wouldn't have had the American Revolution without Boston and Philadelphia. Too often, we focus on Boston, which was the resistance against the tyrannical rule of King

George III. Philadelphia brought us the vision of what America was supposed to be through the Declaration of Independence.

In the climate that we're in right now, we've proven that we can take action and resist, but we have to prove our Philadelphia by giving Americans a vision for what we want America to be going forward. Today's politics are boiled down to two purported competing views, compassion or the rule of law. Compassion and the rule of law are not an either/or proposition. We can do both. That's the winning combination, but we need to show how we're going to accomplish it.

We know we have good policy on our side. Just look at the results of 2019. Americans saw a 6.8 percent increase in household income, the lowest poverty rate on record, the lowest unemployment rate in decades, the lowest black unemployment rate on record, the lowest Hispanic unemployment rate ever.

These are tremendous results. But when explaining our policies, it's one thing to talk about numbers, but we also have to focus on four pillars that the policies for which we advocate are about: community, compassion, opportunity, and self-reliance. At the end of the day, these four pillars are what the policies we push are about.

We want to build community. We are compassionate to people's needs. We want to make America a land of opportunity for all. We want our citizens to be self-reliant. We can tie almost every policy back in these pillars. These four pillars embody the concept of self-government. That's the legacy the Founding Fathers left us.

Looking Ahead

The results of the 2020 election also showed that Biden is already a lame-duck president. Biden is far too moderate for today's Democratic Party, which shows how far to the Left it has drifted. He's also too old. Remember, aides close to Biden suggested that he would only serve one term.[8] Already the oldest president ever elected, he

---

8   Ryan Lizza, "Biden signals to aides that he would only serve a single term," *Politico,* Dec. 11, 2019. https://www.politico.com/news/2019/12/11/biden-single-term-082129

would be eighty-two years old when he runs for re-election in 2024. Ultimately, this is Harris's Democratic Party.

The fight to preserve the republic wasn't resolved in the 2020 election. There's no question that Joe Biden and Kamala Harris will do some damage, particularly through the regulatory process. We have to be ready to battle the Biden administration in these fights.

Over the next several years, however, we can expect Harris's Democratic Party to do a full frontal assault. They won't learn much from their down-ticket losses. They don't realize that the high-water mark for progressive politics in our era was 2018. They're still going to push for Medicare-for-All, universal basic income, free college, getting rid of the Electoral College, and other Leftist policies. They'll continue to try to pit us against each other through identity politics.

The good news is that we're set up well for the long term.

The fact that Republicans had significant gains in the House in 2020 and control the redistricting process in so many states because they held state legislatures means that they are well-positioned to take back the House in 2022. Republicans will have challenges in the Senate in the 2022 midterm election. They have seats up that they currently hold in Florida, Iowa, North Carolina, Pennsylvania, and Wisconsin.

The races in these states will be tight, but if Republicans begin building on the successes of the 2020 election, each of these are winnable. What Republicans should come up with is a new Contract with America that shows a strong message on the recovery from COVID-19, health care, education, immigration, and reducing the budget deficit.

The reason that Republicans performed better with minorities was because they had tangible evidence that the economy was growing before COVID-19. They were benefiting from a good economy. We still have to win back suburban women, and we can do that by honing in on a message of inclusion, patient-centered health care, and promoting sound education policy.

As Republicans continue to expand into minority communities with a message of opportunity and prosperity and begin to win back suburban women, we're seeing the beginning of the end of identity politics. One need only look at the in-roads with minority voters to see that.

The people reading this book are the source of optimism. With all the troubles that the country faces, the people like you who have made it this far in this book are committed to taking action. You are the ultimate source of my optimism in the future of this great country—not politicians, people like you.

The Vast Left-Wing Money Machine

O ne of the striking stories of 2020 was the absolute onslaught of money in politics. Cash records were smashed. Because this money was all given by Leftist donors to Democratic candidates, the media didn't talk about it much. It's important for a book coming out after the 2020 election to take a look at the Left and its sources of funding.

I have a lot of friends who are centrists or even leftists. When I get into conversations with them, all I hear is Koch brothers, Koch brothers, Koch brothers. One of my friends from the Left says to understand politics, all you need to do is follow the money. Well, all the money is on the Democratic and "progressive" side. The perceived shift to the political left in America isn't by accident. Leftist donors with very deep pockets have invested in this.

After the House voted in May 2017 to repeal and replace Obamacare, Mother Jones boasted that "progressive groups are basically printing money."[1] The printing presses never turned off. In July 2020, Politico noted that Democrats and so-called "progressive" organizations raised a record

---

1   Tim Murphy, "Progressive Groups Are Basically Printing Money After the Health Care Vote," Mother Jones, May 5, 2017. https://www.motherjones.com /politics/2017/05/grassroots-democrats-ahca-fundraising/

$392 million through ActBlue.[2] *A co-founder of one group said, "Donald Trump is the single greatest fund-raising tool that Democrats have ever had." The surge in funding continued after the death of Justice Ginsburg. CBS News reported that the Left had shattered fund-raising records.*[3]

In 2019, I put on 250 thousand air miles. FreedomWorks raised a combined $17 million. The FreedomWorks budget is insignificant to most progressive organizations. It's frustrating when I hear Democrats complain about the Koch brothers and money in politics. It makes me angry when FreedomWorks is accused of being a "dark money" group. Why do they say people never say anything about George Soros, Tom Steyer, or Michael Bloomberg? There's a lot of hypocrisy.

With all of this in my mind, I decided that I needed some help with this chapter, so I called my friend and FreedomWorks's counsel, Cleta Mitchell, and asked her to author it.

In case you don't know Cleta or her work, she is a brilliant mind and a great attorney. She has represented so many conservative politicians, candidates, and organizations over the years. In June 2015, Cleta testified in front of the House Oversight and Government Reform Committee on the targeting of conservative groups by the Internal Revenue Service. She has studied the Left and its tactics, which make her expertise invaluable.

During the battle over the confirmation of Amy Coney Barrett to the Supreme Court, Senator Sheldon Whitehouse of Rhode Island droned on about supposed "dark money" from conservative foundations that fund conservative and libertarian organizations.[4] *He sounded like Charlie from* It's Always Sunny in Philadelphia *going on about Pepe Silvia. That scene has become a meme often used to mock conspiracy theorists.*

---

2   Elena Schneider, "Record cash floods Democrats, Black groups amid protests and pandemic," *Politico*, July 1, 2020. https://www.politico.com/news/2020/07/01 /actblue-june-protests-coronavirus-347492

3   LaCrai Mitchell and Sarah Ewall-Wice, "Progressive groups shatter fundraising records in battleground states," *CBS News*, September 21, 2020. https://www.cbsnews. com/news/progressive-groups-break-fundraising-records-election-2020-battleground-states/

4   Senator Sheldon Whitehouse, "Senator Accuses 'Dark Money' of Influencing Barrett's Nomination," Oct. 13, 2020, *Reuters*, video clip posted on Youtube. https:// www.youtube.com/watch?v=NtuJYSv95xI

Whitehouse's rambling was absurd. Thankfully, Senator Ted Cruz brought up dark money on the Left and hit right back at Whitehouse.[5]

Unfortunately, the media ignores the money funneled to the Left. But Cleta explains it in this chapter in great detail to arm you with the facts about the money flowing into Leftist groups.—Adam Brandon

The liberals/progressives/Democrats/media (LPDM)[6] have long screamed loudly about "dark money" and "monied corporate interests," vilifying donors to conservative groups and Republican candidates. The LPDM are obsessed with decrying "money in politics" and are fixated on a narrative about the "wealthy special interests" that fund the "vast right-wing conspiracy."[7]

The LPDM narrative for decades has been that there are buckets of "dark money" supporting and promoting conservative causes and candidates and the poor, defenseless leftists are wholly outmatched.

That "vast right-wing conspiracy"? With bazillion dollars? Nothing could be more laughable or further from the truth.

The simple fact is this: the LPDM has been spouting this false narrative endlessly, all the while building and funding networks upon networks of interconnected organizations, projects, and entities to reshape the country in ways large and small, in hopes of fulfilling the LPDM's dream of a "progressive" America.

---

5   Senator Ted Cruz, "Senator Ted Cruz brings up 'dark money,' SLAMS Joe Biden during questioning of Amy Coney Barrett," Oct. 14, 2020, *The Hill*, video clip posted on Youtube. https://www.youtube.com/watch?v=q4PWeWVIkGs

6   Some might quarrel with the inclusion of "the Media" as part of the defining infrastructure described in this Chapter. The 'legacy media', including the *Washington Post, New York Times, USA Today*, network news, and the now unwatchable cable networks CNN and MSNBC, and the hundreds of copycat media entities and the so-called journalists who populate those enterprises are part and parcel of the hierarchy of the Liberal/Progressive/Democratic movement. No discussion of the LPD is complete without the M, which is a cornerstone of the LPDM's success and its threats to America's founding principles.

7   The phrase 'vast right wing conspiracy' was popularized by Hillary Clinton, who famously blamed " . . .this vast right-wing conspiracy . . .conspiring against my husband . . ." for the Monica Lewinsky affair. See "Hillary Clinton speaks out on Lewinsky allegations," *The TODAY Show*, Jan. 27, 1998, 10:40. https://www.msnbc.com/today/watch/hillary-clinton-speaks-out-on-lewinsky-accusations-44498499720

And they are doing so with the darkest of "dark" (undisclosed) funding from leftist millionaires and billionaires nationwide and, in some instances, from across the globe.

A thorough accounting of all the LPDM's money would require its own book, not just a chapter in a larger story, such as this one.

For the LPDM, process is policy and to truly change America, the existing rules of political engagement must be unwound and rewritten, thereby resulting in wholly different policy outcomes— and, ultimately, a "new and improved" America.

2004: A Watershed Moment for the LPDM

Before there was Trump Derangement Syndrome, there was Bush Derangement Syndrome,[8] arising from the battles in Florida waged by Democrats to wrest the presidential election victory in 2000 from President George W. Bush. Following the 2002 midterm elections, Republicans actually *gained* eight seats in the House and two Senate seats—giving Republicans unitary control of the White House and both houses of Congress.[9]

The 2002 election outcome caused at least one well-connected liberal strategist, Rob Stein, to decide that there must really be a "vast right-wing conspiracy" and that the LPDM needed to fight back.

Stein prepared a PowerPoint for LPDM donors and traveled the country over the next two years, arguing that a "vast left-wing conspiracy" was needed. Underscoring Stein's alarms to the LPDM was a particular watershed event: President Bush's re-election as President in 2004. John Kerry's loss in the presidential campaign wasn't for lack

---

8   "Bush Derangement Syndrome" was first coined by the late Charles Krauthammer, in a column in which he defined the term as "the acute onset of paranoia in otherwise normal people in reaction to the policies, the presidency—nay—the very existence of George W. Bush." Townhall.com, Dec. 5, 2003. https://townhall.com/columnists/charleskrauthammer/2003/12/05/bush-derangement-syndrome-n940041

9   US House of Representatives, "Statistics of the Presidential and Congressional Election of November 2, 2004," http://clerk.house.gov/member_info/electionInfo/2004election.pdf

of trying and funding. George Soros, Peter Lewis, and other wealthy LPDM donors spared no funding of an independent effort outside the Kerry campaign and the Democratic National Committee in their quest to defeat Bush.

America Coming Together (ACT) was a massive and well-funded coalition of leftist groups and labor unions dedicated to defeating Bush for re-election.[10] Founded by an elite group of top left-wing operatives,[11] ACT raised and spent over $137 million during the 2004 cycle, much of it from Soros.[12] Eventually, not content to simply give money to ACT and other groups, Soros himself embarked on a separate, $3 million, twelve-city tour, and ultimately he spent over $27.5 million of his own fortune in his zeal to defeat Bush in 2004.[13]

It did not succeed. The LPDM's goal of making Ohio the Florida of 2004 didn't happen, because the margin of victory in Ohio between Bush and Kerry was too great for a legal challenge. Democrats always have a strategy of trying to create election outcomes that are within the 'margin of litigation', election contests sufficiently close to allow their lawyers to swoop in and litigate their candidates' way to victory. Think Al Franken, who was awarded the US Senate race in Minnesota in 2008 after being down by 725 votes on election day,

---

10   ACT's founders included former AFL-CIO Political Director Steve Rosenthal, EMILY's List founder Ellen Malcom, Sierra Club Executive Director Carl Pope, and future Planned Parenthood President Cecile Richards, among others. *ActForVictory. org*, https://web.archive.org/web/20040930224235/http://www.actforvictory.org/act.php/home/content/about

11   David Tell, "Who's Afraid of George Soros?" *Washington Examiner*, Mar. 8, 2004. https://www.washingtonexaminer.com/weekly-standard/whos-afraid-of-george-soros

12   ACT's top two donors were the Joint Victory Campaign ($18.3 million, largely funded by Soros) and Soros Fund Management ($7.5 million). "America Coming Together," OpenSecrets.org, https://www.opensecrets.org/527s/527cmtedetail_contribs.php?cycle=2004&ein=200094706 . "Soros Fund Management," OpenSecrets.org, https://www.opensecrets.org/527s/527cmtedetail_contribs.php?cycle=2004&ein=450526614 Accessed Sept. 4, 2020

13   Oliver Burkeman, "Soros goes on tour to do his bit to defeat Bush," *The Guardian*, Sept. 30, 2004. https://www.theguardian.com/world/2004/sep/30/uselections2004.usa

and after eight months of successful legal defenses that overruled plentiful evidence of fraud and miscounted ballots.[14]

On August 24, 2020, former presidential candidate Hillary Clinton confirmed as much when she advised presidential candidate Joe Biden that he " . . .should not concede under any circumstances. Because I think this is going to drag out, and eventually, I do believe he will win . . ."[15]

That had been the Democrats' plan in Ohio in 2004. However, on the ballot in Ohio in 2004 was a referendum defining marriage as a union of one man and one woman . . . and evangelicals flocked to the polls to vote for the referendum...[16] and in the process, they also cast their ballots for Bush, pushing the margin of victory beyond the capacity for post-election shenanigans by Democratic lawyers.[17]

Following the 2004 loss to President Bush, a number of leading Democratic operatives, strategists, and donors decided that Stein had a point. It was time to "build" a national, left-wing infrastructure. Control of higher education, Hollywood, big media, and increasingly the K-12 education system wasn't enough. It was time to do more.

---

14 Examples of inconsistencies included hundreds of felons voting illegally and similar ballot errors being counted differently for Franken than for the incumbent Republican Senator Norm Coleman. See: John Fund and Hans von Spakovsky, *Who's Counting?*, Encounter Books, 2012, pp. 13-24.

15 Megan Henney, "Hillary Clinton says Joe Biden should not concede on election night 'under any circumstances.'" FoxNews.com, Aug. 25, 2020. https://www.foxnews .com/politics/hillary-clinton-joe-biden-should-not-concede-on-election-night

16 James Dao, "Same-sex marriage issue key to some G.O.P. races," *The New York Times*, Nov. 4, 2004. https://www.nytimes.com/2004/11/04/politics/campaign/samesex-marriage-issue-key-to-some-gop-races.html

17 Bush won Ohio in 2004 by a margin of over 118,000 votes, 50.8%-48.7%. Ohio Secretary of State website, https://www.ohiosos.gov/elections/election-results-and-data/2004-elections-results/president--vice-president-november-2-2004 / Accessed Sept. 10, 2020.

2005: The Democracy Alliance Is Born

Stein's thesis, which he shared in a PowerPoint presentation titled "The Conservative Message Machine Money Matrix,"[18] was that conservatives had pieced together a well-organized infrastructure of legal, political, and scholarly organizations dedicated to shaping public opinion on a variety of important social and political issues. He further claimed that a few well-connected, wealthy clans—in particular, the Scaife, Bradley, Olin, and Coors families—had provided funding for those groups on a scale that had no equal on the left side of the political spectrum.[19]

In January 2005, a group of LPDM leaders gathered to form the Democracy Alliance, which became (and remains) the central platform through which the LPDM built and funded countless networks, projects, and organizations to reshape the country in the LPDM's ideal image. Others have arisen since as described in this chapter. But the Democracy Alliance was a key to the LPDM's financial juggernaut we witness today.

What *is* the Democracy Alliance?

The Democracy Alliance is a charitable, for-profit corporation, registered in the District of Columbia. As a for-profit corporation, it files no public reports that would be required if it were a non-profit corporation. For the Democracy Alliance, there is zero disclosure: no information about donors, income, disbursements, programs, activities, board members, officers, members, partners . . .nothing. It's the darkest of dark money.

That fact, of course, doesn't bother the LPDM. Only when conservative donors give, or conservative groups receive contributions

---

18   Matt Bai, "Wiring the vast left-wing conspiracy," *The New York Times*, July 25, 2004. https://www.nytimes.com/2004/07/25/magazine/wiring-the-vast-left-wing-conspiracy.html

19   "Rob Stein," *DiscoverTheNetworks.org*, https://www.discoverthenetworks.org/individuals/rob-stein/ Accessed Sept. 10, 2020

not subject to public disclosure, does the LPDM's collective hair catch fire.[20]

To be part of the Democracy Alliance, a donor must agree to contribute a set amount to them annually, with an additional funding commitment to projects, investment funds, or organizations supported, endorsed, or organized by the Democracy Alliance.

Membership dues and other financial obligations of the participants are not disclosed or published by Democracy Alliance. However, information inevitably dribbles out. The most recent membership commitment available publicly was in 2014 and reflects the financial commitments to which members (partners) of the Democracy Alliance must agree in order to be and remain part of the group.

The members/partners give, with no charitable tax deduction, annual dues, as well as a separate "giving commitment" in support of various groups, activities, projects or funds established or endorsed by Democracy Alliance, as follows:

Annual Dues

Individual	$35,000
Family	$70,000[21]
Institution (non-foundation)	$1,000,000[22]

---

20 One must merely think of the Left's obsession with the Koch brothers and their "dark money" during Obama's presidency, which rose to such a fever pitch that Senate Majority Leader Harry Reid even devoted an entire floor speech just to railing against the Kochs' spending "to rig the American political system to benefit the wealthy." "User Clip: Harry Reid's Senate Speech on the Koch Brothers," *CSpan.org*, Mar. 13, 2014. https://www.c-span.org/video/?c4487887/user-clip-harry-reids-senate-speech-koch-brothers

21 The annual Democracy Alliance membership dues for individuals and families are known to have increased from $30K and $60K to $35K and $70K, respectively as of 2017. See: Ruby Cramer, "Democracy Alliance Raises Members Fees and Re-tools to Fight Trump," *Buzzfeed News*, Jan 26, 2017. https://www.buzzfeednews.com/article/rubycramer/democracy-alliance-raises-member-fees-and-retools-to-fight-t

22 Though institutional and family fund-raising quotas are likely to have increased as well, those numbers were last leaked to the public in 2015. Politico.com, accessed via the Internet Archive Wayback Machine, Sept. 11, 2020. https://web.archive.org/web/20181126150252/http://images.politico.com/global/2015/06/22/da_membershipoptions_04-2014.pdf

Annual Giving Commitment

Individual Member	$200,000
Family or institution partner	$1,000,000

In other words, an individual member agrees to at least a $235,000 annual commitment to be part of the Democracy Alliance; a family agrees to give $1,070,000 per year. Every year.

The result is that, between its founding in 2005 and 2018 (the last year for which information has been able to be determined), the Democracy Alliance alone steered and directed $1.83 billion to nearly a thousand leftist and Democratic Party-aligned groups.[23]

Remember that the ostensible reason for the creation of the Democracy Alliance was Rob Stein's PowerPoint presentation in which he described the "massive" funding sources on the right, referencing in particular the Scaife Foundation, the Bradley Foundation, and the Coors Foundation.

Between 2006 and 2018, these largest conservative grant foundations, along with the once-formidable John M. Olin Foundation, which awarded its last new grants in 2005 and dispersed, spent the following:[24]

• Sarah Scaife Foundation	$254 million
• Lynde and Harry Bradley Foundation	$507 million
• Adolf Coors Foundation	$79 million
• John Olin Foundation	$8 million

In total, compared to just the Democracy Alliance's $1.8 billion to left-wing causes over the same period, these foundations funded about $860 million in grants to conservative and free-market organizations.

---

23   Joe Schoffstall, "Confidential Memo: Secretive Liberal Donor Club Plots $275 Million Spending Plan for 2020," *The Washington Free Beacon*, Apr. 11, 2019. https://freebeacon.com/politics/confidential-memo-secretive-liberal-donor-club-plots-275-million-for-2020/

24   All totals from IRS form 990s filed by these foundations, posted online by ProPublica.org and SourceWatch.org.

Whatever "advantage" conservatives may have had insofar as funding for conservative projects, organizations, and entities that Rob Stein perceived in 2005, it has long since vanished, if it ever existed at all. It has been well overtaken by the wealthy LPDM machine he built with Democracy Alliance—and which has since mushroomed almost beyond calculation.

Before There Was the Democracy Alliance There Was the Tides Foundation

Stein's premise of the massive outlay of conservative funding compared to some paltry left-wing money, even in 2005, was based on fairly flimsy evidence—or no evidence at all. Stein no doubt failed to mention in his now-famous PowerPoint the Tides Foundation, which has been a force for the LPDM movement since 1976 and has directed over $3 billion to approximately 1,400 LPDM projects, organizations, and activities since its inception.[25]

According to its website, "Tides is a leader in global grant making and social change work, having made over $158M in domestic grants and over $65M in international grants since 2016. Tides also provides comprehensive fiscal sponsorship to over 150 social ventures based in the United States."[26]

In 2018 alone, the Tides family of non-profits reported multiple funding sources supporting a variety of left-wing programs and activities totaling more than $211 million dollars:

- Tides Center: $147,810,417
- Tides Advocacy Group: $38,747,831
- Tides Canada Foundation: $3,714,587
- Tides Network (Nonprofit Group) $21,515,777

---

25 Tides Foundation, "Tides, a force for social good," Tides.org, accessed Sept. 9, 2020. https://www.tides.org/about/

26 Tides Foundation, "Our Partners and Impact," Tides.org, accessed Sept. 9, 2020. https://www.tides.org/impact-partners/

In addition to its significant funding of various LPDM programs and groups, the Tides Foundation has pioneered the creation of a group of for-profit investment funds. Tides describes this program as a way to marry traditional grant-making with financial investment whereby left-wing donors "break down the silos" to effect "social change" through their investment strategies.

According to Tides, "donors are also learning that they can go beyond making grants, using charitable dollars to invest directly in promising for-profit funds and social enterprises seeking to generate both financial returns and social impact," creating what Tides calls a "double bottom line," which uses investment and/or charitable capital called "impact investing."[27] As of 2018, Tides claimed an "impact investment" portfolio worth over $438 million[28] and offers investment options that offer returns on investments in causes ranging from "green jobs" to "gender equity" to "wealth gap elimination."

Indeed, "impact investing" has mushroomed into a major component of investment portfolios of traditional investment advisors as well as spawning multiple boutique firms specializing in the "making money while supporting social justice" theme.[29]

The real bottom line is that Tides is a leviathan. All by itself.

So. Much. Left-Wing. Money.

It's difficult to wrap one's mind around the vast left-wing money machine. Influence Watch, a project of the Capital Research Center,

---

27 Tides Foundation, "Investing for Impact," Oct. 31, 2019. http://www.tides.org/wp-content/uploads/2020/06/Tides-Investing-for-Impact-2019.10.31-2.pdf

28 Tides Foundation, "Daring Change: 2018 Overview," Tides.org, accessed Sept. 10, 2020. https://www.tides.org/wp-content/uploads/2019/10/Tides-2018-brochure.pdf.

29 The Forum for Sustainable and Responsible Investment estimates that "sustainable and impact investments" grew over 40% just from 2016 to 2018, potentially accounting for over a quarter of all US "professionally managed assets." The Forum for Sustainable and Responsible Investment (USSIF), "Sustainable and Impact Investing: Overview," accessed Sept. 11, 2020. https://www.ussif.org/files/2018%20Infographic%20overview%20(1).pdf

has developed and maintains an ever-expanding amount of information on over 7,500 "public policy influencers," including:[30]

- 4,261 left-wing nonprofit entities and donor funding sources
- 311 for-profit entities and funding sources
- 264 labor unions
- 1,626 donors to and leaders of left-wing groups
- 626 sponsored left-wing projects
- 159 political committees (other than candidates)

The number of LPDM groups carrying out countless projects, programs, and activities to move America ever further to the left has grown exponentially since 2005, with the dramatic increase in funding sources over the past fifteen years.

It's impossible to identify them all in this chapter, so attention will be devoted to some of the wealthiest and most active. But the most comprehensive list with significant background information exists at www.influencewatch.org.

Funders Committee for Civic Participation

One of the ways the left has moved to dramatically increase funding available for LPDM causes and organizations is by creating networks of donors and funders. The Funders Committee for Civic Participation is a perfect example.

A collective of approximately one hundred liberal foundations and funders, its budget in 2017 was $40 million. It counts as members the who's who of left-wing funding sources, including the George Soros Open Society Institute, Democracy Alliance, Neo Philanthropy, the AFL-CIO, the Tides Foundation, and TWO Rockefeller foundations/funds.[31] Its "mission" is almost entirely

---

30   Influence Watch, https://www.influencewatch.org, Accessed Sept. 9 2020

31   Funder's Committee for Civic Participation, "Member Organizations," accessed Sept. 24, 2020. https://funderscommittee.org/about/#member-organizations

devoted to "process" issues that will—these funders believe—change policy outcomes if adopted. Their code for the political process is "civic engagement," which encompasses such things as "expanding the electorate, protecting voting rights, political participation, training young leaders, strategic litigation, research and narrative, [and] reaching underserved communities."

What exactly do these words mean? The LPDM understands the verbiage. It essentially involves supporting the massive changes in election laws, the myriad lawsuits filed by various leftist groups to force such changes when legislatures don't do their bidding, fighting against election integrity and voter identification, and constant research to develop words and terms to advance the LPDM narrative.

Just one project funded by the Funders Committee involved recruitment of fifty-eight 501(c)(3) "table partners" to support the Win Florida plan, which is part of State Voices, one of the Funders Committee's national efforts. The goals for State Voices, which serves as fiscal sponsor for many of the state specific efforts, are "civic access" and "civic engagement"—all designed to create an electorate sympathetic to progressive/LPDM goals for America.[32]

NEO Philanthropy

Launched in 1983 as Public Interest Projects (PIP), NEO Philanthropy is a 501(c)(3) public charity committed to building strong social justice movements. Its founder, Donald Ross, served for a number of years on the board of Greenpeace and is considered one of the early environmental activists. Between 2015 and 2018, NEO Philanthropy received $216,589,128 from left-wing foundations and donors. It does not engage in its own programming; rather, it serves as an intermediary to "bridge the gap that often exists between funders

---

32 "Our Network: Florida," statevoice.org, accessed Aug. 20, 2020. https://statevoices .org/state-tables/florida/

and organizations doing the work," and operates "collaborative funds, fiscal sponsorships, donor services and capacity building."[33]

According to NEO Philanthropy, "Over the past five years alone, funders have used NEO as a platform through which to make nearly 1,400 grants totaling about $115 million to some 480 distinct groups in almost all 50 states."[34] One of the entities for which NEO Philanthropy serves as fiscal sponsor is the Funders Committee for Civic Participation. Some of the key issues advanced by NEO Philanthropy include:

- "welfare and advocacy for illegal immigrants, ease school discipline, oppose immigration law enforcement"
- "Ease voter registration, fight conservative election reform, advocate for early voting and same day registration"

NEO Philanthropy proclaims that it "builds movements." Its goal of "easing school discipline" is a case study of the far-reaching impact of projects advanced by this and other left-wing funders. NEO Philanthropy reports that "for five years the Just and Fair Schools Fund (JFSF) supported grassroots organizing initiatives that worked to eliminate harsh school discipline policies and practices."[35]

The grassroots efforts paid off and became national education policy during the Obama Administration.[36] Broward County, Florida (the sixth-largest school district in America) was recognized and awarded by the Obama Administration for its "success" in easing school discipline and reducing punishment of students. Max Eden, a senior fellow at the Manhattan Institute, made the argument lax school discipline standards could have dangerous outcomes when

---

33 "About Us," NeoPhilanthropy.org, accessed Aug. 25, 2020. https://neophilanthropy.org/about/.

34 Ibid.

35 "Archived: Just and Fair Schools Fund," Neophilathropy.org, accessed Aug. 25, 2020. https://neophilanthropy.org/collaborative-funds/archived-just-fair-schools-fund/

36 Danielle Wiener-Bronner, "Obama Administration Asks Schools to Drop Zero-Tolerance Approach," *The Atlantic*, Jan 8, 2014. https://www.theatlantic.com/national/archive/2014/01/ending-zero-policy-discipline/356812/

testifying before the US Commission on Civil Rights, where he blamed the guidance for creating "a school climate catastrophe and puts more students at risk."[37]

Arabella Advisors

One of the interesting new wrinkles in the vast funding from left-wing donors to LPDM groups, enterprises, and projects is the concept of "for-profit" ventures to finance the progressive movement, such as the Tides Funds and "impact investing" earlier in this chapter. Those are actual investment funds joined with a progressive, left-of-center agenda.

Another type of LPDM for-profit undertaking is Arabella Advisors, which has created its own network of entities. As a self-described "charitable," for-profit, consulting company, Arabella manages and provides services to four non-profit, tax-exempt corporations that serve as "incubators and accelerators" for a range of other left-of-center projects, entities, and non-profits.[38] Arabella describes and has named each of the non-profit corporations "funds": The New Venture Fund, the Hopewell Fund, the Windward Fund, and the Sixteen Thirty Fund. New Venture, Hopewell, and Windward are all 501(c)(3) public charities and the Sixteen Thirty Fund is a 501(c)(4) social welfare organization. Each of the four non-profit corporations serve as fiscal sponsors to other leftist projects, activities, and undertakings.[39]

A January 2020 profile of Arabella Advisors' network by Inside Philanthropy noted that the company "handles over $400 million in

37 Lauren Camera, "Civil Rights Spat Takes Center Stage in Election," *US News*, Dec. 8, 2017. https://www.usnews.com/news/education-news/articles/2017-12-08/civil-rights-spat-takes-center-stage-in-education

38 Influence Watch, "Arabella Advisors," accessed 15 Aug., 2020. https://www.influencewatch.org/for-profit/arabella-advisors/

39 Arabella Advisors, "Fiscal Sponsorship: Freeing You to Focus on the Mission," accessed Aug. 23, 2020. https://www.arabellaadvisors.com/expertise/fiscal-sponsorship/

philanthropic investments and advises on several billion dollars in overall resources.[40]

The New Venture Fund serves as a platform involving more than half of the fifty largest US grant-making foundations, including eight of the top ten, who have funded projects at New Venture.[41] Similarly, Windward "incubates and hosts initiatives which pursue bold solutions to environmental challenges," using Windward's platform that "allows donors to convene and collaborate on . . . issues . . . in order "to make the most of their resources."[42] The Hopewell Fund helps "donors, social entrepreneurs, and other changemakers quickly launch new initiatives. Hopewell offers a nimble, quick-to-market platform for incubating and testing innovative ideas."[43]

Translated into plain English, Arabella is a for-profit enterprise that provides the management, communications, strategic planning, and other administrative functions, support, and services for these "funds," which are actually 501(c)(3) public charities. These entities provide a platform for coordinating with like-minded progressive donors and activists and are structured in such a way as to be able to quickly create, incubate, manage, and deploy 501(c)(3) projects under the rubric of the funds.

The fourth fund managed and supported by Arabella is the Sixteen Thirty Fund, a 501(c)(4) organization which provides the platform and support for projects involving non-501(c)(3) activities, such as lobbying and political activities. The most significant of these projects sponsored by the Sixteen Thirty Fund is Demand Justice, established in 2018 to oppose the confirmation of Justice Brett Kavanaugh, and which has expanded greatly since that initial undertaking.

---

40   Philip Rojc. "Big Builds: A Look Inside Arabella Advisors." Inside Philanthropy. January 14, 2020. https://www.insidephilanthropy.com/home/2019/1/14/big-builds-a-look-inside-arabella-advisors ^

41   New Venture Fund, "Who We Are," accessed Aug. 23, 2020. https://newventurefund.org/who-we-are/

42   Windward Fund, "About Us," accessed Aug. 23, 2020. https://www.windwardfund.org/about-the-fund/

43   Hopewell Fund, accessed Aug. 23, 2020. https://www.hopewellfund.org/

The confirmation of Justice Kavanaugh did not end the Demand Justice activities. Demand Justice has been engaged in a myriad of progressive causes and issues. And that is just one of the nearly five dozen additional left-wing projects funded and operated by the Sixteen Thirty Fund—that we know of.[44]

The LPDM Focus on Changing the Political Process

There are a number of political issues to which the LPDM is devoted: climate change, abortion rights, protecting public employee unions, opposition to school choice and educational reform, immigrant rights, rewriting American history, and on through the LPDM agenda.

What isn't as well understood outside the ranks of leftist donors and activists is the LPDM holy grail of changing America's political processes, including everything from laws governing elections, voting, campaign finance, lobbying, etc. What can be referred to collectively as the political rules of engagement in America. The LPDM believes that if the process is changed, the outcomes will be different and leftist-progressive-Democratic and media driven policies will become reality, thereby transforming America.

Each of the funding sources described earlier in this chapter has as one of its priority issue areas projects devoted to who votes, how we vote, changing how we vote, changing the structure of voting, or eliminating historically and constitutionally established systems such as the Electoral College.

For example, Democracy Alliance funds half a dozen organizations in the space it calls "defending democracy and voting rights."[45] One of those, America Votes, has year-round projects in twenty

---

44   Influence Watch "The Sixteen Thirty Fund," accessed Aug. 25, 2020. https://www.influencewatch.org/non-profit/sixteen-thirty-fund/

45   Democracy Alliance, "Recommended Organizations," accessed Sept. 6, 2020. https://democracyalliance.org/investments

states, focused on "progressive policies, winning elections, and 'modernizing' voting."[46]

The Funders Committee for Civic Participation (FCCP) is comprised of nearly one hundred leftist foundations and funding sources committed to the goals of "expanding the electorate, protecting voting rights, enhancing political participation, training young leaders, funding strategic litigation, and reaching underserved communities in the election process." What began as the "Ad Hoc Funders' Committee for Voter Registration and Education" soon crystallized into the Funders' Committee for Civic Participation when the organization was officially founded in 1983.

From advancing voter registration efforts in the 1980s, to supporting campaign finance reform in the 1990s, to investing in new voting technologies and election administration reform in the 2000s, FCCP has served as a catalyst for leftist philanthropy's expansive activities in the area of elections and voting.[47]

NEO Philanthropy has established as one of its key strategic initiatives the "State Infrastructure Fund," which advances four goals related to voting and elections and moving us to a direct democracy.[48]

One of the achievements of which NEO Philanthropy's State Infrastructure Fund boasts is its involvement in the 2016 federal court litigation filed by the Public Interest Legal Foundation (PILF) against Broward County Florida Elections Supervisor Brenda Snipes for corrupt voter rolls and her repeated failure to clean the voter rolls as required by federal law.[49] PILF sued Broward County because it "had more registered voters on the rolls eligible to cast a ballot than citizens alive."

---

46   America Votes website, accessed 25 Aug, 2020. https://americavotes.org/

47   Funder's Committee for Civic Participation, "About Us," accessed 25 Aug, 2020. https://funderscommittee.org/about/

48   Neo Philanthropy, "State Infrastructure Fund," accessed Aug. 25, 2020. https:// neophilanthropy.org/collaborative-funds/state-infrastructure-fund/

49   Public Interest Legal Foundation, "Broward County Sued in Federal Court over Corrupted Voter Rolls," June 27, 2016. https://publicinterestlegal.org/blog /broward-county-sued-federal-court-corrupted-voter-rolls/

The complaint stated that, according to public data, "over the past several election cycles the voter rolls maintained by Defendant Supervisor of Elections for Broward County have contained either more total registrants than eligible voting-age citizens or, at best, an implausibly high number of registrants. According to the data, at the time of the 2014 general election, approximately 103% of the citizens of voting age were registered to vote and could cast a ballot in Broward County."

After a trial in which multiple leftist organizations, funded at least in part by NEO Philanthropy's State Infrastructure Fund, joined with Snipes to oppose cleaning the voter rolls, an Obama-appointed federal judge sided with Snipes and her leftist allies, denying PILF's petition to order the updating of the voter rolls.[50]

In 2020, Arabella Advisors announced four new initiatives in response to COVID-19, one of which is to "ensure the safe and democratic implementation of the 2020 elections and make future elections more representative of the country." Arguing that because of the pandemic, administration of the 2020 elections will be "disrupted" and that "[c]rowded polling sites will present real public health concerns," one of the new Arabella projects is for the purpose of expanding early voting and vote-by-mail.

These are but a few (but certainly not an exhaustive list) of the projects and efforts to which the massive amounts of left-wing money is being spent with regard to voting, election laws, and election administration, leading up to the 2020 general election.

And to be clear, these projects do not include the multi-billion dollars raised for Democratic candidates and leftist causes, organizations, and charities through ActBlue.[51]

This discussion also does not scratch the surface when one considers the networks upon networks of leftist organizations that receive support and funding and literally metastasize year after year,

---

50 Demos.org, "Historic Decision in Broward County is a Win for Eligible Voters," Mar. 30, 2018. https://www.demos.org/press-release/historic-decision-broward-county-win-eligible-voters

51 Sarah Mathey and Maggie Quick, "Q2 2020 Recap," ActBlue blog, July 20, 2020. https://blog.actblue.com/2020/07/20/q2-2020-recap/

devoted to election and voting procedures and laws. One such network is Unite America, which is a network of twenty-one other
groups, focused exclusively on political process issues, including such
ideas as eliminating one person – one vote in favor of "ranked choice
voting,"[52] support for open primaries,[53] voting by mail,[54] eliminating
the political parties,[55] and similar issues.

One of the most astonishing events leading up to the general
election in 2020 was the flow of money from the massive leftist funding sources into election administrator offices in targeted areas of the
country. In August 2020, Philadelphia received a $10 million grant
from the Center for Tech and Civic Life for various costs associated
with the 2020 general election.[56] The grant is but one of several
involving millions of dollars being provided to election offices in
targeted states and communities.[57]

The Center for Tech and Civic Life has long promoted leftist election law changes, and secures substantial funding from the
Democracy Fund, which was founded and is principally funded by
eBay Founder and former chairman Pierre Omidyar.[58] Other significant contributors to the 2020 election office funding effort? Google.
Facebook. The Rockefeller Brothers Fund, which is also a member of
the Funders Committee for Civic Participation,[59] just to name a few

---

52   FairVote website, accessed Aug. 26, 2020. https://www.fairvote.org/

53   OpenPrimaries website, accessed Aug. 26, 2020. https://www.openprimaries.org/

54   The National Vote at Home Institute, accessed Aug. 26, 2020. https://voteathome
.org/

55   Unite America website, accessed Aug. 26, 2020. https://www.uniteamerica.org/

56   Jonathan Lai, "Philly is about to get $10 million for mail ballot drop boxes, early
voting, and raises for poll workers," *The Philadelphia Inquirer*, Aug. 26, 2020. https://www
.inquirer.com/politics/election/philadelphia-2020-election-funding-20200826.html

57   Ibid.

58   The Democracy Fund contributes primarily to center-left and left-wing media
organizations, groups seeking to limit campaign speech rights, left-of-center voter
registration organizations, and nominally non-aligned public policy groups. See:
Influence Watch, "The Democracy Fund," accessed Aug. 23, 2020. https://www
.influencewatch.org/non-profit/democracy-fund/

59   The Funder's Committee for Civic Participation, "Member Organizations,"
accessed Aug. 25, 2020. https://funderscommittee.org/about/#member-organizations

of the left-of-center donors providing millions of dollars to election offices.[60]

In short, the massive amount of LPDM money isn't only flowing into the "social justice" or pro-choice or environmental movements, although there are literally billions of dollars going to such groups and causes. Untold amounts of funding are devoted to changing the ways in which America conducts elections, casts ballots, chooses and elects candidates, and similar political process issues. It has come to a neighborhood near you.

LPDM Can Transform America

There is a reason that the 2020 platform of the Democratic Party and the candidates and thought leaders of the party are hardly recognizable as the Democratic Party of the 1990s. The vast left-wing money machine has driven the party and seeks to drive the country to a "transformed" America, one that revives socialism, Marxism, collectivism, worships at the altar of big government and is utterly unrecognizable.

The goals are a wish list of the most progressive left-wing ideas ever proposed, which would impact every American's life in countless ways. The LPDM make no secret of their intentions or their wish list for the rest of us. And most frightening of all is that they have the money to make it happen.

America is a center-right nation, but there are a lot of people from the Left investing hundreds of millions of dollars on grassroots. Elections aren't won in an election year; elections are won in the year before it. These wealthy so-called "progressives" know that they need to invest in these issue sets in the off-election years to set the table for elections. The Republican consultant complex simply can't compete and remains at an extreme disadvantage.

---

60   The Center for Tech and Civil Life, "Key Funders and Partners," accessed Aug. 26, 2020. https://www.techandciviclife.org/key-funders-and-partners/

Acknowledgments

First, I need to thank Skyhorse Publishing for their patience. This book was defined by 2020. COVID-19, social turmoil, and the election outcome shapes this book. With the world changing so rapidly around us, there were many late nights, revisions, and rewriting of chapters to get this book where it is. Skyhorse Publishing was flexible with me as I got where I wanted to go.

I needed a lot of help to get this book done, and so many of my FreedomWorks colleagues contributed through research and editing.

This book would not have been completed without the dedication and late nights of my friend and FreedomWorks colleague, Jason Pye. Jason took incomplete notes, random ideas, and barely spell-checked manuscripts and turned them into a coherent final product. When it looked like the book was broken, all it took was meeting up with Jason for a few hours of pool and a bottle of Woodford Reserve to get the book back on track.

To Parissa Sedghi Fornwalt, you've been telling me to write a book for years. Without your persistence (and fund-raising prowess keeping FreedomWorks chugging), this book might have never been a reality.

Thank you to Noah Wall for pushing me to get this book written and finding a publisher and to Paul Sapperstein for quarterbacking the book to the finish. Josh Withrow made sure every fact is backed up and cited. Mac Stoddard is the finest line editor in the land. I also want to thank Jack Hunter and Jackie Bodnar for their invaluable help on the first and second drafts.

To my Walsh Jesuit High School alum group text of Paul Bodnar, Tom Grealis, Dave Hoinski, Judd Deppisch, and Justin Bibb, so many of the ideas and paragraphs were lifted directly from our multi-day threads.

How can I also not say thanks to my parents, Dr. Edward and Charlotte Brandon. The Cleveland ethics are strong within you and you have supported me every step of the way. And to my amazing wife, Jacqueline Brandon. As we say in Ohio, I really "out-kicked my coverage" marrying that one.

Finally, to Pierce Brandon. You will be born in six weeks, and I can't wait to meet you. Dad is looking forward to teaching you about the ongoing tragedy that is Cleveland pro sports, the joy of reenacting the Revolutionary War, and the greatness and honor of being born an American.

All proceeds from the book will go directly to support our work at FreedomWorks. I hope I represented our institution and activist community well as we get ready for the battles ahead and saving this great republic.

About the Author

Adam Brandon is the president of FreedomWorks, the largest free-market grassroots advocacy organization in the country, which helps over six million activists. He has been published in and quoted by, among others, Fox News, *The Wall Street Journal*, *The New York Times*, *The Washington Post*, *Forbes*, and *The Hill*. He earned a BA from George Washington University and master's degrees from Georgetown University, George Washington University, and Jagiellonian University in Krakow, Poland. When he's not in a suit, he can be found watching the Cleveland Browns with his wife.